──── FINDING THOREAU

FINDING THOREAU

The Meaning of Nature
in the Making of an
Environmental Icon

RICHARD W. JUDD

UNIVERSITY OF MASSACHUSETTS PRESS
Amherst and Boston

Copyright © 2018 by University of Massachusetts Press
All rights reserved
Printed in the United States of America

ISBN 978-1-62534-389-5 (paper); 388-8 (hardcover)

Designed by Jen Jackowitz
Set in Crimson Text
Printed and bound by Maple Press, Inc.

Cover design by Rebecca S. Neimark, Twenty-Six Letters
Cover art: *Portrait of Henry David Thoreau,* woodcut by Felix Vallotton, c. 1896.

Library of Congress Cataloging-in-Publication Data
Names: Judd, Richard William, author.
Title: Finding Thoreau : the meaning of nature in the making of an
　environmental icon / Richard W. Judd.
Description: Amherst : University of Massachusetts Press, [2018] | Includes
　bibliographical references and index. |
Identifiers: LCCN 2018019149 (print) | LCCN 2018026249 (ebook) | ISBN
　9781613766361 (e-book) | ISBN 9781613766378 (e-book) | ISBN 9781625343895
　(pbk.) | ISBN 9781625343888 (hardcover)
Subjects: LCSH: Thoreau, Henry David, 1817–1862—Knowledge—Natural history.
　| Thoreau, Henry David, 1817–1862—Criticism and interpretation. | Nature
　in literature. | Nature (Aesthetics) | Environmentalism in literature.
Classification: LCC PS3057.N3 (ebook) | LCC PS3057.N3 J83 2018 (print) | DDC
　818/.309‹dc23
LC record available at https://lccn.loc.gov/2018019149

British Library Cataloguing-in-Publication Data
A catalog record for this book is available from the British Library.

*To Kieran for his patience and good humor
during our many, many discussions of Thoreau,
and for his contributions to the project.
And to Henry with apologies.*

CONTENTS

Preface   ix

Chapter 1: A Prophet without Honor, 1817–1862   1

Chapter 2: Thoreau in the Age of Industry, 1862–1890   25

Chapter 3: The Cult of Nature and the Age of Progress, 1890–1917   56

Chapter 4: Thoreau for the Ages, Thoreau for the Times, 1920–1960   85

Chapter 5: Thoreau in a Changing Political World, 1960–1970   107

Chapter 6: An Environmental Icon   133

Epilogue: Thoreau in the Millennial Age   160

Notes   171
Index   215

PREFACE

When Henry David Thoreau died in 1862, he was relatively unknown as an author and frequently disparaged by critics who read his work. As he rose to prominence in the later nineteenth century, critics and scholars struggled to disentangle him from this earlier appraisal and evaluate him in his own right. Under a more appreciative critical eye, he became many things to many people, but nineteenth-century critics failed to achieve a common understanding of his message or meaning. And so the quest for the "real" Thoreau continued, as scholar after scholar plunged into his considerable corpus and emerged with what each thought to be a definitive understanding of the man and his work. The search itself is eminently useful—indeed, the very definition of scholarship—but it must seem apparent by now that his quintessence will continue to elude us.

This book attempts a different quest. By focusing not on Thoreau but on the numerous attempts at finding him over the ages, it asks how this author, so obscure in 1862, could be appraised a century later as one of America's most widely recognized writers. Few authors have enjoyed such a spectacular reversal of fortunes at the hands of critics and biographers, and understanding how this happened is a fascinating story in itself. But this is ancillary to another perhaps more important inquiry: What might we learn by studying these successive literary interpretations in the context of their times? To put this question another way, how did Americans in different ages react to Thoreau, and what insights might we gain about American culture by tracing the history of this commentary?

Thoreau was unique among American authors in that the bulk of his work was published after his death. His journals, for instance, did not appear in complete form until 1906, with a final "lost" volume surfacing in 1956, and even as late as 1993 typesetters were preparing yet another unpublished manuscript for print. Each new issue from this horde of manuscript materials was greeted by another round of critical appraisal. In this and other ways, each generation of scholars, journalists, nature writers, and biographers was induced to take up Thoreau's ideas and interpret them for their own readers. These interpretations shifted repeatedly over the generations, and the degree to which they varied from age to age tells us the first thing we need to know about Thoreau's writing: as a symbolic figure in American literature, he was remarkably adaptable, given his unique personality, writing style, and philosophic temperament. His malleability was partly self-willed. As a transcendentalist, he aimed at abstraction and used coy metaphors to shake readers free of superficial thinking. His often outrageous paradoxes functioned as "verbal shock-treatment," in the words of Joseph J. Moldenhauer, bolting readers out of their conventional habits. "He turned the world upside down," Saul Padover explained, in order to offer readers an entirely new perspective.[1] More than this, he seemed to take personal pleasure in self-contradiction, indulging an impish sense of humor that literary critics too often overlook in trying to make sense of him. Thoreau, in short, could support any number of wildly different interpretations, and each generation, according to its own cultural needs, aspirations, and anxieties, took advantage of this. He became a symbol for the times—repeatedly—from the Industrial Revolution on into the environmental era.

The methods I use to assess this shifting literary reputation are essentially historiographical, following an approach surprisingly rare in Thoreau scholarship, given his prominence in American history. Almost all we know about him comes from literary biographers, literary scholars, and nature essayists. Roderick Nash, an intellectual historian, placed him at the center of his classic *Wilderness and the American Mind,* and environmental historian Donald Worster, in his *Nature's Economy,* analyzed his contribution to the science of ecology. But both authors treated him essentially as a benchmark in the history of ideas rather than as a window into the culture of his times. This was also true of Paul Brooks's *Speaking for Nature: How Literary Naturalists from Henry Thoreau to Rachel Carson Have Shaped America* and Hans Huth's

Nature and the American: Three Centuries of Changing Attitudes. Like Nash and Worster, Brooks and Huth highlight Thoreau's contribution to the idea of nature, but neither explains how his thoughts resonated through society in his time or ours.

Thoreau's popularity, of course, depended a good deal on the popularity of nature as a literary motif. It is hard to overstate the importance of this point. As William Bradford stood on the deck of the *Mayflower* on that bleak December day, looking out across a hideous and desolate wilderness, his thoughts by necessity turned to the meaning of nature in the new land, and from that moment on, nature has been a defining theme in American culture. The idea itself has changed many times over since 1620, and the way to understand this in historical context, I argue, is not by scrutinizing the great literary minds in each age but by considering the scholars, critics, biographers, journalists, writers, and essayists who interpreted these seminal writings for their own readers. This vast and varied stratum of middling writers played a far more important role in defining American culture than most scholars acknowledge. It is in this sense—as a focus of this ongoing literary conversation—that Thoreau becomes a window into American culture.

Historians now recognize that the shape of nature varied not only from age to age but also according to the point of view of specific groups, classes, races, and genders in each of these ages. A tighter focus on a specific time and place would bring these voices to light, but a broad survey such as this blurs these distinctions. If this approach fails to represent all voices in a single age, it does represent nicely the pageant of change over time. Separately or together, these neglected writers—upper class or lower, man or woman, highbrow or middlebrow—reveal in their struggle to find Thoreau the day-to-day mechanics of defining nature for America.

The first chapter of this book offers a brief biography, highlighting the personal and literary characteristics that would become a focus of Thoreau commentary in the decades after his death. Chapter 2 follows his reputation from 1862 through the 1890s, reviewing a number of dramatic changes in the idea of nature and a parallel shift in Thoreau's literary fortunes. The third chapter assesses his reputation in the Progressive Era, a period marked by rising popular interest in nature study, outdoor recreation, and conservation. The fourth chapter focuses on Thoreau in the decades between 1920 and 1960, when his reputation as a nature writer was eclipsed by his timeliness as a social critic. Chapter 5 describes the struggle to define Thoreau in a confusing and conflicted world of civil protest and environmental concern, and the final chapter caps his odyssey from obscurity to renown by tracing his rise as an environmental icon.

The commentary described in these chapters is pieced together from sources that range from scholarly tome to newspaper filler. I have distinguished between these various forms of assessment where the differences are suggestive, but frequently the voices blend together as a single message. When this is the case, I treat them more or less as the unified pronouncement of an age, keeping in mind, however, that scholars and journalists spoke to different audiences. In order to provide visual relief from the attribution of these multiple sources, I generally combine notes at the end of each paragraph. Where authors are not identified in text, I link them to specific citations parenthetically in the notes.

Much of this information comes from newspapers, and although I have not so indicated in each citation—again to avoid verbal clutter—the newspaper quotes are accessible in one of three databases: America's Historical Newspapers, Making of America, and New York Times Historical. The attributions will be apparent to those familiar with these databases. A second key source of information is the magnificent collection of Thoreauviana left to the Thoreau Society by Walter Harding, the nation's leading authority on Thoreau. I attribute this source specifically in each citation. The Harding Collection is now housed at the Thoreau Institute in Lincoln, Massachusetts, and for help in accessing this archive I owe a great deal to Jeffrey S. Cramer, a prolific Thoreau scholar who curates the institute's collections. I am also deeply indebted to the many bibliographers, past and present, who brought to my attention even the tiniest bit of Thoreau ephemera. I also benefited from the materials collected by Mary Sherwood and housed as the Thoreau Fellowship Records in the Special Collections Department at the University of Maine's Raymond H. Fogler Library. I owe a debt of thanks to the library's Mel Johnson, who launched me on my quest to find Thoreau in the library's considerable collection of databases. Audiences at several formal and informal presentations commented on my work in progress, and my colleague Mark J. McLaughlin provided valuable feedback on the epilogue.

And last but certainly not least, I would like to thank Pat and Kieran, who with patience and good humor put up with several years of Thoreau babble at the dinner table. May they take comfort in knowing that their ordeal is nearly over.

Richard W. Judd
November 2017

FINDING THOREAU

CHAPTER 1

A PROPHET WITHOUT HONOR, 1817-1862

On July 12, 1917, one hundred years to the day after Henry David Thoreau's birth in Concord, Massachusetts, a newspaper editor in Fort Worth reported with amazement that "so far as we know, no public celebration of Thoreau's centennial of any consequence is being held in America." That same day the *Boston Journal* noted that the town of Concord, home to "one of the . . . most celebrated writers that New England has ever produced," seemed to have "forgotten that he ever lived." Although a few hundred admirers paid homage at the author's grave site, the town's leaders, like the rest of America, let the occasion pass without official observance. The Fort Worth editor speculated that recent entry into the European war had "diverted our thought from such things," and Edward Emerson, son of the Sage of Concord, explained that his committee postponed the Concord commemoration until October, when townspeople had returned from their summer excursions. Unconvinced, the Boston reporter concluded the story with a familiar biblical irony: "A prophet is not without honor save in his own country."[1]

The ambiguity that surrounded the 1917 centennial was typical of Thoreau's status as an American writer. Contrary to what we might expect, he was not widely received as an author in his lifetime, and he remained virtually unknown throughout most of the nineteenth century. While he lived, his reputation hinged on the spectacularly unsuccessful *A Week on the Concord*

1

and Merrimack Rivers, the somewhat more widely read *Walden,* a series of unevenly reviewed lyceum lectures, and a few articles appearing in obscure journals. "Given this history of publication," literary critic Townsend Scudder wrote, "and considering the peculiar man himself, there was bound to be a confusion of appraising voices—a babble taking years to blend into anything which approximates a chorus."[2]

Some attribute this obscurity to an extraordinarily harsh retrospective written two years after his death by James Russell Lowell, considered at that time America's most renowned literary critic. Thoreau's reputation languished after this attack, but in the 1880s his surviving friends burnished his memory by publishing excerpts from his manuscripts and a series of adulatory biographies. Distressed by Lowell's commentary, they ignored Thoreau's complex philosophy of life and emphasized his seemingly simple descriptions of nature, precisely at a time when Americans were becoming enthusiastic converts to nature study and outdoor recreation. The nature study movement quickened Thoreau's entry into the American canon. Wendell Glick, who published an anthology of literary criticism in 1969, noted that by the time his reputation had recovered from Lowell's attacks, the latter was receding "into the dusty recesses now occupied by his Brahmin contemporaries." Unimpressed by the poetic justice in Glick's account, Richard Rutland argued that "if Thoreau's story needs a villain, let it be the nation itself that lacked the requisite self-knowledge to understand what literature it needed and to acknowledge what literature it got." But all this reasoning raises an opposite question: What accounts for his near-universal recognition as an American writer in the century that followed? As Edward O. Wilson put it, how did an "amateur naturalist perched in a toy house on the edge of a ravaged woodlot became the founding saint of the conservation movement"?[3] The dynamics of Thoreau's reputation have never been satisfactorily explained.

Thoreau's literary odyssey is one of the least known but most intriguing stories in the history of American literature. As Lawrence Buell points out, Thoreau was one of the first authors to be added to the American literary pantheon, and for this reason the history of his reputation "makes an unusually interesting window onto American literary history." He is also one of the few American writers to achieve fame as a folk hero—a "patron saint of American environmental writing," as Buell puts it. He stands, then, as iconic not only in American literature but in popular culture as well. Surely, the arc of his reputation begs an explanation.[4]

The matter becomes somewhat clear if we consider his work in its historical context. *Walden* challenged all Americans to march to the beat of a different drum, but at the time of its publication in 1854 the gigantic mills at Waltham and Lowell were demonstrating the power and productivity of regimented effort, and as Thoreau lay on his deathbed in Concord in spring 1862, the spectacle of troops moving in unison across the battlefields of Virginia testified to the importance of united purpose. But if the Civil War generation rejected individualism, turn-of-the-century Americans embraced it, seeking a firmer sense of self in communion with nature. In like manner, each successive generation redefined Thoreau in order to find something meaningful in his life and works. Summarizing a century-long search for the true Thoreau, biographer Walter Harding mused that he had been, at one time or another, America's greatest satirist, its greatest conservationist, its greatest prose stylist, its greatest theorist of civil disobedience, and its greatest philosopher. And for each superlative conferred, there was an equally exaggerated condemnation waiting in the wings. Literary critic V. F. Calverton observed that Thoreau's writing indeed possessed "powerful magic, or there would not be such a need to . . . canonize the shade, or weight it down in the earth under a cairn of rocks."[5]

Mark Sullivan, who surveyed graphic representations of Thoreau over the century after his death, found it astonishing "to see the number of ways in which . . . his facial features have been used to convey different messages, or to fit different purposes." Each image, as Sullivan pointed out, reflected a Thoreau for the times. This malleability stems in part from Thoreau's enigmatic writing style. When *Walden* was first published, a reviewer expressed his frustration at finding a meaning in the book: "The author has Carlyle's hatred of shams and Carlyle's way of showing it; he has Sir Thomas Browne's love of pregnant paradox and stupendous joke, and utters his paradoxes and his jokes with a mysterious phlegm quite akin to that of the Medical Knight who 'existed only at the periphery of his being.'" All this and more he mixed together "without regard to abstract consistency."[6] Thoreau's illusiveness frustrated critics like this, but it explains, more perhaps than his stylistic brilliance, his popular status today.

This legacy of conflicting interpretation complicated the quest for the true Thoreau. Shortly before the turn of the twentieth century, Thomas Wentworth Higginson, who knew him well, reflected on his friend's literary persona. We have to look at literary figures like Thoreau, he wrote, "not merely as they now seem, but as they appeared in their day, and we must calculate their parallax." Vexed by the same enigma, Sandra Harbert Petrulionis introduced a volume of Thoreau criticism in 2012 with a query: "How can we disentangle Henry Thoreau from the myriad causes and ideas now synonymous with his name?" The quest for the true Thoreau is indeed fraught with uncertainty; perhaps, after all, there is no solid bedrock beneath the writer and the written. Perhaps, rather than winnow away the false Thoreaus, we should consider the full range of past interpretations, no matter how broad the spectrum. If we cannot disentangle the true from the transient, perhaps we can learn something from the very nature of this entanglement: How did Americans in successive ages respond to his writing, and what, in turn, do these responses tell us about American culture over this long century of criticism?[7]

The Idea of Nature in America

"Thoreau has taught countless Americans to see nature," historian R. D. Richardson wrote in 1986, and indeed his writing tells us a great deal about this core cultural value. As *New York Times* writer R. L. Duffus pointed out in 1931, nations define themselves mainly through their literature; people write, read, and react to the writing of others, and in the process they forge a national culture. In America that culture is inseparably linked to the idea of nature. To the Puritan, nature was a howling wilderness; to the romantic, a symbol of transcendent truth; and to the modern, a fragile system of ecological interactions. Lewis Mumford saw this complicated bundle of ideas as one of the "chief creations of the civilized man." In technologically simple societies, the idea of nature is "scarcely visible," he pointed out, but as society learns to manipulate its environment, it elaborates, and as these manipulations increase in scale, the idea of nature takes on additional layers of meaning.[8] Ironically, the more society is separated from nature by its technology, the more completely its members need to define it. As both Duffus and Mumford suggest, the idea of nature is far from static; each age defines it on its own terms.

But if we set aside Richardson's vision of Thoreau as the voice of nature in America, a broader prospect comes to light: an ongoing critical conversation about his philosophy of nature sustained for more than a century by scholars, literary critics, essayists, journalists, and biographers who took up Thoreau's ideas and translated them into the idiom of their own times. Defining nature was not an act of individual genius but rather a collective cultural project. Great literary figures do, of course, participate in the construction and reconstruction of nature, but only as part of a larger process. By their very genius they are extraordinary; they rise above historical circumstance and convey a transcendent interpretation of nature. But as Thoreau's reputation demonstrates, each age reacts on its own terms to these transcendent interpretations, and thus the meaning of nature in each age—its personal, recreational, spiritual, and therapeutic value—is better represented by its own critics and writers than by the seminal authors themselves. Collectively, this commentary was more widely read than was Thoreau himself, and it was composed by men and women who were close observers of their own times—who appreciated how their readers were likely to react to Thoreau's message. Using Thoreau as inspiration, these midlevel intellectuals interpreted the organic world beyond their doorstep, and, accordingly, they become the focus of our story. In following them as they create this American icon, we get to the very essence of nature as an evolving cultural construct.

Young Thoreau

David Henry Thoreau, known later in life as Henry, was born in Concord on July 12, 1817, third of four children. His grandfather had emigrated from the Isle of Jersey, and when Henry was born his father was maintaining a small farm in Concord that belonged to his wife's mother. Casting his lot as a merchant, John Thoreau moved the family from Concord to Boston, Chelmsford, and back to Concord. Perhaps too withdrawn for this trade, he remained poor—a "small, deaf, and unobtrusive man." Thoreau's mother, Cynthia Dunbar Thoreau, was by most accounts assertive, outgoing, and talkative; together they were a study in contrasts. Thoreau spent almost all his life living at home, and like everything else about him, this family background has been folded into the ongoing discussion of his literary reputation. Early biographers emphasized his Jersey privateer heritage on one side and his Scots and Puritan lineage on the other. Later critics singled out the contrast between his parents and highlighted the supposed tensions in these family circumstances. Neither father nor mother offered an appropriate model, they surmised, and Thoreau's writing reflected this psychic conflict. In fact, family life seems to have been happier than these psychobiographers make it out to be, but these circumstances have been a focus of critical commentary from the first posthumous assessments on.[9]

A methodical tinkerer, John Thoreau eventually went into pencil making with his brother-in-law, and the business prospered modestly. Again, biographical accounts vary. In some, the family's continuing economic uncertainty explains Thoreau's withdrawn personality; in others, the parents maintained the cultural standards of their lineage. To make ends meet, the Thoreaus took in boarders and crowded the household with older relatives. Of the latter, most were, by all accounts, prudish and provincial. This stultifying atmosphere helps explain not only the iconoclasm that marked so much of Thoreau's writing but also the Puritan-like adherence to principle that punctuated his social philosophy.[10]

In 1833 Thoreau entered Harvard College. Although he later claimed these Harvard years were wasted, the school gave him the solid grounding in classics, modern literature, philosophy, and natural history that made his later writing so distinctive. He put his academic credentials to use briefly in 1838 when he and his older brother, John, opened a private academy in Concord. The endeavor was successful, but when John's health declined in 1841 they closed the school and Henry returned to the pencil shop and helped the family perfect a formula for using graphite in the electrotyping process.[11] Henry was close to his brother, John, and it was in the context of brotherly relations that his first and only well-documented affair of heart unfolded. Seventeen-year-old Ellen Sewall arrived in Concord for a two-week visit in 1839, and since the two families were long acquainted, the five children—Sophia, Helen, Henry, John, and Ellen—spent time together. At age twenty-two, Henry fell in love. He seems to have stepped aside to allow John to court Ellen, and John asked her to marry him. She accepted, but her father opposed the union. Henry then proposed and met a similar fate, and thus the romance ended.[12]

Again the arbiters of his literary reputation read much into a seemingly simple episode. Townsend Scudder speculated that marriage would have undermined Thoreau's individualism, a foundational principle in his writing, and thus Ellen "played her unconscious part" in the making of an American literary icon. Others exaggerate or dismiss the episode in order to bolster their own theories on Thoreau's sexual bearing or to suggest that he subsequently sublimated his romantic inclinations in his worship of nature. Perhaps so, but his biographer Walter Harding cautions against such inferences. "It must not be forgotten that he was raised in an atmosphere of prudish bachelorhood and spinsterhood. Neither his brother nor his sisters ever married—nor Aunt Jane, nor Aunt Maria, nor Aunt Louisa, nor Aunt Sally, nor Aunt Betsey, nor Uncle Charles—and all of these were at one time or another members of the Thoreau household." For whatever reason, it does seem that after the episode he resigned himself to life as a bachelor.[13]

Thoreau's Concord

The setting for Thoreau's brief romance was a town of some two thousand inhabitants strung out along several roads converging on a tree-shaded central square. Concord's rivers were too listless to inspire the visions that transformed nearby Waltham and Lowell into industrial cities, and among its neighbors it was known as Sleepy Hollow, an image that helped form Thoreau's own impression of the good society. Its economy had been built around grain and livestock production, but by Thoreau's time this traditional way of life was beginning to break down. The village stood at the center of a manufacturing belt stretching from the Connecticut River on the west to the Charles and Merrimack on the east, and as the regional industrial workforce grew, the market for locally produced agricultural products expanded. In 1844 Concord gained a rail connection to Boston, and this opened opportunities for producing perishables like butter, eggs, milk, fruits, and vegetables—a market that impelled Thoreau's neighbors into the world of abstract prices, impersonal transactions, and distant financial arrangements.[14] Like other Concord transcendentalists, Thoreau was unsettled by the new conditions of production. The countryside was becoming "denaturalized," he thought, suffering from a growing separation between poetry and life. As his confidence in society dissolved, his faith in nature grew.[15]

Despite these changes, Thoreau was firmly rooted in Concord. The town's thin, sandy soils discouraged agricultural expansion, and thus it remained more forested than most in the Boston area, and for this and other reasons it offered an ideal setting for the unique mix of philosophical reflection and scientific observation that made up so much of his writing. Concord bent to the winds of market capitalism sufficiently to give purchase to his critique of commercialism, yet at the margins it preserved the slower pace that inspired his lofty thinking. From this experience he extracted an amazing array of meanings, giving the whole town an allegorical cast unique among literary settings.[16]

Thoreau's other grounding in Concord came in sharing his thoughts with some of the most brilliant minds in America. Standing head and shoulders above Concord's literati was Ralph Waldo Emerson, whose magnetic personality and stimulating insights drew others like him to town. Emerson was America's foremost intellectual in the antebellum decades, founder of the transcendental movement and famous for lofty musings and lectures in which he conveyed his thoughts with a rhythm and diction that electrified listeners, even if they only vaguely understood him. He withdrew from the ministry in 1832 to write and lecture and settled in Concord in 1834, staying for a time with his grandparents at Old Manse. Concord, he found, distanced him from the Cambridge theologians who censured his break with orthodoxy. Its people, if no more tolerant, were at least less sensitive to the nuances of his religious views. There, surrounded by friends and sympathetic thinkers, he sailed boldly into the uncharted waters of post-Puritan spirituality.[17]

Emerson drew other philosophers and writers to Concord, and each arrival increased the gravitational pull of the town's intellectual culture. "The world Thoreau entered when Emerson opened the doors of his house could be matched in few other times or places," Townsend Scudder observed. Along with Emerson, Thoreau became friends with Bronson Alcott, Ellery Channing, and Thomas Wentworth Higginson and conversed with Margaret Fuller, George William Curtis, George Ripley, Elizabeth Peabody, John Sullivan Dwight, Jones Very, Orestes Brownson, and James Freeman Clarke, all of them familiar faces in Concord. He was also in touch with a number of women who, if not literary figures in their own right, were powerful contributors to the town's intellectual climate: Sophia Peabody Hawthorne, Ellen Fuller, Elizabeth Hoar, the wife and daughters of Edmund Hosmer, Emerson's aunt Mary Moody Emerson, and indeed many of those in Thoreau's own extended family.[18] Coming to maturity in this vibrant intellectual climate, he set his sights on becoming a writer.

Each of these transcendentalists was unique, but in some ways, Concord philosophizing was a collective project, an intense and perpetual round of discussion that circulated each idea across the entire community. Bronson Alcott described a day typical among these friends: "Pass the forenoon with Thoreau. We walk by 'The Cottage' and discourse reclining on the hillside near the Indian meadows by the riverside. Afternoon with Emerson. We walk to Walden and bathe. Emerson reads me the introductory paper to his book *Representative Men*, now nearly ready for the press, and we discuss Plato,

Goethe, Swedenborg, and some others of his Representatives of the race." Thoreau's closest companions were Alcott and Ellery Channing, who like Thoreau took their inspiration from nature. With these two he could engage in open and spontaneous conversation, but even here Thoreau could be frustrating. Alcott struggled to understand his approach: "His sagacity," he wrote, was "like a bee and beaver, the dog and the deer . . . the peer of the backwoodsman and Indian." Their kinship rested less on a mutual understanding than on an intense intellectual curiosity and disregard for social convention. "It may be that there are men now as quaint and original as were easily accessible in those days," Thomas Wentworth Higginson recalled in 1898, "but if so, I wish some one would favor me with a letter of introduction."[19]

To a young man of retiring personality, these often intense conversations were emotionally exhausting, and he read into them far more than others might. Because he asked so much of these friendships, he was frequently disappointed. "How happens it that I find myself making such an enormous demand on men and [am] so constantly disappointed? Are my friends aware how disappointed I am? Is it all my fault? Have I no heart?" Biographer Mary Elkins Moller identified numerous journal entries that reveal a visceral desire for solitude and no small hint of misanthropy, but she notes that these expressions were balanced by others indicating a "strong sense of belonging to a community." Desperate for friendship, and desperate to avoid it, he learned from these Concord transcendentalists, but he also learned from their failings.[20]

In 1841, when the brothers' Concord Academy closed, Emerson, who traveled frequently on lecture tours, invited Thoreau to move into his household as a gardener and handyman. Thoreau spent two years with the Emerson family and while there began publishing poems in the *Dial,* a short-lived periodical that served as an outlet for transcendentalist thought. Margaret Fuller, who edited the journal, found his writing rich in ideas but short on technical skill—"so choked with mystical symbolism, as to make painful reading." When Emerson became editor, he published more of Thoreau's work but like Fuller found it troublesome. "We must mend him if we can," he wrote to Fuller in 1840.[21] Emerson's friendship was crucial to Thoreau's literary development, but the weight of the older man's imposing personality bore down on the young disciple. A Concord companion noted that Thoreau so imitated Emerson in tone and gesture that it was "annoying to listen to him," and another remembered that in the company of both, it was difficult to discern who was actually speaking. Aware of Thoreau's close relationship to Emerson, critics debated for decades the authenticity of his style and philosophy.[22]

Thoreau himself grew troubled by his lack of independence, and on Emerson's advice in 1843 he moved to Staten Island, where he spent ten months tutoring the son of Emerson's brother and looking for an outlet for his essays. Thoroughly homesick, he returned to Concord in early 1844, age twenty-seven and still casting about for a career. Living at home, he pursued an assortment of income-producing jobs and spent his afternoons sauntering, a task he approached with all the seriousness of a chosen profession. He simplified his needs to match this disparate income and spent most of his time pursuing his calling as Concord's "self-appointed inspector of snow-storms and rain-storms."[23]

Romanticism and Transcendentalism

The philosophy that united Thoreau and the other Concord intellectuals was transcendentalism, a native offshoot of the European romantic movement. Romanticism challenged the rationalist interpretation of reality inspired by the scientific revolution and the materialistic ethic of the dawning industrial age. It preached simple pastoral virtues in an era of complex industrial organization and promised spiritual satisfaction in lieu of material reward. In this struggle of values, romantics were no match for the forces of science and industrial progress, but they captured the allegiance of Europe's intellectual elite, and their influence spread quickly across the Atlantic.[24]

Transcendentalism mixed together French romanticism and German idealism, but its direct antecedent was the English romantic movement, particularly the writings of William Blake, William Wordsworth, and Samuel Taylor Coleridge, who saw nature as an archetype of spiritual harmony. On long walks through the Lake District, Coleridge described plants and animals in the naturalist tradition but viewed farmsteads and villages as though they, too, were spontaneous natural creations. His colleague William Wordsworth wrote of the humble dwellings of the Lake District as having "risen, by an instinct of their own, out of the native rock." Romantics like these saw the pastoral world as a metaphor, a lesson in essential human relations absent the corrosive effects of the Industrial Revolution. In the European tradition, the idea of nature was symbolic; in the hands of America's poets and philosophers, it was firmly grounded in the physical environment.[25]

Romanticism crossed the Atlantic at a time when writers like Emerson, Hawthorne, Whittier, Melville, Dickinson, Whitman, Bryant, Cooper, and Longfellow were creating an American literature almost de novo. These were exciting times for American writers. Print culture—books, journals, newspapers, magazines—was growing, aided by advances in education, printing, papermaking, and eyeglass manufacture. Literacy was on the rise, and Americans were hungry for cultural self-improvement.[26] This awakening was nationwide, but it was most intense in New England, where Boston minister William Ellery Channing was brokering the synthesis of evangelical Christianity and Enlightenment thinking that brought Unitarianism into the mainstream of New England religious life. Transcendentalism combined the Unitarian message of divine benevolence and free will with the romantic celebration of human emotion, and like the European romantics, transcendentalists accepted nature as a source of this spiritual awakening. Symbols of universal law were embedded in nature, and by reading these symbols the observer transcended reality and gained access to divine truths.[27]

American transcendentalists were more grounded in nature than European romantics, but Thoreau took this perspective even further. Unlike Emerson, who descended from eight generations of Puritan clergymen, Thoreau was a first-generation intellectual, and he was determined to live his transcendental philosophy deliberately rather than vicariously. Having grown up among versatile Concord farmers in a craft-making family, he was too much the workingman to simply idealize nature; he smelled, tasted, and lived it. Thoreau described a world Emerson and other transcendentalists never really understood. They distrusted the raw power of wild nature, and thus they never fully trusted Thoreau.[28]

Walden Interlude

Having returned from New York with no publication prospects, Thoreau began mulling over options that would eventually lead him to the cabin at Walden Pond. As with other aspects of his life, the experience became the focus of ongoing controversy among biographers and critics. The two-and-a-half-year stay at Walden, Clifton Johnson wrote in 1910, was "so unusual a proceeding on the part of a man of his education and cultured tastes [that it] could not help attracting much curious interest." As Johnson intimates, the event defined Thoreau for later scholars, but the idea of living the primitive life in a rural retreat was not unusual among romantics, and in fact several of Thoreau's friends had done as much.[29] Thoreau embraced the romance of self-sufficient living, but there were more prosaic motives behind the move to Walden. Thoreau's own household was crowded with family, boarders, and a constant round of visitors, and he needed a quiet place to write. "He had wanted for years to be independent," biographer R. D. Richardson added; he was twenty-eight and living at home without money, job, or prospects. Higginson put the matter simply:

> A young man . . . having a passion for the minute observation of nature . . . takes it into his head to build himself a study . . . in the woods, by the side of a lake. Happening to be poor, . . . he takes a whimsical satisfaction in seeing how cheaply he can erect his hut, and afterwards support himself by the labor of his hands. . . . He goes to the village every day or two, by his own showing, to hear the news. He . . . makes more close and delicate observations on nature than any other American has ever made, and writes the only book yet written in America, to my thinking, that bears an annual perusal. Can it be really true that this is a life so wasted, so unpardonable?[30]

Thoreau had been looking for a place to settle since moving in with the Emersons in 1841, and a solution presented itself when Emerson purchased land on the pond, intending to build a summer house. The hut provided solitary space and allowed him to remain in his beloved Concord—all at minimal cost. He did not discourage visitors, but the distance from Concord ensured that only a self-selected class of walkers would cross his threshold.[31]

According to Richardson, the two years at the pond "produced more writing of higher quality over a greater range of subjects . . . than in any other period of his life." But what made his time in the woods distinctive was his inclination to dress his behavior in the mantle of moral truth. As he wrote later in his book, "I went to the woods because I wished to live deliberately, to front only the essential facts of life, and see if I could not learn what it had to teach, and not, when I came to die, discover that I had not lived." He recognized that he was making a virtue of his impecunious life circumstances, but there was a philosophical lesson to be learned: simplifying helped him understand the true worth of living. "The poorer I am, the richer I am."[32]

Biographers see the Walden years as a watershed in Thoreau's writing. While there he completed the manuscript for *A Week on the Concord and Merrimack Rivers,* and according to William Condry, his subsequent writing reflected "the optimism and self-assurance he had gained in the leisured solitude of Walden life." Robert Kuhn McGregor argued it was during the

Walden years that he chose to dedicate his life not to the transcendentalist specter of nature but to the real thing. Having sorted out this relationship, he returned briefly to the Emerson household and then moved back to his parents' home in 1847. "I left the woods for as good a reason as I went there," he wrote at the end of *Walden*. He learned that he could survive—indeed, thrive—without the trappings of civilization, and this led him to the great lesson of his widely read book. In proportion as one simplified life, "the laws of the universe will appear less complex, and solitude will not be solitude, nor poverty poverty, nor weakness weakness."[33]

It was also during the Walden years that Thoreau began seriously composing the journal he had begun in 1837. His practice was to record virtually any suggestive encounter in the field and craft the best of these into lectures and essays. Early entries recorded simple moral lessons drawn from nature and human nature, but later he became more expressive, documenting his progress toward the exquisite relation to nature that became the hallmark of his writing. As Emerson did in his own journal, Thoreau loaded his entries with seemingly unconnected thoughts to see if they would, by some feat of analogy, cohere. This epigrammatic approach fragmented his writing, but it also gave readers an inexhaustible supply of pithy quotes useful for virtually any occasion—perhaps his greatest source of popular recognition in the century after his death.[34]

Thoreau Private and Public

Well before his hermitage at Walden, Thoreau had become the stuff of local legend, and the anecdotes that echoed through the village during his lifetime bore heavily on his reputation in the later nineteenth century. In the compass of their small town, Concord people had more than their share of eccentrics, but even among these Thoreau stood out. Ungainly and standoffish, he dressed in rough, unfashionable clothes and walked with a "long, swinging step of a man who is used to walking great distances." Celia Frease, a schoolgirl when Thoreau was a young man, recalled his ill-fitting clothes, wrinkled coat, and unpolished boots. "Every hair of his head seemed to have an individuality of its own, and at war with every other hair creating a painful discord." The artist N. C. Wyeth, who grew up in a town near Concord, remembered these neighbors harboring a "strong distaste" for him. One old-timer claimed that he "never had much use for that loafer," and another summed him up as a "sort of hermit boor." Few would have grasped the irony in Emerson's remark that Thoreau was "a very industrious man, and setting, like all highly organized men, a high value on his time, he seemed the only man of leisure in town."[35]

Thoreau did little to correct these impressions. Defensive and uncomfortable in most social settings, he had great difficulty reasoning out the behavior of those he did not know well, and he devoted hundreds of journal entries to his frustrations with those he did. In 1852 he wrote in his journal that "what men call social virtues, good fellowship, is commonly but the virtue of pigs in a litter, which lie close together to keep each other warm." He was not averse to sharing this opinion with others. An old farmer once remarked, "If he would rather visit with woodchucks than with me and my wife, I haint nothing to say except that it is a little hard on the woodchucks.'" Or as a friend of Margaret Fuller once remarked, "H. Thoreau imitates porcupines successfully."[36]

Thoreau's personality is one more enigma in the makeup of the man and his work. While some villagers described him as aloof, others found him cheery and entertaining. John Albee remembered "a very pretty picture . . . of Thoreau leaning over the fire with a fair girl on either side, which somehow did not comport with the subsequent story I heard of his being a hermit." He could entertain children for hours with stories, tricks, and huckleberry expeditions, and in hundreds of journal entries he described pleasant conversations with older citizens who helped him understand the town's natural and human history. He related easily to these folksy men, as he did to his transcendentalist colleagues, but he largely ignored those outside these two circles. As a childhood friend related, "There was a great intermediate class between Emerson and the Canadian woodchopper who would have gladly aided Thoreau if he had been a little more human in his dealings with them." Literary critics collected these stories, both positive and negative, and found them helpful in understanding his thoughts. Thoreau's personality beamed through the critical commentary and, like it, changed with the times.[37]

Thoreau's public lectures left a similarly inconsistent image. By some accounts, he was a poor lecturer. He read his notes without animation, seldom looked up, and lacked the charm and conviction of a seasoned circuit lecturer. He refused to cheapen himself, as he said, by explaining his thoughts, and thus he remained incomprehensible to those a journalist described as "slow plodders." In other instances, however, he seemed positive and animated. A *Portland (ME) Transcript* reviewer pointed to an outpouring of images that kept the audience attentive: "He bewilders you in the mists of transcendentalism, delights you with brilliant imagery, shocks you by his apparent irreverence, and sets you in a roar by his sallies of wit."[38] In either case, editors across the country reproduced the reviews, carrying Thoreau's reputation beyond the New England lecture circuit.

Thoreau's reputation was also complicated by his curious habit of imitating Emerson in mannerism, voice, and thought. According to Moncure Conway, this resemblance was "a quiet joke in Concord," and James Russell Lowell immortalized it in his *Fable for Critics,* published in 1848:

> There comes———, for instance; to see him's rare sport,
> tread in Emerson's tracks with legs painfully short;
> How he jumps, how he strains, and gets red in the face,
> To keep step with the mystagogue's natural pace!

Lowell's satire dogged Thoreau on the lecture trail. A disappointed Worcester reporter remarked after one lecture that the audience "had looked for a bold, original thinker" but instead was offered up "a better *imitation* of Emerson than we should have thought possible, even with two years' seclusion [at Walden Pond] to practice in." Townsend Scudder believed the characterization was true only while Thoreau was "still groping" his way to maturity, but whatever the case, it was a long-standing barrier to Thoreau's literary success.[39]

Literary Forays

Thoreau's first major literary success came in writing about a topic that had little reference to the transcendental philosophy he learned at Emerson's feet. In 1846, during his second summer at Walden, he traveled to Bangor, Maine, and joined a cousin on a timber-surveying expedition up the Penobscot River. He made a second trip to Maine in the fall of 1853, this time to Moosehead and Chesuncook Lakes, guided by Penobscot Native Joe Aitteon. His third trip in 1857 took him to the headwaters of the north-flowing Allagash River and back down the Penobscot East Branch, paddling with Penobscot guide Joe Polis.[40] Mindful of a growing popular interest in wild America, he pitched his account of these three trips to a middle-class audience looking for vicarious adventure in remote places. As in all his writing, he described the colors, scents, sounds, and taste of the woods, but he also worked into his descriptions his thoughtful reflections on the wildness of the human spirit.[41]

Thoreau published the first of these three essays in the *Union Magazine of Literature and the Arts* in 1848, and for this he had Horace Greeley of the *New York Tribune* to thank. Bayrd Taylor, who was managing the magazine at the time, remembered Greeley arriving in his office with a thick manuscript under his arm proclaiming, "Now you *must* do something for this young man. His name is Thoreau; he lives in a shanty at Walden Pond, near Concord, on $37.21 a year, and he must be encouraged." Considering Thoreau's frugality, Taylor offered him $75 for the manuscript, "as it would meet the latter's expenses for two years to come." In 1864 the three essays were combined and published as *The Maine Woods*.[42]

Another literary endeavor was less successful. Having completed *A Week on the Concord and Merrimack Rivers* at the pond, in 1849, on the advice of Emerson, he underwrote its publication. He introduced the book, which describes a boating adventure with his brother in 1839, with a compelling narrative image: "The weeds at the bottom gently bending down the stream, shaken by the watery wind . . . were objects of singular interest to me, and at last I resolved to launch myself on its bosom and float whither it would bear me." From the title and the opening lines, *Week* might have appeared a familiar New England pastoral composition, but rather than evoke images of folk and nature, Thoreau mixed into the travel narrative a combination of nature facts, local lore, poetry, and vaguely connected commentaries on philosophy, classical verse, theology, and the human condition. He was, as biographer Laura Dassow Walls said, "experimenting wildly with form," combining thoughts on nature with a radical critique of religion, slavery, industrialization, and war. Natural history supplied the imagery and transcendentalism the message, but as a biographer put it, the rivers in the title were "often little more than a dimly fluvial backcloth for the endless flow of the author's philosophical reflections."[43]

Week brought Thoreau's first round of critical reviews, and some were indeed laudatory. English writer Sophia Dobson Collet, an expert on Eastern mystic religions, considered the philosophic digressions a tribute to American individualism, and James Russell Lowell found the combination of nature study and literary discourse compelling. But even Lowell, no stranger to ponderous thought, found the digressions tedious. The sections on Buddha, Persius, friendship, "and we know not what," he insisted, were "like snags, jolting us headforemost out of our places as we are rowing placidly up stream or drifting down." Horace Greeley assigned the *Tribune*'s review to Unitarian minister George Ripley, a man of broad influence who might have helped cement the loose blocks of Thoreau's nascent literary reputation. Unfortunately, Ripley found the book troubling. He favored its general tone but raised two themes that would resonate through critical commentary over the next half century. First, the philosophy seemed "second-hand, imitative, often exaggerated"—a reference to Thoreau's association with Emerson. Second, he found Thoreau's transcendentalism a poorly disguised form of "Pantheistic egotism." Others echoed Ripley's pronouncement on the book's impiety. Thoreau's blunt observation that "when one enters a village the church, not only really, but from association, is the ugliest looking building in it" appeared in numerous reviews.[44]

Of a run of 1,000 copies, Thoreau sold only 219, partly because his publisher made no effort to advertise or distribute it. His friend Franklin Sanborn insisted that Thoreau "rejoiced in the slow sale of his first book," since this left him free from solicitations for lectures. No doubt Thoreau expressed these face-saving sentiments, but in fact the book's fate left a deep impression. Praise for the passages on the river itself convinced him to shift his attention from arid philosophizing to nature description in subsequent essays, while the harsh criticism of the rest of the book delayed publication of *Walden* for nearly a decade. Partly because of the book's failure, Thoreau's relation with Emerson cooled considerably in the early 1850s. Thoreau had written *Week* in order to live up to Emerson's philosophical expectations, and its diffuse structure was patterned after Emerson's own writing style. Emerson encouraged him to seek a publisher, and when none could be found, he suggested Thoreau underwrite the production costs. The book's failure dashed Emerson's hopes for a great American transcendental poet, and it saddled Thoreau with the cost of publication. Thoreau's subsequent journal entries became increasingly literal, inspired less by Emerson's quest for transcendence than by Harvard naturalist Louis Agassiz's field methods.[45] In contrast to Emerson's idealism, Thoreau grew increasingly grounded in nature. In addition, the young handyman-scholar had developed a close, albeit Platonic, relation to Emerson's wife, Lidian, while he was living in the Emerson household, and this may have played a part in the rupture. Thoreau resented Emerson's long absence in view of Lidian's delicate health, and as Robert Sattelmeyer says, the "inevitable suggestions of Lancelot and Arthur could not have been long out of his mind."[46]

Walden

Compared to *Week*, Thoreau's second book was a success; all but 256 copies of *Walden*'s original run of 2,000 sold in 1854, the first year of publication. The book was not reissued during his lifetime, but a second printing appeared in 1862, immediately after his death, and a third and fourth in 1863 and 1864. With *Walden,* Thoreau had the benefit of a more aggressive publisher. James T. Fields of the Boston firm Ticknor & Fields brought to the book an extraordinary talent for marketing. At a time when most Americans instinctively turned to Europe for their reading material, Ticknor & Fields was transforming its listing—Emerson, Hawthorne, Longfellow, Stowe, Lowell, Holmes, Whittier—into an American literary renaissance, and Thoreau was an important beneficiary of this achievement.[47]

Thoreau claimed to have written the book to satisfy his neighbors' curiosity about what he ate and what he spent, but his true purpose was much more serious. Having simplified his needs during his time alone in the woods, he could see that his neighbors were blinded by a compulsive drive to accumulate. This burden led him to *Walden*'s most famous passage: "The mass of men," he wrote, "lead lives of quiet desperation"; people had become "so occupied with the factitious cares and . . . coarse labors of life, that its finer fruits cannot be plucked by them." Although he made his point by satirizing his Concord neighbors, *Walden* was a genial book with fewer of the blunt, iconoclastic statements that colored the reception of *Week*. His critique was not so much aimed at material things themselves as the motives behind their acquisition. "Simplicity, simplicity, simplicity!" he advised. "I say, let your affairs be as two or three, and not a hundred or a thousand; instead of a million count half a dozen, and keep your accounts on your thumb nail." Again, this was not a goal in itself but rather a means to achieve higher goals—leisure, nature, contemplation, spiritual awakening, or true friendship.[48]

Reaction to *Walden* suggests a promising young writer, but the book was not heralded as the literary masterpiece it would become at the hands of twentieth-century critics and scholars. The *Portland Transcript* dismissed it as the "quaint . . . production of a crooked genius," and the *Worcester Palladium* added that the book's odd insights left the reader "no wiser in the end." Neither wholly pastoral nor completely transcendental, *Walden* was difficult to describe. A *New York Times* critic situated it in the eighteenth-century genre of English jest books: comic satires that made light of virtually anything held sacrosanct, without expressing a hint of compassion. Others interpreted it more literally as an adventure story written by a man who lived like a king on hoe cakes and water. "He ... builds his own house, cooks his own victuals, makes and mends his own clothes, works, reads, thinks as he pleases, and writes this book to chronicle his success in the experiment." The "Economy" chapter raised a great deal of skepticism, the common impression being that "anybody could live on six cents a day when mother's cupboard was close at hand and well stocked."[49]

Those who considered *Walden* a proposal for reform were equally confused. The idea that simplicity could resolve the great social issues of the day seemed unconvincing, and in an era when most social engineering depended on collective action or moral persuasion, Thoreau's emphasis on the individual seemed "repulsively selfish." No one, a reviewer admonished, "has a right to live for himself alone, away from the interests, the affections, and the sufferings of his kind."[50] With industrialization at full flood in the 1850s, readers were not prepared for *Walden*'s antimaterialist message. Jesse Clements, writing in the *Western Literary Messenger,* saw Thoreau "at war with the political economy of the age." In Clements's view, the lust for material goods was the very engine of progress. "To give a man a new want is to ... conquer his habitual rust and idleness." There was nothing virtuous in homespun and linsey-woolsey, a Boston *Daily Atlas* reviewer added; the preference for "clean, well made clothes over dirty, ragged ones, scarcely argues any moral degradation or idle folly."[51]

Nor did *Walden* fit easily into the transcendentalist genre. Thoreau forced together Emerson's optimistic message of spiritual redemption and his own reclusive cynicism, and the mixture was often self-negating. The descriptions lacked the pietistic overtones usually attached to a study of this sort, and Thoreau evaded the classic romantic formula that saw the adventurer returning from the wilderness reassured of humanity's goodness and God's greatness. The stay at Walden Pond seemed to sharpen rather than assuage his cynicism. There were essential truths in *Walden,* a Boston reviewer observed, but there was "not a page, a paragraph giving one sign of the liberality, charitableness, kind feeling, [or] generosity" that would make it a true celebration of human freedom. In a widely reproduced review in *Knickerbocker Magazine,* an anonymous writer compared *Walden* to a recent autobiography by P. T. Barnum. Both were written by "bold and original thinkers," one who retreated into nature to escape civilization and another who reproduced nature's curiosities to bring civilization to his doorstep. Barnum had conceived an elaborate sham to satisfy his lust for of possessions, and Thoreau had conceived an equally elaborate sham—the Walden experiment—to expose the error of lusting after possessions. Neither had any idea of "laboring very hard with their hands for a living," and both were determined to support themselves principally through a "skillful combination of nature with art." One "sneers at and ridicules the pursuits of his contemporaries with the same cheerfulness and good-will that the other cajoles and fleeces them." Both were artists, both skilled at self-advertising, both capable of making "large contributions to the science of human nature," and both, finally, "humbugs—one a town humbug and the other a rural humbug."[52]

The book garnered an impressive collection of positive reviews as well, again reflecting the shifting cultural currents in these antebellum years. According to historians Bradley Dean and Gary Scharnhorst, "By the end of August 1854, *Walden* had in fact been praised in over thirty newspapers and magazines from Maine to Ohio." Most commented on the accuracy of his nature descriptions, and at least a few complimented *Walden* as a sincere attempt by a spiritually grounded writer to "find the minimum due to his body, and the maximum due to his soul." Given the weight of these positive reviews, *Walden* marked a turning point in Thoreau's reputation. In the years after 1854, followers appeared in Concord, seeking him out as they sought out Emerson, and they brought with them what Alcott called "the disciple's faith in their master's thoughts." After his death this following would congeal into a cadre of defenders anxious to draw him out into the literary limelight, and this impulse would play an important part in his rise to fame in the closing decades of the century.[53]

Civil Disobedience

Even as Thoreau was gaining stature as a nature writer, he was being drawn in another direction by the national debate over slavery, an embroilment that would contribute significantly to his reputation as a principled contrarian. Thoreau's abolitionist expressions drew from a tradition of early reformist ideals. In 1828 William Ladd of Maine had founded the American Peace Society, predicated on the principles of nonresistance, and in the 1840s utopian reformer John Humphrey Noyes transformed religious perfectionism—the possibility of living free of sin—into a way of life at his communities in Vermont, New York, and Connecticut. In the same decade, William Miller convinced thousands of men and women in rural New England and New

York that the Second Coming of Christ was eminent. Abolitionist William Lloyd Garrison emerged from the same apocalyptic mold, believing like Noyes that the state had to be destroyed before the nation could be redeemed. Thoreau, already the village rebel, absorbed these idealistic convictions—passive resistance from Ladd, religious perfectionism from Noyes, and apocalyptic change from Miller and Garrison—and became the spokesman for the abolitionist ideas of his transcendentalist friends and family.[54] The Walden experiment demonstrated the power of the deed, and he applied this lesson in his abolitionist activism. When Congress authorized war with Mexico in 1846, he stopped paying his poll tax, and the Concord sheriff, after weeks of badgering, locked him in jail. He was released the following morning, but as at Walden he gave this simple act a philosophical justification steeped in American revolutionary ideology. In the essay that recounts his night in jail, originally titled "Resistance to Civil Government," he argued that the state was created purely for the convenience of the citizenry and had no right to force moral obligations on those who created it. In higher matters, it was conscience, not the state, that served as the citizen's guide.[55]

The essay reached only a limited audience during his lifetime, but the same thoughts gained notoriety when he voiced them in public. The 1850 Fugitive Slave Law, which directed northern states to return refugees from slavery caught in their jurisdiction, brought the issue of slavery home to Massachusetts, and in May 1854 Anthony Burns, a victim of the law, was tried in Boston along with those who attempted to shield him. Thoreau participated in the public outcry that ensued, delivering a series of speeches in which he denounced not only the law but also the commonwealth that enforced it. His indignation was tinged with philosophic anarchy and a hint of utopian perfectionism: "Heroes can live on nuts, and freemen sun themselves in the clefts of rocks, rather than sell their liberty for this pottage of slavery. We, the few honest neighbors, can help one another; and should the state ask any favors of us, we can take the matter into consideration leisurely, and at our convenience give a respectful answer." During these years Thoreau published other social and political essays, and his fiery tone gave the public a new Thoreau persona. Even the *Antislavery Standard* raised its editorial eyebrows at the incendiary rhetoric produced by a man who was "understood to inhabit a small hut, in an out-of-the-way place, in Concord, Mass."[56]

Thoreau became more involved in abolitionist activities when Franklin Sanborn introduced him to Kansas radical John Brown in 1857. Thoreau, Emerson, and Alcott were unaware of Brown's plans for a raid on the

Harpers Ferry Armory, but they admired his devotion to principle, and when word of the incident spread north, Thoreau commemorated Brown in a speech delivered in Boston before an audience of twenty-five hundred. At a time when most Americans considered Brown a traitor, Thoreau lionized him. One Boston commentator characterized the speech as a mix of "just and striking remarks" and "foolish and ill-natured ones" and reminded readers that "the lecturer was cultivating beans and killing woodchucks" at Walden while more committed partisans were laboring to turn public sentiment against slavery.[57] In December 1859 Brown was hanged for treason, and after filling his journal with indignant prose, Thoreau rang the town church bell to gather a crowd and delivered a plea, as he said, not for Brown's life "but for . . . his immortal life." Quite possibly, Thoreau was the first American to speak publicly in defense of Brown, and again newspaper coverage was extensive. The events of that fateful fall and winter fueled Thoreau's cynicism. In October he wrote in his journal, "I speak to the stupid and timid chattels of the north, pretending to read history and their Bibles, desecrating every house and every day they breathe in!"[58]

Reconciliation

Although his views on society grew darker in the shadow of the slavery issue, Thoreau's status as a member of the Concord community improved in his last years. Almost inadvertently, his lectures, writing, and surveying earned him a respectable living, and when the family business shifted from pencils to high-quality powdered graphite, its finances stabilized. As demand for his services as lecturer and as surveyor grew, Thoreau assumed yet another persona. "Managing success," Walls writes, "was a new and disconcerting prospect." Those who earlier viewed him as Emerson's shadow found, as William Lyon Phelps wrote in 1924, that "his chief imitation of Emerson was in his absolute originality and independence, qualities common to both teacher and pupil." And in a rare moment of enthusiasm, Thoreau reciprocated in his journal: "How I love the simple, reserved countrymen, my neighbors. . . . For nearly twoscore years I have known, at a distance, these long-suffering men . . . and now feel a certain tenderness for them, as if this long probation were but the prelude to an eternal friendship."[59]

Thoreau's health began declining in 1855 when an unexplained paralysis left him debilitated for months. By 1857 he was feeling the effects of chronic tuberculosis, a disease common in his family. During the summer of 1861 he spent eight weeks in Minnesota, attempting to improve his health. His recovery was temporary, and by winter he had accepted his fate. In these last months he lay in the front room in his mother's house and with his sister Sophia's help began revising his Maine woods essays. He received a great deal of sympathy and seemed to realize, perhaps for the first time, that his neighbors genuinely cared for him. "He came to feel very differently toward people," George Hoar remarked, "and said if he had known he wouldn't have been so offish." Amid a stream of visitors he worked on the essays. On May 6, 1862, at age forty-four, he died "without pain or struggle . . . his last audible words being 'moose' and 'Indian.'" In a letter to Nathaniel Hawthorne's wife, Mary Mann described his last days as peaceful, leaving his family "so fully possessed of his faith in the Immortal Life that they seemed almost to have entered it with him."[60]

In many ways, Thoreau's literary odyssey began with his death. Neither of his books had circulated widely while he was alive, and the obituaries in the press highlighted his strength of character and skills at plant identification rather than his writing. Locally, he was remembered as a "man of simple tastes, hardy habits, and of preternatural powers of observation," who chose to live "without the least ambition to be rich, or to be popular, and almost without sympathy in any of the common motives of men around him."[61] Thus his reputation stood in 1862.

He was fortunate, however, in having left behind devoted friends conversant with the literary world and a mountain of unpublished manuscripts—a near lifetime of thoughts on nature, individuality, and the state.

Over the next half century, this legacy fueled an ongoing and vigorous stream of commentary as his manuscripts were published, reviewed, and interpreted. But despite his growing recognition, he remained, as this brief biography suggests, an enigma. His unorthodox but suggestive life choices and his provocative literary legacy left biographers and critics without firm footing. "And so we have Thoreau in one after another Protean disguise," literary historian Ethel Seybold wrote as late as 1951, "Thoreau the hermit; Thoreau the naturalist; Thoreau the scholar, student of the classics, of oriental lore, of New England legend and history, of the life of the North American Indian; Thoreau the primitivist, the 'apostle of the wild'; Thoreau the man of letters, writer of perfect prose; even Thoreau the walker." Each of these guises was fostered by a scholar or critic who believed that in the welter of contradiction there lurked an essential Thoreau, and finding him became the holy grail of Thoreau scholarship—one of the great quests of American literature.[62] After a century and a half of criticism, it is safe to say that this essential Thoreau is knowable only in the context of the time in which he is read.

But despite these conflicting incarnations, perhaps the critics and scholars are right. Thoreau loved nature, and in nature he discovered his true self, and this was the lodestone that drew together all the seemingly contradictory impressions of the man. According to Daniel Mason, Thoreau trusted the insights that came to him through nature, and he was rewarded with an extraordinary ability to communicate these intimations to others. "He was as fresh and happy as the morning he walked through; as brave and gallant as the dawn-heralding chanticleer, whose song he celebrated." Knowing nature, he knew himself; knowing himself, he knew nature. This was the essential Thoreau, and this was the quality that made him a bellwether of America's search for the meaning of nature.[63] This is how we shall assess the strange and meandering legacy of his life and writing in the decades after May 6, 1862.

CHAPTER 2

THOREAU IN THE AGE OF INDUSTRY, 1862–1890

In February 1862 Bronson Alcott, having spent the night with the ailing Henry Thoreau, wrote Daniel Ricketson that their mutual friend was growing "feebler day by day." Anticipating the loss that would come in just three months, Alcott eulogized his friend as "the most . . . wonderful worthy of his time"—an extravagant claim that raises two questions. First, why were acquaintances like Alcott and Ricketson so adamant about Thoreau's greatness? Other authors gained champions after their death, but Thoreau, as a commentator put it, "became the property of a cult," officiated by a cadre of friends who were "sensitive to every slight upon their Henry, and determined to make his name prevail."[1] Alcott's eulogy hinted at the near deification that inspired this small group of defenders, who in the decades to come would play a major role in resurrecting Thoreau from the obscurity that closed in over his grave in spring 1862.

Equally puzzling is the fact that so few outside this Concord cult showed a similar confidence in Thoreau. In 1864, just two years after his death, Moncure Conway wrote an essay titled "The Transcendentalists of Concord" in which he recounted a walk with Emerson to the shores of Walden Pond, a setting, as Conway mused, that had inspired more poetry than any place of comparable size on earth. Standing on the shore, the two men discussed Thomas Carlyle, Theodore Parker, and Louis Agassiz but curiously gave little or no thought to the poet who had so recently made his home in the nearby woods. In Conway's mind, it was Emerson who gave Walden its mystical associations. A half century later, a *Boston Transcript* correspondent approached a number of bathers at the pond and discovered that Thoreau was virtually unknown at this epicenter of his reputation. "I met in each instance with uncomprehending glances, and replies that plainly revealed the ignorance of the bathers concerning the Concord writer." "So he was allowed to die quietly as he had lived," Charles Adams wrote in the *Yale Literary Magazine* in 1865, and this, to the broader public, seemed to be the end of things. He had been an Emersonian at the "very heyday of Transcendentalism" and an abolitionist at the apogee of the antislavery crusade; that he failed to connect with the reading public on either account boded poorly for his reputation postmortem.[2]

In part, this was Thoreau's own doing. He had no taste for fame, a critic observed, being a "kind of scribbling Timon, who, disgusted with men, had abandoned human society, and taken to the woods." He dressed in drab clothing in order to meld into nature, and in so doing he faded from society. He made no attempt to promote a coherent creed, and for this reason his lectures and essays failed to build on one another. They would, some thought, be plundered for epithets but never elevate him to the rank of philosopher. And as Thomas Wentworth Higginson delicately put it, he had none of the "personal charm" that might have carried his reputation beyond the bounds of Concord. "We find it difficult to separate his traits as an author from his qualities as a man," one critic noted a year after his death. Terms like *egotistical, cynical, misanthropic,* and *solitary* appeared in the press whenever a new Thoreau book was released.[3]

Thoreau's approach to religion marred his reputation as well. Most natural historians treaded lightly around biblical interpretations of divine creation, but Thoreau seemed oblivious to the delicacy of this issue, and indeed he flaunted his iconoclasm. "I have no sympathy with the bigotry and ignorance which make . . . puerile distinctions between one man's faith . . . and another's," he wrote. This troubled readers, as did his fascination with pantheism and Eastern religion. "That such a book as this has been written and published in the vicinity of Boston, is a fact to be pondered," one amazed reviewer asserted. Even his nature writing seemed irreligious. "Bald in comparison with the glowing word-painting of many lovers of Nature," his prose seemed a denial of nature's sublimity.[4] On top of that, the decades after his death brought a series of devastating retrospectives of his life and work by some of the most respected critics of the day—significant at a time when his reputation was at best still formative. And finally, Thoreau's obscurity was attributable to an unreceptive cultural milieu. In an age of industrial ascent, material progress seemed vastly more important than the ideals he espoused.

In the course of events, however, the world would come to view Thoreau as the most wonderful worthy of his time. When Ticknor & Fields published an anthology of his essays in 1863, the *New York Times* predicted that this was "probably the last relics that the world will receive of Henry D. Thoreau," but within a few years five more volumes reached the public, and Alcott declared confidently that the unpublished manuscripts contained material "for as many more." In fact, five more did appear over the next three decades, along with four biographies issued in America and two in England. Coincident with the rise of American literature itself as an academic discipline, *Walden* assumed full canonical status at the turn of the century and went on to become a world classic, perhaps the most popular book in American literature.[5]

How did this happen, and what does it tell us about the idea of nature in America? In his 1939 biography, Henry Canby argued that Thoreau's reputation grew steadily simply because the brilliance of his prose broke through the crust of unjustified criticism. In a sense he was correct, not so much because Thoreau's writing had irrepressible literary appeal but because cultural currents were aligning: in many ways, Americans' enthusiasm for industrial capitalism stood in dialectical opposition to their reverence for nature, and by the mid-1880s the luster of the former had been tarnished by a series of labor uprisings, titanic economic mergers, and deep-set financial panics. Americans, as Alexandra Krastin put it, "began to realize that the machine age had brought with it some unforeseen repercussions." Ambivalent about their new economy, Americans turned to nature for relief. This shift triggered a revival of interest in Thoreau that no one, not even his closest friends, could have predicted or orchestrated.[6] This chapter explores the complicated interaction between Thoreau's ascendancy and the changing cultural milieu in the later nineteenth century and the way this ascendancy reflects the changing place of nature in America.

Literary Assassination

Surprisingly, it was Thoreau's mentor, Ralph Waldo Emerson, who set the tone for this first generation of unsympathetic critics. At the apex of his career as America's leading literary authority, Emerson delivered a eulogy at Thoreau's graveside in 1862 and published it in the *Atlantic Monthly*, and the following year he composed a biographical sketch to accompany the anthology issued by Ticknor & Fields. Emerson had never been wholly comfortable with his protégé's literary style. "The trick of his rhetoric is soon learned," he wrote in his journal. "It consists of substituting for the obvious word & thought its diametrical antagonist. He praises wild mountains & winter forests for the domestic air; snow & ice for their warmth; villagers & wood choppers for their urbanity and the wilderness for resembling Rome & Paris. . . . It makes me nervous & wretched to read it, with all its merits." In his correspondence, Emerson communicated this point of view to others, and in his biographical sketch he again drew attention to the ironic reversals that "defaced" Thoreau's writing.[7]

Nor was he comfortable with Thoreau's personality. "It seemed as if his first instinct on hearing a proposition was to controvert it, so impatient was he of the limitations of our daily thought. This habit, of course, is a little chilling to the social affections." More directly, Emerson criticized Thoreau's aloofness. With the nation plunged into civil war, the solitary life seemed, in retrospect, irresponsible. "Bred to no profession," Emerson wrote, "he never married; he lived alone; he never went to church; he never voted; he refused to pay a tax to the State; he ate no flesh, he drank no wine, he never knew the use of tobacco." He was, Emerson concluded, a mere "bachelor of thought and Nature" who failed to live up to his intellectual potential. "I so much regret the loss of his rare powers of action, that I cannot help counting it a fault in him that he had no ambition. Wanting this, instead of engineering for all America, he was the captain of a huckleberry-party." These words, spoken by someone perceived to be Thoreau's closest friend, spread through the press at a point where Emerson might have dwelled with greater enthusiasm on his young disciple's literary contribution. A *New York Times* editor noted Emerson's eulogy and drew his own conclusion that Thoreau was "a strange elfish creature—'King of the Gypsies,' as Emerson was wont to call him—shutting himself out from human concourse and sympathies, and holding weird revels with birds and beasts, fishes and flowers, in preference."[8]

Emerson damaged Thoreau's reputation in a less obvious way as well. In 1864 he compiled a selection of Thoreau's letters for Ticknor & Fields as a sampling of classical thought in America and a reflection of the writer he had wanted Thoreau to be. But as Thoreau's friend and biographer Franklin Sanborn later remarked, Thoreau's correspondence on the whole was "much more affectionate, and less pugnacious than would appear from the published volume." Sophia Thoreau persuaded Fields to insert a few domestic letters in the collection, but the compilation nevertheless confirmed public impressions that there was "no trace of emotion" in Thoreau's personality. Higginson, who reviewed *Letters to Various Persons,* complained of the lack of "private history" in the selections and of the fact that Emerson included so little of Thoreau's "beloved science of Natural History." Others saw in the correspondence only what they expected from Thoreau: wise thoughts "mixed up with the queerest and oddest conceits" and satire with a "more or less an eccentric twist." But with transcendentalism and nature appreciation on the wane, the letters contributed to the impression that Emerson's disciple "belonged to another era."[9]

If Emerson damned with faint praise, James Russell Lowell, an equally renowned critic, was openly hostile. In 1865 Lowell picked up the seven volumes of Thoreau's work then in print and published a retrospective in the *North American Review,* a journal he edited. He began by applauding those writers in Thoreau's generation who cast off the burden of European tradition. It was not until "Emerson cut the cable and gave us a chance at the dangers and glories of blue water" that American belles lettres flourished. Lowell then offered a few words of praise for the imagery Thoreau crafted to advance this literary liberation. An essayist himself, Lowell considered his subject a formidable stylist in the American tradition of pure, simple presentation. But this brought him to a critique common among early reviewers: there was no philosophical continuity in these brilliant stylistic flourishes. The phrases and sentences, so elegantly crafted in their own right, failed to connect. Thoreau's flashes of insight gave the reader "the feeling of a sky full of stars,—something impressive and exhilarating certainly, something high overhead and freckled thickly with spots of isolated brightness; but whether these have any mutual relation with each other, or have any concern with our mundane matters, is for the most part matter of conjecture."[10]

Where it was discernible, Thoreau's message was unconvincing. As an exercise in self-reliance, the Walden experiment was, in Lowell's eyes, a hoax: he "squatted on another man's land; he borrows an axe; his boards, his nails, his bricks, his mortar, his books, his lamp, his fish-hooks, his plough, his hoe, all turn state's evidence against him." *Walden* merely glorified Thoreau's own failures. "Was he poor, money was an unmixed evil. Did his life seem a selfish one, he condemns doing good as one of the weakest of superstitions." And finally, Thoreau's natural history was nothing more than pretension. "He thought everything a discovery of his own, from moonlight to the planting of acorns and nuts by squirrels."[11]

The reason for Lowell's animus is important, first because the review had a profound effect on subsequent criticism, and second because it illustrates the vast differences between Thoreau's work and the midcentury literary mainstream that Lowell so brilliantly represented. Most biographers attribute Lowell's tone to an 1858 incident involving an essay Thoreau published in *Atlantic Monthly,* also edited for a time by Lowell. Describing a pine rising up out of the Maine woods, Thoreau wrote that it was "as immortal as I am, and perchance will go to as high a heaven, there to tower above me still." Lowell found the passage impious and struck it out. This prompted an angry response from the author, and there is reason to believe this influenced Lowell's opinion of Thoreau. The two had been on friendly terms at Harvard, and Lowell's review of *A Week on the Concord and Merrimack Rivers* in 1849 suggests that early on he thought highly of Thoreau's writing. The editing incident seems to have soured this relation, and given Lowell's stature as a literary critic, his revenge was sweet.[12]

In the background, however, were more fundamental differences that suggest Thoreau's dissonant relation to midcentury cultural trends generally. At Harvard Lowell had been a young literary radical aspiring to break free of Calvinist norms and embrace a more cosmopolitan literary world. The journal *Anthology,* first published in 1804, encouraged writers like this, and the *North American Review,* founded in 1815 as its successor, continued to explore secular literary topics. But by the time Lowell became editor, the journal had become a bulwark of propriety and a hedge against freethinking philosophies such as those espoused in Concord. As a member of the Boston elite and a Harvard professor of modern languages, Lowell "stood like a colossus bestriding the narrow world of criticism" and had "no compunctions about advertising his aristocratic views." America, in his opinion, had transcended its boorish frontier origins after two centuries of settlement and had entered the court of world civilizations. Thoreau's celebration of simplicity and his "life in the woods" struck at the heart of this genteel complacency. As Townsend Scudder wrote, Thoreau "stamped on the corns of worthy, public-spirited, philanthropic, hard-working, respectable men," and none represented this class more forcefully than James Russell Lowell.[13]

Lowell was also signatory to a subtle rivalry between Harvard academics and Concord transcendentalists that hinged in good part on the latter's celebration of nature's divinity. In 1838, during his last year at Harvard, he had been suspended for several months for failing to conform to the prescribed curriculum, and his parents sent him to Concord to "rusticate." Lowell was "philosophically slothful," as a later scholar put it, and understood very little of what the Concord transcendentalists wrote. Although more secular than the Harvard divines who vilified Emerson, he distrusted the transcendentalists' revolt against convention and their emphasis on nature. In his critique of Thoreau, he wrote, "We look upon a great deal of the modern sentimentalism about Nature as a mark of disease." His dismissive phrases were repeated in the press, underscoring a general understanding that simple descriptions of nature were unacceptable in genteel literary circles. With the publication of Lowell's 1865 essay, "the pattern was set," Lewis Leary wrote nearly a century later. Thoreau had become, in the eyes of the critics, "an eccentric, antisocial, a hermit, good perhaps as a diarist of woods and stream, but hardly to be taken seriously."[14]

Following on the heels of Lowell's essay, Unitarian minister and literary critic William Rounseville Alger reviewed Thoreau's published works in a curious book titled *The Solitudes of Nature and of Man*. Like Lowell, Alger had been kinder to Thoreau while the latter was alive. In an earlier essay on friendship, Alger quoted him at length, claiming that his commentary on this subject in *A Week on the Concord and Merrimack Rivers* was "a composition which every one enamored of the theme should peruse and ponder." Ten years later, in 1866, Alger wrote in the *Monthly Religious Magazine* that Thoreau's friendships were in fact "few and feeble" and his expressions of disgust for humanity legion. In *Solitudes*, published that same year, Alger, like Lowell, discredited Thoreau's nature writing, but where Lowell's scorn was veiled, Alger's was unmistakable. "Few persons have cherished a more preposterous idea of self than Thoreau. . . . This poisonous sleet of scorn, blowing manward, is partly an exaggerated rhetoric; partly, the revenge he takes on men for not being what he wants them to be; partly, an expression of his unappreciated soul reacting in defensive contempt, to keep him from sinking below his own estimate of his deserts." Playing on fresh memories of the Civil War, Alger pointed to a satire in *Walden* detailing a battle between red and black ants. What might have been a clever metaphor suggesting the transience of current events became an inexcusable slight to America's wartime sacrifice. Whether motivated by religious, cultural, or personal animus, Alter's message was clear: Thoreau's preference for nature over society amounted to a "scornful depreciation of others."[15]

A fourth challenge to Thoreau's reputation came in 1880 from Robert

Louis Stevenson, writing in London's *Cornhill Magazine.* Unlike Lowell and Alger, Stevenson endorsed Thoreau's life in the woods. As Emerson said, he "pulled the woodchuck out of its hole by the tail; the hunted fox came to him for protection; wild squirrels have been seen to nestle in his waistcoat." Still, the Walden recluse failed to measure up to the Scots writer's standards. His relation to nature was a matter of "womanish solicitude" rather than outdoor adventure. "There is apt to be something unmanly, something almost dastardly, in a life that does not move with dash and freedom, and that fears the bracing contact of the world." The Walden experiment might have been an affirmation of the American pioneering spirit—"a man's work"—but instead Thoreau wasted his time befriending animals.[16]

Stevenson's critique, published in 1880, shows the lasting influence of Emerson and Lowell, but it also hinted at a change in the idea of nature in the closing decades of the century. For critics informed by Emerson, Lowell, and Alger, nature held no magic as a literary form. In 1880, however, there were signs of change. Late-Victorian Americans, too young to have participated in the westward movement or the Civil War, were ready to view the Walden experiment not as a desertion from duty but a test of self-reliance and reaffirmation of manhood. Although Stevenson's essay was easily as caustic as those of Lowell and Alger, it suggests that the concern over Thoreau's retreat into nature seemed less odious.[17]

Thoreau in the Machine Age

These retrospectives were the product of personal motives, but they were also coincident with larger cultural and economic factors. The carnage on the battlefields of the Civil War suggested an unfathomable savagery latent in American civilization, nurtured, perhaps, in the long confrontation with raw nature in a wilderness setting. In the midst of the horrifying reports of death and destruction at Shiloh, Antietam, and Fredericksburg, the *Atlantic Monthly* published Thoreau's "Autumnal Tints," a celebration of nature in New England. A *New York Times* review of the essay began by praising the richness of Thoreau's imagery but quickly turned satirical: "'King of the Gypsies' he was called while he lived, the forest was his home, and birds and herbs his most familiar companions. He was on talking terms with oaks. The aspen forgot to tremble in his presence, the mimosa to shrink at his approach." A few years later, a Portland editor reacted similarly to Thoreau's writings: they "relate chiefly to Nature and its objects, [and] . . . to his own crooked phylosophy [sic] of life and such things." The dismissive tone in reviews like these underscores the war's effect on nature-related imagery, and in this context Thoreau's life of "simple savagery" in the Walden woods was singularly unappealing. His Puritan forebears held to the idea that too much raw nature coarsened the soul. Midcentury romantics overturned this notion, but after the Civil War the old coin of Puritan antiprimitivism again gained currency. As John Burroughs said a half century later, Thoreau's "sudden plunge into the great ocean of primal energies . . . gave readers . . . a chill from which they are still sneezing."[18]

The reform spirit that animated so much of Thoreau's writing had dissipated as well. The Civil War ended the nation's great national ignominy, and those looking for meaning in the great battlefield catharsis wanted to believe that the nation had been finally and conclusively cleansed. The idea of perfecting existing social institutions gave way before an alternative vision: the spectacle of industrial progress. From this vantage, Thoreau's pronouncements on slavery, society, and government seemed all too impatient and imperious. Nor was transcendentalism in the air. Preoccupied with industrial growth and westward expansion, Americans had become less pietistic and idealistic, putting their faith not in the power of ideas but in the idea of power. "In a society that regarded chaos as natural, that made greed a virtue, that placed financial achievement before personal integrity, culture was not likely to flourish," the literary historian Granville Hicks wrote. In 1888 Oliver Wendell Holmes pronounced his era's judgment on transcendentalism: there had been "too much talk about earnestness and too little real work done." The Concord philosophers lacked commitment to "the common duties of life"—a charge easily laid on Thoreau's doorstep.[19] Industrializing America had little time for *Walden*'s relentless criticism of material values and still less for a self-proclaimed idler. Larger factories, faster locomotives, and new industrial technologies quickened the flow of material goods, and the rise of commercial advertising encouraged consumers to express themselves through acquisitions. The nation, as Alexandra Krastin wrote in *Saturday Evening Post*, was "lusty and growing" and "hardly in the mood for a pungent philosophy extolling the unfathomed richness of a simple life."[20]

In the midst of the Industrial Revolution, the transcendentalist faith in individual salvation dissipated. The words in Emerson's essay on self-reliance— "trust thyself: every heart vibrates to that iron string"—had captured the mood of a post-Puritan age grounded in the inestimable worth of each individual soul, but they seemed vaguely threatening in a society where people marched to the rhythm of the machine. Holmes expressed these subtle reservations: "It may well be imagined that when Emerson proclaimed the new doctrine . . . to his young disciples . . . of . . . trusting to intuition, . . . without reference to any other authority, he opened the door to extravagances in any unbalanced minds, if such there were, which listened to his teachings." Emerson's commitment to self-reliance echoed the individualism of the pioneering West, and with the saga of manifest destiny drawing to a close, Americans were thinking of themselves as a society rather than an aggregation. "We are all linked together," E. C. Gale wrote in the *Yale Literary Magazine.* "Man and man, nation and nation, by bonds indissoluble, although invisible. It is madness to attempt to stand alone." Industrial discipline, trade union organization, and partisan politics all seemed to bear out the need to be part of something larger. One Thoreau was admirable a *New York Times* critic observed; a nation of Thoreaus would mean "a return to the habits of his favorite Indians."[21]

Industrial capitalism stripped the idea of individualism of its dangerous antinomian implications and transformed it into a philosophy of business self-promotion, synonymous with speculative boldness, unabashed opportunism, and shrewd competition. At a personal level, the new industrial economy demanded self-discipline rather than self-reliance, and middle-class families read this into their strictures on good manners, hard work, and suppressed self-gratification. Evangelical preachers delivered the same message to working-class families, raising sobriety, punctuality, responsibility, and respect for property to the rank of high virtues. Temperance, which had strong roots in the 1840s reform ferment, became more than a crusade against rum; it was, as Daniel Walker Howe notes, a "new secular code of conduct promoted by the market place and practiced by people in their everyday lives."[22]

Thoreau's prose style, like his thoughts on individualism, seemed outmoded in the postbellum world. Granville Hicks summarized the heady renaissance spirit that energized Thoreau's writing in the 1850s:

> Emerson had hacked away at Puritanism, slashing off this and salvaging that, tempering what remained at the forge of German idealism, until the very essence of Protestantism stood forth hard and sharp and bright in his essays. Thoreau had stripped from the pioneer spirit the husks of materialism, reducing it to an inexorable demand for independence of soul. Hawthorne, brooding over the consequences of pride and isolation, had conceived darkly beautiful allegories of sin and death. Melville had found in the harsh reality of Nantucket whalers and navy frigates a vision of the undying struggle against cosmic evil.[23]

By the 1870s American writers had settled into a new role as genteel entertainers bent on sentimentalizing social problems and, according to Hicks, sheltering readers "from sordid contacts with the facts of the fierce industrial struggle." These tastes would change again with the appearance of literary realists like Mark Twain, William Dean Howells, Rebecca Harding Davis, and Bret Harte, but the hallmark of the 1870s was gentility, erudition, abstraction, circumlocution, euphemism, and a predictable message that reassured more than it aroused. In this climate Thoreau's sparse but heavily loaded phrasing seemed, as Canby put it, "too staccato, . . . and his subjects too homely." Henry James, literary spokesman for the age, considered Thoreau's prose to be "imperfect, unfinished, inartistic; . . . [and] only at his best . . . readable." Middle-class readers "cared for truth," Daniel Gregory Mason wrote in 1897, "but they preferred the comfortable variety; and this lightening bolt, trying to purify the air, gave them a headache." Thoreau pestered more than he reassured.[24]

In this new social climate, the essays on nature and society issued posthumously by Ticknor and Fields met a somewhat cold reception. *Cape Cod*, published in 1865, won a number of favorable reviews praising Thoreau's freshness, but they did little to change the overall impression that he despised society, and *A Yankee in Canada,* published a year later, again generated mixed reviews. When *Anti-slavery and Reform Papers* appeared, also in 1866, Alcott wrote in his diary that the essays would "come at the fitting moment and be widely read," but in fact the message only confirmed Thoreau's reputation for cynicism. His stirring memorialization of John Brown, his antigovernment pronouncements, and his personal secession from the commonwealth ran counter to the longing for reconciliation between North and South and solidified the impression that he was too doctrinaire for the more pragmatic and chastened postwar mood. For these and many other reasons, the 1870s was a low point in Thoreau's reputation as a writer.[25]

Resurrection

The weight of the 1870s cultural milieu pressed on Thoreau's literary record, but there were countervailing forces that kept him in the limelight, if not as a literary genius, at least as a fascinating study in one man's relation to nature. Although very few of the eulogies that followed his death in 1862 celebrated his genius as a writer, they suggest a lingering fascination with his character.

He "lived and died in that little New England town," according to one, "a puzzle to those around him while alive, an object of rather confused encomium, now that he is dead." Although evasive about his literary merit, these memorials carried the seeds of a kinder reception. "Thoreau was the most thorough child of nature which our age has produced," the *Boston Recorder* reported in 1863. "Every thing he wrote has the scent of the wild woods." Thomas Wentworth Higginson found his departed friend's most endearing trait to be "his veneration for every little songster of the wood." In celebrating this sense of compassion, the eulogies anticipated the manner in which Thoreau's reputation would be resurrected in the coming decades.[26]

Thoreau's relation to nature would be the basis of this resurrection, but it was brought on in part by the fact that even though he published little in his lifetime, he wrote a great deal. Shortly before he died, Thoreau gave his unpublished manuscripts to his younger sister, Sophia, who took this as a mission to bring them to the attention of the world. Sophia's accomplices in this project were Alcott, Emerson, and James T. Fields, junior editor of the Boston firm Ticknor & Fields. As Robert Sattelmeyer points out, Thoreau "enjoyed the good will of two of America's most enterprising figures in literary publishing and promoting": Fields as his publisher and Horace Greeley of New York as his informal literary agent. With encouragement from Fields, Greeley, Alcott, Channing, and Emerson, Sophia prepared *Excursions* in 1863, containing several of his Concord essays, along with *Maine Woods* and *Cape Cod* in 1864, *Yankee in Canada* in 1865, and *Anti-slavery and Reform Papers* in 1866. Fields reissued *Walden* shortly after Thoreau's death, and in 1871 he purchased the remaining copies of *A Week on the Concord and Merrimack Rivers* from Sophia, removed the title page bearing the Munroe imprint, and replaced it with his own, listing it as a second edition. In the 1880s excerpts from Thoreau's journal began appearing under the imprint of Fields's successor, Houghton Mifflin.[27] This amazing stream of new works in print suggests the decisive role of Thoreau's friends and publishers in burnishing his reputation, but again each successive publication saw light in a popular culture more receptive to nature writing. Each prompted another round of critical appraisal, and each moved Thoreau closer to the center of a growing national discussion of the importance of nature to American civilization.

Thoreau's first popular endorsement came not in America but in England, a country with a tradition of nature writing dating back at least to Gilbert White's 1789 *Natural History and Antiquities of Selborne*. Thoreau's descriptions of Concord were heavily influenced by British romantics like William Gilpin and William Wordsworth, and these affinities resonated with readers in that country. Author George Eliot, who used pastoral settings in her novels, introduced Thoreau to British readers in 1856 with an announcement in *Westminster Review* identifying *Walden* as a "bit of pure American life." Other reviews followed, stressing Thoreau's characteristically American independence and portraying him as "a kind of half-wild man of the woods" who confirmed the British readers' disdain for America's materialist bent.[28]

Where Gilpin and Wordsworth wrote about nature mostly for upper-class readers, Thoreau's unadorned style and simple love of nature appealed across class lines. In Thoreau British working people found a set of values that challenged industrial capitalism and offered an alternative to England's machine-dominated culture. Rank and file in the Labour Party, according to Henry Canby, carried copies of *Walden* as pocket pieces "and knew it by heart." He was particularly popular among Christian and Fabian socialists, whose interpretations gave him a modern cast. British socialists saw their country stripped of its virtue by luxury-loving aristocrats and self-satisfied capitalists, and they looked to *Walden* as a vision of living a pure and temperate life free of the compulsions of modern industrialism. In his *England's Ideal*, Edward Carpenter titled a chapter "Simplification of Life," and Robert Blatchford, author of *Merrie England*, praised Thoreau for pointing the way to a more natural society.[29]

America's reluctance to shower similar acclaim on Thoreau inspired his friends to greater efforts. At least since 1863, Bronson Alcott had been planning a reminiscence about the great literary figures he had known in and around Concord, and in 1871 he began holding monthly "parlor conversations" with fashionable Boston folk about these authors. Nearly eighty years old, he used his perspective on literature to rank them according to achievement. Least significant was Oliver Wendell Holmes and just above him James Russell Lowell. Next in Alcott's estimation were Longfellow, Whittier, and Alcott's neighbor Hawthorne. Margaret Fuller was a "coming woman," ranking just below Theodore Parker, and Ellery Channing was near the top of his list—an "almost unknown but a peculiar genius." Next came Thoreau, and at the top of the list, of course, was Emerson. Alcott's recollections drew interest, and this encouraged him to compose a "Book of Characters," as he called it, "just as it fell from his lips, having all the interest of biography with the added conversational charm which biography cannot have." His *Concord Days,* published in 1872, touched on all the writers he had known, but he was especially careful in drawing out the endearing qualities in his friend Henry Thoreau.[30]

Concord Days was forthright. Anxious to establish critical distance even while demonstrating an intimate knowledge of his friend, Alcott wrote that Thoreau was "over-confident by genius, and stiffly individual, dropping society clean out of his theories." Thoreau's preference for nature over society had been a matter of disagreement between them, but Alcott did his best to distinguish this as Thoreau's most enduring literary accomplishment. "His style of thinking was robust, racy, as if Nature herself had built his sentences and seasoned the sense of his paragraphs with her own vigor and salubrity."[31] The praise was heartfelt but hopelessly enmeshed in confusing stylistic constructions. Trained as a poet and Neoplatonic philosopher, Alcott had difficulty mastering the mundane biographical details that supported his defense of Thoreau. As Hawthorne's son Julian observed, "The man couldn't write." His prose was "figurative and epigramatical," according to naturalist Wilson Flagg, and however appropriate this was to poetry, it was not suited for biography. Thoreau, Alcott wrote, was "suffused with an elegiac tenderness, as if the woods and brooks bewailed the absence of their Lycidas, and murmured their griefs meanwhile to one another,—responsive like idyls." *Concord Days* was clearly more supportive than Emerson's eulogy, but it did little to cut through the misconceptions that stood in the way of a more positive reception for Thoreau.[32]

Other intimate biographies followed. Shortly after Thoreau's death, Ellery Channing had confided in Franklin Sanborn that the two of them had been entrusted with "the care of [Thoreau's] immediate fame," and before the end of the century both would write biographies of Thoreau, each as confusing as Alcott's. In 1862 Channing borrowed Thoreau's journal from Alcott and recorded extracts enough to expand his own thoughts on Thoreau into a book-length study. As luck would have it, Sanborn was editing the *Boston Commonwealth* at the time, and in this Channing published his "Life of Thoreau" in weekly installments in 1863–64.[33] Ten years later—a year after *Concord Days* appeared—he published *Thoreau, the Poet-Naturalist: With Memorial Verses.*

Like *Concord Days, Poet-Naturalist* was openly defensive. Chipping away at an image hardened by years of denigration in the press, Channing gave Thoreau a human face. He was not a misanthrope; he simply "claimed the right of choosing his own company, wherein he differed little from other people, save in being more select." The long essay on friendship in *Week* showed that he gave human relations deep and serious thought, and he was affable and even affectionate with his close friends. Aware of the pitfalls in Thoreau's social philosophy, Channing reduced these complex thoughts to a sentimental common denominator: "to live rightly, never to swerve, and to believe that we have in ourselves a drop of the original Goodness besides the well-known deluge of original sin."[34]

Biography was not a well-recognized genre in the 1870s, and in any case the task of redeeming Thoreau was daunting. Like Alcott, Channing was far too disorganized to paint a coherent image of someone this complicated. To render a solitary and event-starved life appealing, he combined his reminiscences of Thoreau with selections from the journal and his own poetic tributes—all tossed together, as a *New York Times* critic put it, "without much apparent reason, except to show that Mr. Channing can write worse verse than prose when he tries." His phrasing, in contrast to Thoreau's own spare and precise constructions, was a blend of affected classical erudition and Victorian sentimentality. As he wrote in one particularly opaque passage, Thoreau's natural history "looked to fabricate an epitome of creation, and give us a homeopathy of nature. . . . Forests whispered loving secrets in his ear. For is not the earth kind?"[35]

The public image of Thoreau as misanthropic was difficult to dislodge, and some reviewers simply selected excerpts from *Poet-Naturalist* that fitted their own preconceptions. "We are unable to find in this memoir, or in Thoreau's books, convincing evidence of that human kindliness which some of his admirers have claimed for him," one wrote. And indeed, Channing's portrait was riddled with ambiguity. A solitary individual himself, he made little effort to explain Thoreau's aloof behavior, and others who knew Thoreau pointed out that Channing actually exaggerated his friend's reclusiveness. Nor was he adept at highlighting Thoreau's nature studies. As a later biographer put it, Channing "served only to emphasize that an age as well as a man was dead."[36]

Yet unlike Lowell, whose essay put words in his victim's mouth, Channing let Thoreau speak for himself. The strategy made sense, given Channing's vastly different writing style. Around three-fifths of *Poet-Naturalist* was made up of quoted matter, the bulk of it from the unpublished journals. "More than most men, Thoreau put himself into his writings," a reviewer explained, "and Mr. Channing, whose power of appreciation we should rate higher than his faculty of expression, has had the art to perceive this at least, and to fashion his work accordingly." In his own voice, Thoreau emerged from the book a compassionate friend of nature and humanity. "One wanders as through a devious woodland path," a reviewer wrote, "wherefrom we emerge with a much better notion, gathered we know not how, of the forest than would ever be obtained in the beaten high road." Thoreau remained an oddity, but his eccentricities at least seemed more human.[37]

Poet-Naturalist also revived a theme introduced earlier by Emerson in his graveside address. "Fishes swam into his hand, and he took them out of the water," Emerson wrote. "He pulled the woodchuck out of its hole by the tail, and took the foxes under his protection from the hunters." Building on impressions of Thoreau as a child of nature, Alcott and Channing stressed their friend's miraculous powers over woodland creatures. Birds, beasts, trees, plants, blossoms, and even reptiles "spoke to him their 'various language,' and found in his pages a faithful and eloquent interpreter." Reviewers, even those skeptical of Thoreau's commitment to humanity, accepted these characterizations. A. D. Anderson wrote in the *Nassau Literary Magazine* that "the first thing to attract our attention is his love for Nature. The birds fluttered about his head as he walked beneath the trees, and the squirrels chattered on as if no human being were near." Shaker spiritualist Leila S. Taylor admired the "strange sympathy [that] drew all animals to him."[38] *Concord Days* and *Poet-Naturalist* aggregated these anecdotes into a new, more romantic image of Thoreau that was beginning to make sense to urban readers pining for the woods their parents or grandparents left behind in moving to the city. The biographies fused Thoreau, Walden Pond, and nature into a single self-reinforcing incarnation, and Americans weary of urban ills and industrial conflict were ready to appreciate this sentimentalized vision.

An early sign that Thoreau's reputation was changing came in 1871, when James Russell Lowell republished his 1865 critical retrospective in an anthology titled *My Study Windows*. The *North American Review* once again deferred to Lowell's "masterly criticism" and predicted that Thoreau's following would "steadily diminish as times goes on," and John Nichol quoted Lowell approvingly in his 1882 *American Literature,* but this time Thoreau defenders were prepared. James Leonard Corning mused that the study windows "must have been a little smoky," and Emerson himself characterized Lowell's critique as foolish and confused. Thomas Wentworth Higginson, speaking with a great deal of personal and literary authority, noted that it was hard "for one who thus knew him to be quite patient with Lowell in what seems almost wanton misrepresentation." Time was "melting away the dross from his writings," Higginson reasoned, leaving his literary legacy secure. "Indeed, it has already survived two of the greatest dangers that can beset reputation,—a brilliant satirist for a critic, and an injudicious friend for a biographer."[39]

The opinions voiced by Emerson and Higginson might have had some effect on Lowell. In 1885, shortly after Emerson's death, he returned to Concord to deliver a lecture on the 250th anniversary of the town's founding. Standing in the place where he had been "bound out" during his Harvard years, he commented on the town's literary legacy. Unable to dismiss Thoreau on this celebratory occasion, Lowell at last raised the Concord naturalist to the level of Emerson and Hawthorne: "If we have stars enough—which I sometimes doubt—to make a whole constellation . . . , then we have in these men of Concord, those three eminent stars which make the belt of Orion."[40]

Concord and the Colonial Revival

It would be convenient to say that Thoreau's friends understood the waning influence of transcendentalism and reinvented Thoreau as a sentimental nature writer. But extracting his reputation from the morass of negative commentary was more complicated than that. The defensive posture in these biographies resulted in "two Thoreaus," as a critic put it, "one that of his admirers, and the other that of his detractors." Some considered him an ascetic and others a selfish epicurean; some found him lazy and others a font of energy. Fellow Harvard classmate John Weiss described him as "repellent, cold, and unamiable," while Thomas Wentworth Higginson remembered him as "guided by a fine instinct of courtesy." Some came away from his writing spiritually uplifted and others convinced he was a heretic. In Emerson's eyes he was a practical failure, but to others he was a prophet of successful living. Whether he would become a giant among American writers or disappear into the underworld of scholarly footnotes was still an unsettled question.[41]

New cultural developments in the closing decades of the century helped bring Thoreau's qualities as a writer into focus. Among these was a cultural movement called the Colonial Revival, fashioned around a heightened interest in old-time architecture, furniture, decor, and lifeways. Although it is difficult to pinpoint the causes of this complex cultural form, it likely originated as a nostalgic reaction to the social disorder of the late nineteenth century. The 1880s brought economic depression, widespread political corruption, working-class upheavals, and an unprecedented influx of European immigrants, all of which shook the confidence of the northeastern

Anglo-American establishment. This in turn triggered a wistful longing for an earlier and more bucolic era. Church steeples, village greens, and meadows fringed with stone walls—places where "every body knows his neighbor and his neighbor's neighbor"—became comforting images against a backdrop of rapid urbanization and demographic change.[42]

With the coming of the nation's centennial in 1876, Concord assumed particular importance in the Colonial Revival. The "rude bridge that arched the flood," immortalized by Emerson, had long since disappeared, but neighbors planted an avenue of pines along the road to the site, adding to the suggestion of a shrine, and in 1875 the town commissioned a Minute Man statue from its own Daniel Chester French, a nationally known sculptor. Visitors streamed into town to stand at the place where New England farmers touched off the War for Independence, and in this and subsequent years locals reenacted the battle to the cheers of onlookers.[43]

A mere eddy in the tide of industrial progress, the Colonial Revival nevertheless offered an opportunity to express misgivings about modernity in culturally approved ways. Harriet Mulford Lothrop, writing in 1888, noted with regret that Concord's colonial meetinghouse had given way to a block of commercial buildings, and other writers simply ignored the town's business economy. In fact, by this time literary tourism had indeed become the town's business. Thousands of visitors each year traced the footsteps of America's literary greats in a pilgrimage that invariably ended at the Authors Ridge in Sleepy Hollow Cemetery. With luck, the "literary prowler" would chance into a conversation with someone who had known one or more of these prominent figures—perhaps even an aging Franklin Sanborn, Bronson Alcott, or Ellery Channing.[44]

Thoreau had spent a lifetime romanticizing the Concord countryside, and his work featured prominently in this new tourist economy. The family home had become an elegant hotel, and local shops carried an inventory of Thoreau memorabilia—plates, inkstands, pen-and-ink portraits, paper cutouts, and sketches of the hut. In light of this, local recollections softened. "Most of Thoreau's towns-people remember him as a serious, blue-eyed, strong-featured man, whom they met occasionally on the streets, or here and there in the woodlands, or on the river," Hannah Hudson wrote in *Harper's* in 1875. He was enigmatic and "possibly a little brusque in manner and language" but nevertheless an American genius. In his *New England in Letters*, Rufus Rockwell Wilson observed that it was "not Emerson or Hawthorne, but Henry David Thoreau of whom one hears most . . . today." Concord's premodern image and Thoreau's doctrine of simplicity melded into a "corrective to the orgiastic excesses of the Gilded Age," as the historian Gary Scharnhorst put it. Person and place, according to the English biographer Henry Salt, were mutually reinforcing, like the association between Wordsworth and the Lake District, Sir Walter Scott and the Highlands, Robert Burns and the Ayrshire Fields, and Gilbert White and the town of Selborne.[45]

Romancing Walden Pond

Careful campaigning by friends and supporters helped cement this association. To ensure Thoreau a role in the remaking of Concord, Alcott, Channing, Sanborn, and Sophia Thoreau linked his memory to Walden Pond and did their best to render both iconic. Barksdale Maynard, in his history of the pond, suggests that it was already considered sacred as early as 1863. While this may be true, it discounts the protracted efforts by Thoreau's friends to cement the connection between person and pond. As late as 1896, Philip Hubert recalled traveling past Walden by rail with an "intelligent-looking fellow passenger" from North Acton who expressed complete ignorance of the pond's literary significance. "Such is fame, or, at all events, Thoreau's fame," Hubert concluded. "Its trump is not heard more than six miles away." In Hubert's sample of one, Walden was just another pond, but elsewhere there were signs that the waters of Walden, as Maynard indicates, were becoming sacred.[46]

Alcott and Channing were doing their best to accentuate this by regularly guiding pilgrims to the site of the hut. The structure itself had been moved to the bean field before Thoreau died and then moved again to the Brooks Clark farm, farther north. It was finally demolished in 1868 and some of the sheathing used to repair outbuildings. At the pond, trees and brush closed in around the cellar hole. "Abby walks with me to Walden," Alcott wrote in his journal in 1863. "We find the old paths by which I used to visit him from 'Hillside' but the grounds are much overgrown with shrubbery, and the site of the hermitage is almost obliterated." That fall Channing walked with Calvin Greene of Rochester, Michigan, to the site. They searched for the cellar hole but "could not fix it."[47] In June 1872 Alcott and Iowa suffragist Mary Newbury Adams visited Walden and commemorated what they supposed to be the site of the hut with a stone Adams brought up from the pond. Alcott saw this as a fitting tribute to Thoreau, and two years after his visit with

Adams he noted in his journal that he, Sanborn, and Charles Dudley Warner of the *Hartford (CT) Courant* had each contributed to what by this time was a noticeable pile of rocks. "The pyramid is insignificant as yet," he wrote, "but could Thoreau's readers add theirs, the pile would rise above the treetops to mark the site of his hermitage." The path to the site, he noted with satisfaction, "bears the marks of frequent footsteps."[48]

In 1866 the Fitchburg Railroad Company constructed a picnic ground and bathing facility on the west shore of the pond and later added a dance platform, lunch tables, swings, merry-go-rounds, wooden horses, seesaws, shaded seats, a football ground, walking paths, dining and boating facilities, and, according to a newspaper correspondent, "other abominations with which all nature's sanctuaries near our great cities are fast being polluted." Amusement parks like this were a common means of boosting revenue for railroad and street-railway companies, but the public response to the railroad's "Lake Walden" resort was revealing. The *New York Tribune* complained that the pond had "degenerated into a resort for picnic parties" from which "all the privacy and wildness" had been destroyed.[49] Sophia Thoreau wrote to Daniel Ricketson, complaining that "associations have rendered the spot so entirely sacred to me, that the music and dancing, swinging and tilting, seemed like profanity almost," and in 1872 naturalist Wilson Flagg expressed dismay that "assemblages of people" visited the pond not for nature observation but "for ice-creams and soda-water, and for repeating in the country the amusements of the city." In 1900 the dance pavilion burned, and the rest of the facility met a similar fate in 1902.[50]

Walden's reputation as sacred and wild crystallized in the protest over its rising recreational use. As Hubert suggested, its meaning had not yet penetrated the popular consciousness, but among those caught up in the Colonial Revival, its waters had become as sacred as the soils of the Concord battlefield. Literary pilgrims sensed the poet's presence as they walked its shores, and in the nearby woods the leaves "rustled the name of Thoreau." Nature writer Hamilton Mabie saw in the pond a likeness of Thoreau: "One gets an impression of distinct individuality from this little sheet of water," he wrote, "which holds itself apart from the wooded heights that encircle it, and rises and falls by some mysterious law of its own." Like Thoreau's writing, the waters were "so clear that the most delicate forms of ether are reproduced in it."[51] Primeval, pure, hallowed, and mysterious, the consecrated pond lent specificity to Thoreau's aery transcendentalism and symbolized the timelessness of his writing.

The Concord School of Philosophy

The Colonial Revival melded Walden, Concord, and Concord's native son into an elaborate symbolic nexus that benefited Thoreau in ways few other authors could claim. His public image was embellished by yet another development in the last decades of the century: a summer philosophic institute run by Concord intellectuals that drew preceptors and students from all across the country. The idea of a "university" conducted by Boston-area philosophers originated as early as 1840 with Emerson, Alcott, and Thoreau. It came to nothing, but three decades later a Platonist, H. K. Jones, held a series of Socratic conversations in Concord that inspired Alcott to organize a similar program at his Orchard House. With help from Emerson, Blake, Sanborn, and Ednah Dow Cheney, he formed a club in 1879 to study the "diffusion of the ideas and tendencies proper to the nineteenth century." The early meetings were informal, but Sanborn, as the school's business manager, widened the focus and recruited transcendentalists, Hegelians, Platonists, Aristotelians, and pragmatists from around the country to participate in a four-week summer session.[52]

Participants viewed the Concord School of Philosophy as a way of rekindling the embers of transcendentalism and keeping Concord at the center of the nation's intellectual life. Emerson offered a suggestion that "the most will say the least," but among a group of philosophers intent on conveying their rarefied comprehension of the infinite, the injunction was futile. A Worcester journalist noted that much of the discussion was "impossible for an untrained person to follow," but he found a "curious charm in listening to what you don't understand . . . and a great satisfaction in knowing that men have come, by pure thought, to absolute faith in a personal God, and in the immorality of the soul." In 1880, with more than 150 people attending from all points of the country, the school moved to Concord's Second Parish Church, and what had initially been a round of ridicule from the press ripened into expressions of praise for a forum on the "great questions of the human mind." In its third year, it drew five or six hundred women and men, mostly teachers, writers, college professors, and clergymen, and the substance of the discussions was widely reported across the country. The sessions were conducted in a bohemian atmosphere, with an unstated consensus that "philosophy begins and ends with Emerson, and eloquence with Alcott, and the art of the romancer with Hawthorne." In addition, each participant "bows and worships at the shrine of Thoreau."[53]

The Concord School of Philosophy once again drew Thoreau into the cultural limelight. His portrait hung over the classroom, and each year the school featured an "evening devoted to Thoreau and his unpublished manuscripts," during which his old friends Harrison Blake and Franklin Sanborn read from the journal and urged the audience to relive "the spirit of Walden." Among the most popular features in the curriculum, the Thoreau readings were ritual-like, with an appreciative Ralph Waldo Emerson sitting close to the podium. Obtuse metaphysical discussions were set aside as the audience listened to Thoreau's refreshingly direct descriptions of the Concord countryside. The selected passages emphasized his kindness, courtesy, and "acute sense for the rights of others." According to one, this threw "new light, or certainly very unfamiliar light, upon the character of this unique author." His reputation began to grow outward from his close circle of admirers.[54]

Friends and publishers kept Thoreau's reputation alive through sheer force of will in the 1870s, but the 1880s brought a more positive dynamic. Writing in 1882, the naturalist John Burroughs expressed confidence that those who disapproved of Thoreau in Lowell's day would eventually come to appreciate his brilliant, if polarized, perspectives on nature and society. "The world likes a good hater and refuser almost as well as it likes a good lover and acceptor, only it likes him farther off." Charles Abbott, another naturalist, agreed: the world was "growing wiser"—becoming more tolerant—and there was no better evidence of this "than the increase in numbers of those who now ponder as seriously over Thoreau's suggestive pages as they were once entertained by the polished periods of Lowell." Speaking for an age beginning to think differently about society and nature, Abbott cryptically reminded readers that "Lowell is tame, Thoreau is savage." In 1862 this would have been an indictment; in 1895 it was an invitation to follow the Concord naturalist into the "haunts of nature."[55]

Nature and Nature's Icon

That the Concord School of Philosophy readings emphasized Thoreau's nature writing was no accident. Blake and Sanborn sensed that after four decades of industrial expansion, the machine age had lost its power to inspire, and urban dwellers were looking back on the pioneering era with a sense of nostalgia. That the search for Thoreau was taking a new turn was evident in a biography published in London and Boston in 1877 by Alexander Hay Japp, a Scots author writing under the pseudonym H. A. Page. Confused by the conflicting views presented by Lowell, Channing, and Alcott, Japp drew together a variety of sources and pieced them into a "consistent view of the man's character." He offered no new information, but his interpretation was original, and like Channing he used long quotes from Thoreau to support his points.[56]

Japp's *Thoreau: His Life and Aims* was indeed a watershed. It was the first biography written by someone not personally acquainted with Thoreau, and because he was not a member of the Concord cult—not even an American— his perspective seemed more genuine. More important, he was the first to confront the conundrum of Thoreau's binary approach to nature and society. Where others stumbled over Thoreau's polarized opinions, Japp saw them as two sides of the same philosophy. First, it was through nature that Thoreau rekindled his love of mankind after battling the alienating forces of slavery, the state, and the industrial system. Second, Thoreau judged society according to the standards he saw in his natural surroundings. Nature was pure and honest, and he expected the same from humans. Third, Japp saw a strain of socialism running through *Walden* and *Maine Woods*. In studying Native culture, he observed, Thoreau learned that the poorest members of a tribe "enjoyed as good a shelter as the richest, and . . . none were starving while others were in luxury." Industrial society could achieve the same if its products were distributed fairly. While Thoreau was in fact no primitive socialist, Japp's interpretation helped modernize his antimaterialism for an age far different from his own.[57] The biography was even more significant as a capstone to the child-of-nature myth. Thoreau's profound spiritual connection to the woods around him reminded Japp of the medieval monk whose life had been recently and piously recorded in Margaret Oliphant's *Francis of Assisi*. Both men, during their wilderness sequester, realized that all creatures were bound in a common calling. Peace with nature, they taught, was a lost legacy of humanity. Japp quoted Robert Burns's "To a Mouse":

> I'm truly sorry man's dominion
> Has broken Nature's social union,
> And justifies that ill opinion
> Which makes thee startle
> At me, thy poor, earth born companion
> And fellow mortal![58]

In living out this Edenic relation to nature, Thoreau authenticated the life of the saint. The similarities, Japp hoped, would kindle interest in a Christian socialism that embraced both humans and animals.[59]

As with Alcott and Channing, the critical reaction to Japp was uneven. The *North American Review,* even without prompting by Lowell, who retired as editor in 1873, remained convinced that Thoreau's influence would "steadily diminish over time," and J. V. O'Connor ridiculed Japp's comparisons in the *Catholic World.* The saint enjoyed "miraculous power" over animals; Thoreau's claim rested on his "ability to bring a mouse out of its hole or tickle a trout." Others, however, found these comparisons intriguing. William Sharp's article in *Encyclopedia Britannica* endorsed the idea that in Thoreau's presence, beasts, birds, and fishes "forgot their hereditary fear of man." To readers searching for a tangible connection to nature in the postfrontier age, Japp's mutually reinforcing references to Thoreau and Saint Francis—both known for their tender hearts, their austerity, their purity of thought, their singleness of purpose, and their unassuming garb—seemed far more convincing than Lowell's characterization of Thoreau as a cynic and fraud.[60]

Japp's biography appeared at a critical moment. The popularity of antebellum authors like Emerson, Lowell, Alcott, Fuller, and Hawthorne was on the wane, and Thoreau no longer derived status from his association with the American literary renaissance. Japp offered a different perspective on his significance. Comparison to Saint Francis, however fanciful, set the stage for Thoreau's entrance into an emerging field of nature studies that combined, as one reviewer put it, the "eye of the naturalist" and the "mind of the poet." Japp stripped Thoreau's reputation of its transcendental accents and presented him as a childlike prophet of nature. As much as Japp accomplished in unlocking the meaning of Thoreau's social cynicism, it was his comparison to Saint Francis that lodged in the public mind.[61] The child-of-nature myth, formulated by Emerson, Alcott, and Channing and crystallized by Japp, turned Thoreau's reputation in a new direction: the saintlike imagery lingered in subsequent accounts of Thoreau's life.

Publishing the Journal

Another turning point in Thoreau's reputation was the publication of selections from the journal, an achievement brought to fruition once again by Thoreau's friends and defenders. As early as 1863, Alcott had proposed a collected works in seven volumes containing a sampling of journal entries arranged according to morals, politics, letters, and poems. All of this was to be completed "when [Thoreau's] . . . editor appears." Alcott, Emerson,

Channing, and Sanborn each considered editing the journal at one time or another, but rendering this immense body of material—forty-seven manuscript volumes—in a form acceptable to readers was a daunting prospect. Emerson warned that it "would require the combination of a Linnaeus and a poet" to complete the project.[62] In any case, Sophia Thoreau, who held rights to the journal, refused to release it. For these reasons, they lay untouched, first in Alcott's attic and then in the Concord Library, for nearly two decades.

In 1874 Sophia returned briefly from Bangor, having moved there a year earlier, and announced her intention to bequeath the journals to a younger executor. She had been, as Thoreau biographer Henry Canby described her, "fanatical in her desire to carry out what she thought would have been her brother's wishes," and when Channing and Alcott published their own biographies of Thoreau, she took issue with the approach. And so it was to a third friend, Harrison G. O. Blake, that she commended the literary rights. Alcott considered Blake a "fitting person to edit selections from them" but mused privately that the "man may not yet be born suited to accomplish this task in a manner worthy of the author and his subjects."[63]

In 1876 Sophia Thoreau—the last in the family line—died in Bangor and was buried in Concord. The manuscripts were sent to Blake in Worcester, who began cultivating interest by reading passages at the Concord School of Philosophy. Shortly after the 1880 reading, a newspaper correspondent mused that "a fresh volume from the hand of this dead writer would send a thrill of joy throughout the reading world." Having dispensed with an earlier plan for sorting the material by subject, Blake decided on seasons as the organizing principle, as it would emphasize the importance of nature in his work. He pared back the philosophical asides to present Thoreau on his best terms, stressing once again the child-of-nature theme. The entries would bring the reader "into closest contact with nature, making him see its sights, hear its sounds, and feel its very breath upon his cheek." *Early Spring in Massachusetts* appeared in 1881, and *Summer, Winter,* and *Autumn* in 1884, 1887, and 1892. Blake, like Alcott and Channing, had fulfilled his long-standing debt to his deceased friend.[64]

The four volumes were not an ideal platform for overcoming entrenched skepticism. The journal entries were fragmentary, like isolated stars in the firmament, as Lowell said earlier, and the result, a reviewer summarized, was "hardly a systematic or philosophic one." The idea of combining passages from a single season over the course of twenty-four years did violence to Thoreau's original intentions, however obscure these may have been. They highlighted his changing style and perspective, but this was both a strength and a weakness. One reviewer marveled at how little he had matured over these years, while another found it revealing to note the differences in style and tone over time. As Isabella King pointed out in the *Harvard Register,* the entries in the early volumes showed "more plainly the actual contact with mankind, while those of later years evince the closer communions with nature, for the love of which Thoreau withdrew, to so great an extent, from the society of his fellow-men."[65]

Reaction to the volumes highlights the uncertainty about nature in the industrial era. As Blake anticipated, critics acknowledged only those entries that confirmed their own preconceived notions. Thoreau's single-minded devotion to nature, according to one, seemed self-indulgent and "absurdly egotistical," and his refusal to publish the journals himself confirmed his disdain for society. Others found the combination of poetry and science appealing. "He wrote something remarkably pretty about water-lilies, and in the next few lines informed the reader that there are seven varieties of lily pads to be found in the Concord River."[66] The reviews were mixed, but the volumes accomplished a great deal in bringing Thoreau into the public eye. They piqued interest in his innermost thoughts—in the logic behind his sometimes bizarre behavior—and they showed that his character invited not so much condemnation as understanding. Perhaps he was a cynic, a reviewer concluded, but "if we cast aside superficial judgments and look deeper we find that he was something more. There is surely a healthy, sane side to this outwardly repellent nature!" The volumes gave face to a still largely unknown author, and to the surprise of many, the face bore a certain charm. The volumes also gave the child-of-nature myth an aura of authenticity. "The lightning is his candle, the woods are his library, the clouds his pictures, the grass his carpet, the foliage his tapestry, berries are his reflection, the opening and shutting of the flowers mark for him the time of day." The portrait of Thoreau in his natural element helped clarify his reasons for abandoning society.[67]

Publication of the journals brought to light another feature of Thoreau's writing that would become increasingly significant over the years. He had mastered, as one biographer said, the "brief gnomic sentence" that packed "much thought into little room." His terse and often ironic flashes of insight, "sermons in themselves," were classically transcendental, a style he borrowed from Emerson, who used these disconnected thoughts to symbolize the spontaneous expressions of the soul. But they were also convenient capsules of Thoreauvian thought, eminently useful to newspaper editors searching for filler copy. They were as innocuous as they were timeless, valued by editors because they enlightened all readers and offended none. Scattered through the press and across the nation, these sentimentalized insights into nature and human character became building blocks in Thoreau's reputation.[68]

In 1890 Blake selected a series of thoughts on nature to publish as a pocket version of the four volumes. Designed as a "traveling companion" for those on trains or in hotels, it provided a generous sampling of the brand of inspirational aphorism so appealing to late-Victorian readers. Sensing a market in nature-based sentimentalism, Blake claimed they were certain to lift the reader "above the world of care and sadness into that fairer world which is always waiting to receive us." Without bothering to contradict the old notion that Thoreau was a cynic, he wrote that it was his friend's "personal character which gives such power to his words." During the year in which *Selections from the Writings of Henry David Thoreau* was published, Henry Salt observed "quite a carnival of Thoreauism" in the press, stimulated in good part by Blake's efforts.[69] *Walden* went through six American reissues between 1889 and 1902 on its way to becoming a literary classic; Thoreau's collected works were published in 1894 in eleven volumes and his entire corpus, including the journal in its entirety, in 1906.

A Bevy of Biographers

Blake's volumes attracted the interest of several biographers at a critical point in the evolution of Thoreau's reputation. As the *New York Times* pointed out in 1880, "In a few years, the persons who saw most of Thoreau in the flesh will have gone the way of all the earth, and the best things to be said of him by them will then be lost." Most previous critical and biographical studies had been written by those who knew Thoreau, but for this reason they were generally too defensive of their opinions to alter accepted interpretations.[70] In the years after publication of the journals, others tried their hand at chronicling his life, some using firsthand knowledge but others writing from a distanced perspective. Free of the compulsion to challenge or defend Thoreau, these biographers were open to exploring the many ways he fitted the changing mood of late-century America.

The biographies of the 1880s and 1890s were crucial in another sense. They were the first to present Thoreau in light of the new popular appreciation for nature as a counterpoint to a machine-dominated culture that was beginning to seem more oppressive than liberating. The first of these new biographies was Franklin Sanborn's *Henry D. Thoreau*, published in 1882 in Houghton Mifflin's American Men of Letters series. Like earlier biographies written by those who knew Thoreau, the effort suffered from lack of perspective. Perhaps because there were so few dramatic incidents in Thoreau's life, Sanborn packed his biography with disconnected details about "Concord and its famous people" and detoured through a dense thicket of transcendental and utopian thought. He contributed several new anecdotes to the child-of-nature myth, but when it came to the complicated issue of personality, he confused as much as he clarified. Thoreau was cold yet courteous, cynical but also deeply spiritual, withdrawn but forthcoming among friends. He participated in family life, but even around friends he sat stiff and erect and walked with "clenched hands as if deeply intent upon a purpose." A failure at life, he nevertheless offered a vision of successful living. As one reviewer summarized, Sanborn's biography might be "considered as a vindication, a criticism, a eulogy, or a biography," but it was "in no one of these aspects . . . a very successful literary performance." Another reviewer concluded that "as one reads his printed words, and supplements them with such light as his friends throw upon his life, he cannot well escape the idea that in many things Thoreau was a mere wind-bag and a sham."[71]

Still, Sanborn's rambling account helped to humanize Thoreau as only someone who knew him intimately could have done. The reader was treated to a pleasant if erratic tour through the village in the company of "all sorts of Concord people" while awaiting an introduction to Thoreau, who seemed to interact freely and easily with these townspeople. Sanborn also published a selection of letters written while Thoreau was living in the Emerson household, reinforcing the idea that his friend could be charming, domestic, and even gossipy. The correspondence showed, as one reviewer concluded, that "in general, Thoreau's misanthropic bark was much worse than his bite."[72]

In 1890 Henry S. Salt, another British biographer, published *Life of Thoreau*. Clearly the best biography to that date, it was, with the exception of Japp's study, the first written by someone who had not known Thoreau personally. A Christian socialist on familiar terms with George Bernard Shaw and William Morris, Salt was, like many British radicals, intrigued by the ethical implications of Thoreau's principle of simplicity—so intrigued, in fact, that he abandoned his teaching position at Eton, moved to a cottage, and became a disciple of simple living. In his biography, he carefully pared away the decades of criticism, leaving Thoreau less at odds with himself and society. Where Japp compared him to a medieval monk, Salt portrayed him as a modern critic of society. Honing Thoreau's "Civil Disobedience" on the stone of British socialist and trade union ideology, Salt highlighted his description of government as an instrument of oppression. More than any other writer, it was Salt who prepared American readers to think of Thoreau as a critic of capitalism at a time when their passion for industrial progress was waning.[73]

In 1892 Sanborn published a revised edition of his 1882 biography and followed this in 1901 with *Personality of Thoreau*. As the last of Thoreau's intimate acquaintances, he lent his authority one more time to the task of burnishing his friend's image: "I have lived there, off and on, for more than sixty years," he wrote of his home in Concord, "and . . . I have never seen or heard of a more industrious resident. His tasks began before the earliest haymaker or wood-chopper went to his work, and were continued after the latest evening seamstress had set her last stitch." In 1901 Annie Russell Marble released *Thoreau: His Home, Friends and Books,* a classic Colonial Revival piece that wrapped Thoreau in the idyll of Concord country life. By the time Marble wrote, the old shibboleths had been chipped away, leaving readers more intrigued than offended by his "complex nature." Marble made a convincing case that, as British writer Francis Underwood put it, Thoreau's "tender heart for children, woodchucks, ducks, and fishes" was a virtue to be emulated rather than scorned.[74]

In the last decades of the century, Barksdale Maynard noted, "living recollection" yielded to systematic biography, and in the process the old reminiscences, antagonistic or friendly, fell away. Time, like friends, biographers, and publishers, was on Thoreau's side. The legacy of negative criticism lingered, but as Maynard noted, his talents as a writer were beginning to loom larger than his eccentricities as a person. As Horatio Powers wrote in the *Dial,* his cynicism was justified, perhaps, in light of his hatred of slavery, and although he lived free of material possessions, "he was not the fool to think that this course would do for all." He thought highly of himself, but he expressed his egoism honestly and at times humorously. Every good writer, a reviewer reflected, was "more or less of a skulker, or hider of himself," and most were in the habit of "calling a spade a spade." Writing in 1908, Salt proclaimed that "it has taken fifty years to do it, but we are at last beginning to get rid of certain false notions concerning Thoreau by which the minds of his readers have been obsessed."[75]

A Thoreau for Changing Times

The events of the 1880s—the Colonial Revival, the Concord School of Philosophy, the journal publications, the new biographies—provided the circumstances under which Thoreau would become a writer of American classics at the turn of the century. His essays were included in a variety of literary anthologies, and he was on his way to becoming, at least to some, a popular hero. Blake's editions had demonstrated that withdrawing from nature was not an act of cynicism but rather a personal sacrifice that yielded succor for a world burdened by an overbearing industrial system. His literary mission was still not clear—too imprecise to be science and too concrete to be philosophy—but his approach to nature fitted the late-Victorian temper: it was neither rhapsodic, like the images drawn by romantics such as Rousseau and Chateaubriand, nor savage, like the Darwinian struggle so many modern naturalists embraced.[76] Nor did Thoreau's prose seem as unvarnished as it had in the 1870s. During these decades, realism, naturalism, and regionalist literature reinforced the value of spare, vigorous, folksy prose, and this trend gave Thoreau's writing credibility. "The truths of nature quiver in his talk, as color quivers on a chameleon," Donald Mitchell wrote appreciatively in 1899. Likewise, his social criticism resonated with the pessimistic undertones in naturalist and realist novels.[77]

Secularization removed another limitation on Thoreau's reputation. In the 1840s even Emerson, the most gentle of all iconoclasts, had been vilified in the Cambridge-Boston press, and Thoreau, who openly challenged not only Calvinist doctrine but the supremacy of Christianity itself, had come under withering attack. Well into the 1870s his critics condemned the undercurrent of pantheism and Eastern philosophy in his writing, but in the next decade these objections all but disappeared. To late-century critics, Thoreau's passion for nature seemed religion enough. A *Catholic World* correspondent writing in 1878 expressed shock at Thoreau's attitude toward Christianity, but after reading *Week* and *The Maine Woods,* the reviewer found that the "jar and discord of Thoreau's theological opinions melted away in the harmony of the great music which he made us hear among the hills and scenes which he loved so well." In a more tolerant atmosphere, his description of nature loomed larger than his rejection of the church.[78]

In an age marked by political scandal and saddled by bloated corporations, Thoreau's critique of social institutions seemed less troubling than it had in the years after the Civil War. Once considered a solitary cynic standing against the tide of progress, he was joined in the 1880s by a chorus of writers such as Henry Adams, Theodore Dreiser, Frank Norris, and Edith Wharton, whose novels portrayed the demoralizing effects of the new industrial order. Mark Twain and Charles Dudley Warner coined the term *Gilded Age* in 1873 to signify the combination of glitter, greed, materialism, and corruption that characterized their society, and against this backdrop the moral benefits of simple living became clear. S. A. Jones concluded his study of Thoreau with the prediction that "when our latter-day mad race for wealth, only wealth, shall have brought to us the inevitable result . . . , it will be the 'hermit' of Walden, not the Sage of Concord, that will lead them."[79]

In the wake of the Civil War, America was not prepared for the books and essays Thoreau's friends and publishers rushed into print. The devastating critiques by Lowell, Alger, and Stevenson, the waning of the reform impulse, and the fascination with industrial progress diverted them from the satisfactions of a life lived in close communion with nature. By the 1880s, the nation was ready to appreciate Thoreau. In part, this resulted from the persevering efforts of friendly biographers working to repair the damage done by earlier critics. In part, it reflected the mellowing of memory in Concord, as locals found Thoreau an unanticipated boon to the town's tourist economy. But mostly, it came with the vast changes in American culture and society at the end of the century. The Industrial Revolution had distanced the nation from its Arcadian roots. The quiet revere in nature had been eclipsed by the breathtaking vision of a towering Corliss engine thrumming effortlessly astride a giant flywheel or a bustling locomotive traveling at speeds unheard of in the days of horse and wagon. But by the 1880s Americans, for a variety of reasons, were beginning to distance themselves from the machine. An anonymous reviewer in 1888 reflected on Emerson's complaint that Thoreau wasted his considerable engineering talents in conducting huckleberry parties. Perhaps, the reviewer surmised, Thoreau "had undertaken an enterprise more arduous and requiring higher genius than building railways or discovering the North Pole." It had been his mission, the reviewer concluded, to reunite humanity and nature. At the end of the century, critics and biographers were ready to appreciate the audacity—even the necessity—of this cause.[80] Encouraged by a band of dedicated defenders, they welcomed a new writer into the literary galaxy.

CHAPTER 3

THE CULT OF NATURE AND THE AGE OF PROGRESS, 1890–1917

In a December 1899 issue of the *New York Times,* A. S. Clark described a walk he had taken recently from the banks of the Charles River in Boston to the shores of Walden Pond, a classic saunter in the manner of Henry David Thoreau. Pilgrimages like this were familiar newspaper filler at the turn of the century, but Clark included in his narrative of famous landmarks an impression of the nature he encountered along the way. He might have recalled Thoreau's description of Walden Pond in his youth as "completely surrounded by thick and lofty pine and oak woods," but if he anticipated a similar scene, the illusion was dispelled as he walked the path to the pond. The trail was bordered by spindly oak saplings and blackened pine stumps and showed signs of constant use—"the antithesis of those charms which commonly attach to a rural pathway." From the hill above the pond the forest appeared thin and heavily cut, and only a brush-choked clearing marked the spot where trees once shaded Thoreau's hut. Walden Pond was still a "beautiful expanse of water nestling down among the hills," but the ongoing demand for fuel wood and lumber, Clark thought, promised even further desecration. Seventeen years later, Edward Emerson, who had grown up nearby, recorded a similar impression: the forest along the shore had been devastated by fire, gypsy moths, and "rude and reckless visitors," and the shore itself strewn with trash and locomotive cinders.[1]

Others saw the pond differently. In the introduction to a 1910 edition of *Walden,* Clifton Johnson wrote that "the woodland seclusion is almost as complete as it was in Thoreau's time," and Winthrop Packard observed in his 1911 *Literary Pilgrimages of a Naturalist* that it was "much as Thoreau remembered it had been in his boyhood, walled in by dense forests, a place of echoes." The nearby trees, Packard added, need not fear the bite of the woodsman's ax. "The spirit of reverence for its shores . . . should prevent that." C. T. Ramsey found the pond deserted on the day he visited, and the solitude gave the impression of wildness. His pilgrimage, he wrote later, "seemed almost like a dream; for a time I had forgotten the troubled world, and was transported into Elysian fields."[2]

The play of memory, imagination, and evasion in these conflicting interpretations provides a glimpse into the complicated uses of nature at the turn of the century. Americans saw places like Walden Pond as refuges from the rapid pace of modern life, and their anticipations inspired a new class of popular literature dedicated to the natural world. Like Clark and Emerson, writers in this genre understood all too well the need for shielding their Arcadian retreats from a remorselessly materialistic society, and like Johnson and Packard, they were sometimes willing to ignore evidence that society had already enveloped them. These fears and dreams inspired a new way of thinking about America's natural heritage.[3]

In the years between 1900 and World War I, literary scholars accepted Thoreau into the pantheon of American writers, and publishers included him in scores of republications and anthologies. At the same time, he became a symbol of nature in the popular mind. These two standards of judgment were both connected to the emergence of the nature-writing genre. Undiscovered in 1880, he was listed in the *Cambridge History of American Literature* among America's great authors in 1917, and over the next half century *Walden* became a model for countless popular stories of withdrawal and rediscovery, including such classics as Aldo Leopold's *Sand County Almanac* and Henry Beston's *Outermost House.*[4] A literary revival like this is unusual. Typically, writers' reputations diminish over the years, as critics and scholars turn to more contemporary authors addressing more contemporary issues. Buoyed by the surge in nature writing, Thoreau gained rather than lost adherents.

But the convergence of nature worship and Thoreau appreciation was not so simple. As historians of the literary canon point out, he was less a founder of this new genre than a product of it. His posthumous publications had been modestly successful, but the sale of his books lagged far behind other literary classics. Among lay readers, he was but one among hundreds of nature writers available at the turn of the century and not, in most estimates, the most popular. He was unique in drawing philosophical insights from his observations, but his early biographers had done their utmost to hide this distinction, sensitive to the fact that modern readers were less inclined than Thoreau to see nature as a paradigm for asceticism or a mirror of higher truth. Anderson Graham pointed out quite correctly in his 1891 survey of nature books that "more and more we see as time passes the reflected Transcendentalism of Thoreau falls into oblivion, . . . while the study of nature, that was his own peculiar sphere, wins a wider and fuller appreciation."[5] For this reason, readers turned to New York naturalist John Burroughs, who, unlike Thoreau, was sociable in public, amazingly prolific, and attuned to the popular demand for a view of nature that removed, as Millard Davis wrote, "the . . . Spirit from the scene—or from behind it." Most of all, Burroughs presented nature as a walk in the woods: a compelling, if not allegorical or inspirational, narrative of forest life. This was the nature that Clark, Emerson, Johnson, and Packard went looking for at Walden Pond.[6]

Thoreau's reputation certainly benefited from this new, more sentimentalized vision of nature, but it also linked him to a movement with little lasting literary value; by the end of World War I nature study, as a distinct genre, had all but disappeared. How, then, did Thoreau became part of, and transcend, this evanescent literary genre, and what does this tell us about the idea of nature in the early twentieth century?

Walking in the Woods

Nature writing had deep roots in American soil. As the writer Stanton Kirkham observed, colonial settlers, confronting an endlessly varied continental wilderness, became a nature-studying people; there was "scarcely a journal, a diary, or a set of letters . . . in which we do not find that careful seeing, and often that imaginative interpretation, so characteristic of the present day." Wallace Stegner wrote later that finding something new in nature was an "indispensable element in the reports of exploration and discovery."[7] To Europeans, wilderness was an abstract romantic vision; to Americans, it was a vast physical reality bound up in the pageant of westward migration and the formation of national identity.

Nature writing gained coherence as a literary form in the mid-nineteenth century. Folio pictorials like Nathaniel Parker Willis's 1840 *American Scenery*,

George Putnam's 1852 *Home Book of the Picturesque,* and William Cullen Bryant's somewhat later *Picturesque America* included, along with illustrations by some of the nation's most gifted artists, essays that romanticized America as a youthful agrarian republic.[8] Susan Fenimore Cooper's *Rural Hours,* published in 1850, was the first of many seasonally arranged books describing the nearby woods in thoroughly domestic terms. That same year Donald Grant Mitchell, writing as Ik Marvel, published *Reverie of a Bachelor,* a highly sentimentalized reminiscence of his country boyhood. Frederick William Shelton's 1853 *Up the River* explored similar themes along the Hudson, and in *Country Margins* S. H. Hammond and L. W. Mansfield wrote of "beautiful valleys, . . . with broad farms and green fields . . . and . . . a quiet village with church steeples going up from among the clustered houses." Marvel, Shelton, Hammond, and Mansfield were undeniably shallow writers. The literary critic Norman Foerster characterized their work as "a great deal of sensuousness and a negligible degree of spirituality," to which the historian Edward Foster added, "God forbid the intrusion of a startling idea." Still, they were popular in the second half of the century, and together with scores of articles in *Harper's, Scribners's Monthly, Graham's,* and *Godey's Lady's Book* and thousands of prints, lithographs, engravings, and paintings, they represented an emerging market for rural nostalgia.[9]

Scholarly writing about nature changed as well. Transcendental philosophers saw nature mainly as a metaphor for divinity, but in the more secular society of post–Civil War America, authors transformed nature into a belletristic device. Magazines continued publishing essays on nature themes, but these were aimed at readers more interested in literary finesse than in nature itself. The essays would begin with a specific observation about nature and then shift to a broader commentary on the human condition. These thoughts were expressed with appealing literary flair and impeccable taste and typically ended with a clever ironic twist. The master of this literary form was James Russell Lowell.[10]

This use of nature in genteel literature fell out of favor at the turn of the century. In his *Responsibilities of the Novelist,* Frank Norris attributed this to the aridness of the genre and its failure to connect to modern sensibilities. "The New England school for too long dominated the entire range of American fiction—limiting it, specializing it, polishing, refining and embellishing it, narrowing it down to a veritable cult. . . . It is small wonder that the reaction came when and as it did." By the end of the century, as Norris indicated, the pantheon of great American writers was in flux.[11] In the autumn of 1890 the *Springfield (MA) Republican* issued a eulogy on those writers who invoked nature as a framework for stylistic flourish: "These brilliant woods of October, now growing bare and casting on the green sward their carpet of colored leaves, ... fits well with the literature of New England a generation ago as we now look back upon it. There was a verdure and freshness therein,—it adorned the age, it covered and matured much noble fruit which the world has gathered and preserved; but how much of it is like these fallen leaves, splendid and rusting, at our feet,—admired and admirable, but, withal, of the Past." Those who contributed to this renaissance in writing would remain fresh and green, in the author's opinion, only to the degree they conveyed "a keen sense of New England." Those whose approaches to nature were abstract and universal rather than tangible and local were, like the fallen leaves, destined to wither and disappear.[12] And this was indeed Lowell's fate. His poetry, once considered the most decorous in American literature, was too abstruse for end-of-the-century readers. His metaphors, according to the literary critic John Macy, seemed flat and formless; "the music simply does not happen." The dilettante style of subordinating nature to the turn of phrase had run its course. The writer as pure artist, the ideal that drove Lowell's criticism of Thoreau, gave way to the writer as messenger—the muckraker, the progressive—or the outdoor advocate.[13]

The nature-writing genre developed in concert with a turn-of-the-century expansion in outdoor activities like hiking, golfing, bird-watching, fishing, hunting, mountaineering, camping, and bicycling. As early as 1875 the *New York Times* published a series of articles on the "walking mania" sweeping the Northeast, and in the next decade garden clubs, rod and gun clubs, cycling clubs, conservation associations, mountaineering organizations, and private recreational camps and lodges proliferated.[14] The popularity of these outdoor activities signaled a deeper dialectical turn in American culture. In the 1860s and 1870s Americans had been captivated by the panorama of industrial ascent, but over the next two decades this optimistic feeling gave way to an ill-defined disenchantment with economic and cultural trends such as industrialism, urbanism, secularism, and modern science. The University of Wisconsin historian Frederick Jackson Turner's brilliant address on the significance of the frontier in American history underscored the cultural importance of the nation's pioneering past, but even those unaware of his commentary understood that the two-hundred-year push against the western wilderness had shaped American character, and the conclusion of this epic triggered a quest for reaffirming contact with frontier-like environments.

President Theodore Roosevelt celebrated the strenuous life, and millions of Americans heeded his call for robust outdoor activity.[15]

While urban-industrial life provided a motive for withdrawing to nature, railroads provided the means, and common carriers like these became important promoters of leisure travel and park development. In addition, by 1909 America boasted some three million registered automobiles, and the Good Roads campaigns initiated earlier by bicycle enthusiasts yielded state funding for road improvement. "Our highways are reasonably good, our lanes and by-ways . . . inviting," wilderness traveler Maurice Thompson wrote. "There is no good reason why . . . tourists . . . should not explore the pastoral districts where the richest materials for poetry, romance, and art may be had for the taking."[16] These outdoor enthusiasms generated an outpouring of guidebooks and essays on bird-watching, hiking, camping, botany, and gardening, and this in turn transformed the rural picturesque tradition into a new nature-study genre.

Just as transcendentalism grew out of European romanticism, turn-of-the-century nature writing was linked to literary trends in Britain. The nation's huge stratum of gentry, clerics, priests, vicars, and scholars, all with sufficient leisure to pursue pastimes like hunting, angling, rambling, birding, and botanizing, sustained an outdoor tradition dating back to Izaak Walton's 1653 *Compleat Angler*. The tradition culminated in the British naturalist Richard Jefferies, whose *Gamekeeper at Home, Amateur Poacher, Wild Life in a Southern Country,* and *Nature Near London* were widely read in America.[17] Jefferies ascribed to the British tradition of the chase, while American nature writers developed a less adversarial fellowship with nature, and he populated his landscapes with farmers, gamekeepers, huntsmen, poachers, shepherds, mowers, thatchers, and field-workers, while the Americans typically screened humans out of their nature scenes.[18] Still, American writers adopted a narrative style much like Jefferies's, who gave his readers the illusion of moving through a picturesque, almost magical, landscape: "A little farther, and the ground declines; through the tall fern we come upon a valley. But the soft warm sunshine, the stillness, the solitude have induced an irresistible idleness. Let us lie down upon the fern, on the edge of the green vale, and gaze up at the slow clouds as they drift across the blue vault." American writers conveyed this experience as a walk in the woods, and in this sense they had more in common with Jefferies's country embellishments than with Thoreau's symbol-laded descriptions of Concord.[19]

Thoreau aside, there were two writers who bridged the gap between the country-life books of the 1850s and turn-of-the-century nature writing. The first of these was Thomas Wentworth Higginson, who published nature essays in the *Atlantic Monthly* and included them in his *Out-Door Papers* in 1863, at a time when the popularity of nature writing was at low ebb. The first writer in what would later become a genre, he explored the landscapes around his suburban home near Boston and composed a "chatty, anecdotal, half-scientific, half-sentimental" chronicle, as Fred Lewis Pattee said in his history of nature writing, of "semi-rural life." Higginson owed much to his transcendental friends Emerson and Thoreau, but for his book he chose the uncharted territory between sentiment and science. Like the country-life authors, he romanticized "the simple enjoyment that may be crowded into one hour of sunshine," but like the scientific naturalists of his day, he insisted this enjoyment be focused on specifically identified natural objects. "The transition from Thoreau to John Burroughs," as Pattee put it, "was through Thomas Wentworth Higginson."[20]

Wilson Flagg, who wrote of places more natural than Higginson's suburbia, preceded Thoreau into print by about a decade. Flagg attended Harvard Medical School but abandoned medicine for the life of a writer, composing essays for the *Boston Weekly Magazine* in 1839–40 and collecting these in 1857 into *Studies in the Field and Forest*.[21] Flagg's essays combined a keen understanding of nature with a deep love of rural settings. Even the most sublime natural scene, he contended, would be "cold and unaffecting" without the domestic touch—grazing cattle, perhaps, or a humble cottage. His compositions were as sentimental as those of Ik Marvel, but, like Higginson, he was precise and realistic in his depiction of nature, anticipating in many ways the ecological insights of Vermonter George Perkins Marsh's 1864 *Man and Nature*. Also like Higginson, he presented nature in narrative form and tangible detail, using a technique that forecast end-of-the-century trends. Nature appreciation, once the province of wealthy travel writers and literary elites, was becoming democratized.[22]

New Stars Ascending

In 1880 John Burroughs, Wilson Flagg, and Thomas Wentworth Higginson stood virtually alone in sustaining the tradition of nature writing in America, but at the end of that decade they were joined by hundreds of others. "It seems only a few years ago that the few books on outdoor life which had any sort of general circulation got it largely because of their uncommon literary value," a *New York Times* correspondent wrote in 1900. People read Emerson "before their library fireplaces and with no idea of going and doing likewise."[23] End-of-the-century readers demanded a more engaging literature. The average person, by one account, "regarded an interest in letters as a mark of detachment from reality, if not downright frivolity. . . . Robust energies found profitable outlets." Nature writing provided vent for these robust energies; it was filled with practical advice on the location, behavior, and identifying characteristics of plants, animals, and birds and hints on forestry, gardening, or farming. "Let us learn to see and name first," Dallas Sharp told his readers. "The inexperienced, the unknowing, the unthinking, cannot love."[24]

Nature writing fed on the enthusiasm generated by outdoor activities, but it also owed much to bookmakers, who saw market opportunity in these popular recreational trends. During the 1880s Ticknor & Fields of Boston emerged as a colossus in the publishing field, producing elegant but relatively low-priced books by writers such as Emerson, Longfellow, Hawthorne, Whittier, Bryant, Lowell, Holmes, Stowe, Agassiz, Jewett, Dana, Child, and Thoreau. James T. Fields, himself an important arbiter of American literature, took a particular interest in books with nature themes, and as editor of magazines such as the *Atlantic Monthly*, the *North American Review*, *Our Young Folks*, and *Every Saturday*, he regularly included essays on nature. Fields retired in 1870, and in 1880 the firm merged with the publishing house of Henry Houghton and George Mifflin. Houghton Mifflin benefited from the reputation Ticknor & Fields had established in American classics, but by 1880 the center of American book publishing was shifting to New York City. As both writing and publishing diffused away from New England, the Boston firm found it difficult to attract top novelists and essayists, and in response it began cultivating a new crop of writers to meet the demand for middlebrow reading. In 1876 the company published John Burroughs's first book, *Wake-Robin*, and the firm continued to dominate the field of popular nature writing well into the twentieth century, giving the genre, according to the historian Eric Lupfer, a "coherence and cultural prominence that it would not have had otherwise." With Burroughs's popularity on the rise, Houghton Mifflin "saw that it might hitch Thoreau's wagon to Burroughs's star." Thus, as Barksdale Maynard writes, the nature-writing movement "created Thoreau, and not the other way around."[25]

Superficial though it was, the genre filled a void in popular culture. Charles

Darwin's *Origin of Species,* published in 1859, undermined confidence in the fixity and permanence of the natural world, and this void was deeply troubling at a time when society itself seemed to lack a solid center.[26] Novelists such as Jack London, Stephen Crane, and Frank Norris, haunted by the realization that civilization was but a thin veneer over the Darwinian struggle, portrayed social interaction in both urban and rural settings as senseless and futile. Progress was an illusion and morality, as the historian George Cotkin put it, "largely a matter of force."[27]

Nature writers were sensitive to the challenge presented by Darwinism. Dallas Sharp readily admitted that the natural world seemed at times senselessly savage. With the onset of winter, wild creatures, "unhoused and often unsheltered . . . suffer as we hardly yet understand." Yet he quickly turned from these stark images to describe animals tucked securely in their burrows and fortified with an ample harvest of seeds. William Beebe portrayed the coming of winter in equally ambiguous terms: "How pitiful the weak flight of the last yellow butterfly of the year, as with tattered and battered wings it vainly seeks for a final sip of sweets! The fallen petals and the hard seeds are black and odourless, the drops of sap are hardened. Little by little the wings weaken, the tiny feet clutch convulsively at a dried weed stalk, and the four golden wings drift quietly down among the yellow leaves, soon to merge into the dark mould beneath." This image of poignant death translated the Darwinian struggle into sentimental pathos, and the writer was soon anticipating "the keen, invigorating pleasures of winter." Bradford Torrey's approach to the struggle for survival was equally evasive. Plants and animals persevered by "elbowing their rivals out of the way," but these apparently wasted lives served higher purposes. "It must be unsafe to criticise the working of a single wheel here or there, when we . . . can only guess at the grand design itself." Nature writers found ways to reestablish the harmony and stability that seemed so lacking in the Darwinian world and at the same time reignite the spirit of adventure that had gone missing in urban-industrial life. All of this, of course, Thoreau was admirably prepared to do.[28]

The Idea of Nature in the Late Nineteenth Century

Nature writing was a literature of invitation, and by way of example several writers actually abandoned the city, moved to a farm, and wrote pleasant reflections on nature from the perspective of an educated outsider.[29] Birding manuals were another popular form of invitation. Informational in tone, they nevertheless managed to romanticize birds as charming and illusive neighbors. Although no hint of Darwinism appeared in these endearing narratives, they were at least superficially scientific. Frank Chapman's popular *Bird Life* and his *Handbook of the Birds of Eastern North America,* both published in a light, easily handled format with a minimum of technical data, hinted at the emotional side of bird life, and *Citizen Bird: Scenes from Bird Life in Plain English for Beginners* was a spectacularly successful collaboration between Mabel Osgood Wright, a dedicated conservationist; Elliott Coues, a respected ornithologist; and Louis Agassiz Fuertes, one of America's finest illustrators. Florence Merriam's *Birds of the Village and Field* and *Birds through an Opera Glass* likewise struck a balance between scientific fact and appealing anecdote, as did Neltje Blanchan's *Bird Neighbors,* Jenny Stickney's *Bird World,* and Sara Prueser's *Our Dooryard Friends.*[30]

Bradford Torrey, America's best-known bird-guide author, spent his childhood in Boston and learned bird lore on strolls through the Common and Public Garden. At age twenty-one he organized America's first birding organization, the Nuttall Ornithological Club, which eventually became the American Ornithologists' Union. Beginning with a chapter on the Boston Commons, his 1885 *Birds in the Bush* described nests, habits, and songs in precise detail and added charming anecdotes about the romance of birding and bird life. Another urban ornithologist, Olive Thorne Miller, purchased caged robins, blue jays, bluebirds, and other common species and kept them though the winter in her Brooklyn aviary before releasing them. At her desk she studied them as individuals, finding some among the same species selfish and others kind, some optimists and others pessimists. As they grew comfortable in her presence, they revealed their individual "bird tragedies and comedies, bird loves and griefs," which she recorded in a series of graceful and moving sketches that maintained an air of scientific credibility yet took on a fictive quality. This narrative format, with its emphasis on individuality and emotion, fueled the passion for birds that gave rise to Audubon Clubs all across the country.[31]

Writers of plant guides likewise took on the challenge of blending science and romance. Caroline Creevey's *Flowers of Field, Hill, and Swamp,* for instance, described forget-me-nots by quoting Tennyson's ode to the flower and explaining that "they nestle modestly among mosses and galiums, peeping with mild eyes around clumps of onoclea fern." To this library of popular guidebooks, John Henry Comstock added *Insect Life,* containing chapters on pond life, brook life, orchard life, forest life, and roadside life. Phil Robinson's *In Garden, Orchard, and Spinney* detailed the natural history of a small plot of land, similar to Thomas Wentworth Higginson's *The Procession of the Flowers* and Charles M. Skinner's *Nature in a City Yard.* Backyard nature writers, as a reviewer put it, discovered a delightful outdoor world in "a few square feet of homely soil."[32]

Each of these authors had a unique perspective on nature, but there were generalities enough to define them as part of a distinct field, neither mainstream literature nor scientific study. First, the authors built their narratives around personal observation rather than textual research; they at least purported to be eyewitnesses of nature. Second, they wrote to an urban audience they imagined living in sheltered apartments and working in artificial surroundings. Urbanites, as one writer put it, lived in a "snow-choked, smoke-clouded, cobble-paved, wheel-wracked, street-scented, wire-lighted half-day, half-night something, that is neither spring, summer, autumn, nor winter." Having expressed this antiurban bias, writers offered to reacquaint their readers with the exotic world outside the city. Third, in a somewhat contrary fashion, nature writers described places that were not remote and wild but accessible even to the city dweller. Nature was next door, they imagined, to almost every American. William Beebe, for instance, pointed out that any marsh "within a half-hour's trolley ride of any of our cities or town" could host an adventure.[33] Fourth, success in the genre depended on arranging the outdoor experience into a simple but compelling narrative that subordinated scientific knowledge and abstract philosophy to a simple walk-in-the-woods format. This heavily narrative style led one critic to remark that things happened to the nature writer "in the most accommodating way, for they manage to give each story of bird or beast a point, while ordinary mortals do the same things and have no adventures that so pleasantly will round off a chapter." Nature writers aimed at capturing the "spirit of outdoors" and made no attempt at deeper understanding.[34]

Finally, all nature writers were, like A. S. Clark and Edward Emerson at Walden Pond, sensitive to the fact that nature was under siege, and for this reason they were kin to the great conservation figures of the Progressive Era. They were distinct from these conservationists, however, in projecting a sentimental as opposed to utilitarian message. Mabel Osgood Wright and Frank Chapman, the nation's leading bird conservationists, heightened their readers' sympathy for victims of the feather trade by giving them individual personality and emotion. Both were editors of the Audubon Society's

Bird-Lore, which published hundreds of articles romanticizing and anthropomorphizing birds in order to sharpen the society's preservationist tone. While mainstream conservationists made using nature more efficient, these writers made it a matter of the heart. "Let us consider some of the more humble trees about us," Beebe entreated. "Not, however, from the standpoint of the ... scientific forester, but from the sympathetic point of view of a living fellow form, sharing the same planet." Messages like this had far greater popular appeal than the cold logic of economic efficiency.[35]

Thoreau among the Nature Writers

Thoreau's reputation must be viewed in light of this rising popular interest in nature. In the 1880s, as the literary historian Lawrence Buell noted, Houghton Mifflin began anthologizing Thoreau's work in their literary collections and textbooks, "ensuring that [he] ... would become a household word." In all of these selections the company emphasized nature writing, as did the eleven-volume compilation published by Houghton Mifflin in 1893. And with copyrights expiring, new editions appeared more frequently in print, including an issue of *The Maine Woods* from Thomas Y. Crowell with photographs taken by Clifton Johnson along the trails Thoreau followed through the wilderness. Publications like this helped integrate Thoreau into the nature-study movement. After reading the Crowell volume, for instance, the Yale literary historian Henry Beers described Thoreau not as a transcendentalist but as an outdoorsman, listening "with his ear close to the ground, for the voice of the earth."[36]

By the turn of the century the mood of the nation seemed opportune for publishing the entire journal. Sophia Thoreau had passed the volumes on to Harrison Blake, who bequeathed them to Elias Russell, and he in turn sold the rights to Houghton Mifflin for $3,000. In 1905 the *Atlantic Monthly* began printing selections in installments, and these were lauded as "pure beauties of observation and feeling, easily disentangled from all transcendental discourse." Houghton Mifflin contracted with Bradford Torrey to edit the journal, and it was published in 1906 with only minor changes and excisions, making up fourteen of the twenty volumes in Houghton Mifflin's *Writings of Henry David Thoreau.*[37]

According to Buell, the twenty-volume edition marks the departure point for Thoreau's canonization. Buell attributes this event to the *Atlantic Monthly* editor and Harvard professor Bliss Perry, who was intrigued by the journal's literary richness and recommended it to Houghton Mifflin. Indeed, it was rare, as Franklin Sanborn wrote in the *Dial,* to "find the diary of a man published in multiple volumes who was not a president, a traveler, or an interviewer of others"—and this from an author who only a few years earlier had been "generally overlooked or condemned." It was here, then, that academics began looking at Thoreau seriously and here that the twin paths of scholarly discourse and popular opinion began to intertwine. Sluggish sales suggest that popular reaction was at best mixed, and Paul More, literary editor for the *Independent* and the *Nation,* pointed out that "laboring through the fourteen volumes . . . may well appall the sturdiest reader," especially since Thoreau's most memorable reflections were already available in the Blake volumes reissued by Houghton Mifflin in 1894.[38]

Popular and academic opinion also coalesced in reading the journal almost exclusively as a nature study. In his preface Bradford Torrey claimed that "the world in general has agreed to regard Thoreau not as a preacher of righteousness, but as an interpreter of nature." Edward Emerson added that a "whole literature" had sprung up since his day, "unquestionably inspired by him." Had he simply "ruminat[ed] . . . on the eternities," the literary historian Barrett Wendell insisted, "his position . . . would hardly be important. What gave him lasting power was his unusually sympathetic observation of Nature." All this prompted Anderson Graham to demand that "every passage with a precept, a teaching or a doctrine . . . be ruthlessly excised." Thoreau had arrived at the gates of literary fame, but his message had to be thinned considerably to fit the fashion of the times.[39]

This worried some critics. "Why is it, then, that Thoreau the thinker is still knocking at the gate where Thoreau the writer has been admitted?" biographer Henry Salt asked. Daniel Mason complained that "of the philosopher, . . . we hear, strangely enough, scarcely anything at all," and the socialist critic John Macy, who edited the *Nation,* found it ironic that in the age of the robber baron, Thoreau's sobering pronouncements on industrial society had been "discreetly turned to the wall." Others wondered if he could "outlast the sentimentality which was the disease of the movement that called him father." As these critics suggest, Thoreau was incomplete as a writer at this turning point in his literary reputation, and, just as important, he was not yet America's most popular nature writer.[40] A brief look at the authors who best represent the early-twentieth-century love affair with nature brings to light the strengths and limitations of Thoreau's reputation in the age of progress.

John Burroughs

The differences between Thoreau and turn-of-the-century writers are exemplified in the era's two greatest naturalists, John Burroughs and John Muir. Together, they help explain how the nature-study movement transformed Thoreau and how he transcended the genre these two men represented. Burroughs was born in 1837 and grew up on a farm in the Hudson Highlands. While teaching school he read Flagg, Emerson, and Thoreau and began recording his own experiences in the woods. He published his first article, "Expressions," in James Russell Lowell's *Atlantic Monthly* in 1860, two years before Thoreau died. In 1864 he moved to Washington, DC, where he worked in the Treasury Department and as a bank examiner before returning to New York State. His first book, *Wake-Robin,* was published in 1871, and he followed this with a long string of publications that, by the end of the century, ranked him as America's best-known naturalist. He died in 1921 on a train returning to his New York home after spending a winter in California.[41]

Well into the twentieth century Burroughs was, as his biographer Clara Barrus claimed, "more sought after . . . than any other American author." Like other nature writers, he stripped away the philosophical meanings transcendentalists had attached to nature and gave readers a realistic depiction that neither overtaxed their capacity for sentimentalism nor challenged their literary reach. His images conveyed a vivaciousness that Thoreau seldom bothered to cultivate, but, more important, he presented nature on terms familiar to his readers. "When we read Thoreau we are always conscious of Thoreau," Fred Lewis Pattee explained. "With Burroughs we are . . . walking with a delightful companion who knows everything and who points out new wonders at every step." Thoreau loaded his descriptions with transcendent symbols and encouraged readers to go beyond the nature he described. Burroughs simplified nature, employing none of the moody foreshadowing that sometimes occluded Thoreau's compositions. According to W. G. Barton, "What he feels you shall share."[42]

The greatest difference between Thoreau and Burroughs was the meaning each assigned to nature. Thoreau saw it as a philosophic conundrum and Burroughs a walk in the woods. Burroughs cast nature as a setting for nostalgic withdrawal. "You grow old, your friends die or remove to distant lands, events sweep on and all things are changed," he wrote, "yet there in your garden or orchard are the birds of your boyhood, the same notes, the same calls, and, to all intents and purposes, the identical birds endowed with perennial youth." Thoreau demanded that his readers seek higher truths in nature, a condition that was, as Dallas Sharp said, "electrifying, purifying, illuminating, but not altogether conducive to peace." Nor was Burroughs likely to let his social opinions intrude on his nature studies. Like Thoreau, he believed that cities were confining, but he fell short of condemning those who lived there to lives of "quiet desperation." Where Thoreau judged and chided, Burroughs reassured. He left no moral messages, but in an age that saw nature as a place of recreation and therapeutic escape, he was, as William Sloane Kennedy wrote, "predestined to popularity."[43]

A sense of personal inadequacy kept Burroughs from writing his self into his studies: "I think I . . . lack egoism," he wrote. "But this weakness . . . is probably a great help to me as a writer upon nature. I do not stand in my own light. . . . I can surrender myself to nature without effort." Thoreau used nature to define his selfhood; Burroughs abandoned his selfhood to nature. This was the difference, according to Thomas Wentworth Higginson, that put Thoreau's writing "on the level of literature" and that of Burroughs at the "level of journalism."[44]

Burroughs understood these differences. Thoreau, he thought, was less interested in nature than in the meaning behind it, and at times this preoccupation came "at the expense of the truth." Burroughs recorded many misgivings like this, perhaps to accentuate his own virtues as a nature writer, but more likely as a way to step out from Thoreau's shadow into the sunlight of turn-of-the-century nature appreciation. William Sloane Kennedy noted as much: "Burroughs's . . . irritable overhaulings of Thoreau toward the end of his life were partly an attempt, it seems to me, to define his own position. Conscious of being much more deeply veined with humanity than Thoreau, and yet ever-lured by the intense white light of his ethical quality, and of his superior erudition, he wanted . . . to . . . place himself in his own sphere, so all could see the fact."[45] Burroughs nonetheless found much to admire in his predecessor, and at the end of his life he found himself regretting the distance between them. "I was thinking this morning of Thoreau's way of writing, and what a mistake I have made in not heeding it," he mused. "I am afraid I try to say things in too pretty a way. . . . I am too afraid to give the mind a jolt." Successful nature writing, he realized, was not simply vivid description. Thoreau "walks . . . into the land of mythology, ideality, religion—while I just walk in the fields and woods."[46] This distinction would favor him only as long as the enthusiasm for nature study lasted.

Thoreau clearly made mistakes in his species descriptions, but his contemporaries had been less interested in fact than in symbol. If he had been "too intent upon the bird behind the bird," it was because he and his readers saw nature as metaphor more than substance. By Burroughs's time, nature had assumed more concrete meanings, and this put pressure on writers in his generation to accurately identify and describe it. W. G. Barton, writing in 1885 shortly after Harrison Blake published the first of his four volumes of journal entries, captured these changes in an essay comparing Thoreau, the recently deceased Wilson Flagg, and John Burroughs, still rising to the pinnacle of his career. Thoreau was less fluid as a writer than Flagg and less ebullient than Burroughs, who "sees, hears, smells, feels, fancies, thinks, and bursts forth copious and rich." But Thoreau could "bring his reader so very close to that great . . . untamable spirit in himself." This was the essential difference, as Higginson said earlier, between journalism and literature: Thoreau explored his own soul in his visions of nature, and thus his writing gained an element as timeless as the soul itself.[47]

Visions of Wildness
In his musings on Thoreau, Burroughs also described his predecessor as the "first man in this country, or in any other, so far as I know, . . . to announce a Gospel of the Wild." Thoreau's quest for the primal essence of nature left Burroughs awestruck. He "ransacked the country . . . in all seasons and weathers, and at all times of the day and night; he delved into the ground, he probed the swamps, he searched the waters, he dug into woodchuck holes, into muskrats' dens, into the retreats of the mice and squirrels." There was something in this obsessive quest that flavored his writing—something Burroughs could never quite grasp. Channing and Alcott had emphasized Thoreau's gentler, friendlier side, but to later critics he was, as William Sloane Kennedy insisted, best read as a "civilized wild man"—a capricious and unkempt soul. He "craved wildness," George Ellwanger added, "a nature primordial and untrodden by the foot of man."[48]

Burroughs to the contrary, Thoreau's fascination with wilderness was not altogether unique in the mid-nineteenth century. Wilderness adventure books began appearing in the United States as early as the 1840s, when the English journalist Henry William Herbert, writing as Frank Forester, popularized primitive outdoor recreation his *Field Sports, Fish and Fishing,* and *Complete Manual for Young Sportsmen.* By the end of the century Forester had several American imitators, including William Sedgwick Steele, "Adirondack" Murray, Wallace Hoff, Isabella Bird, Lucius Hubbard, and

Willard Glazier. Novelists such as Stephen Crane, Frank Norris, and Jack London used Darwinian motifs in their work, and this inspired nature writers to add a hint of struggle and survival to their own stories. Among them, it was Maurice Thompson who carried this atavistic theme to extremes. Souls "weakened by civilized living," he insisted, could be restored only in contact with raw nature, and this was especially true for those too young to have earned their manhood in the Civil War or by pioneering in the West. Thompson's own masculine affirmation came in plunging his canoe "down between the dank, fantastically grooved jaws of the gorge, till the mist and darkness blended into one, and the thunder of the stream in its agony was appalling." W. H. Hudson likewise entered an "instinctive or primitive state of mind" in the face of danger. Layers of self-deception fell away, leaving him in touch with his core consciousness. "I have met men whose talk was spicy and aromatic," he wrote, "from whose lips simple words fell with a new, racy meaning." Writing for a generation concerned about the sedentary state of urban life, Thompson, Hudson, and writer-adventurers such as Clarence King and Enos Mills made nature a test of stamina, manhood, resourcefulness, and moral fiber.[49]

Burroughs and others like him abandoned the symbolic and literary associations that so ornamented Thoreau's work and presented nature as a nostalgic retreat. Those who found this approach too shallow discovered in the West, with its vast, unfathomed wilderness, a new set of transcendent meanings. Stanton Kirkham's 1911 *East and West: Comparative Studies in Nature in Eastern and Western States,* perhaps the first nature book predicated on auto travel, searched out nature in both familiar and unfamiliar places. The ancient landscapes of the East, he discovered, were wild in their own way, but the West, a land still in its birth throes, appealed to the "primitive untrammeled man . . . who is not content with hills and brooks but demands mountain chains, the forest, and the desert for his portion." In the West Kirkham found himself in touch with the "cryptic depths of the subconscious mind of the race."[50] Nature—challenging, energizing, affirming—regained its transcendent symbolism.

This new emphasis on wilderness gave Thoreau a more outdoorsy persona. W. H. Hudson praised his willingness to "take a ranker hold on life and live more as the animals do," and the Iowa naturalist W. T. Worth observed that anywhere but in the woods he was "like a creature caged. Writing in *Frank Leslie's Popular Monthly,* Lincoln Adams paraphrased Emerson's eulogy for Thoreau: "He could find his way in the woods at night as easily as by day. He could see as through a spyglass; hear as with an ear trumpet, and each track upon the earth or in the snow revealed to him the creature which had gone before." At a time of "luxurious living and artificiality," Adams thought, this was the model of true manhood.[51] Academics highlighted his wild qualities as well. Dalhousie University's Archibald MacMechan, who wrote a chapter on Thoreau for the *Cambridge History of American Literature,* described *Walden* as "the struggle of primitive man to obtain food and shelter," and Norman Foerster remarked that Thoreau's "lust (hardly too strong a word) for rainstorms and swamps" was evidence of his "ardent yearning for wildness."[52]

Here again, Thoreau differed from turn-of-the-century nature writers. The wilderness they typically described was resistant to the intimate forms of kinship that characterized so much of his writing. Mary Austin, writing at the turn of the century, crafted a lyrical tribute to the sparsely settled desert region east of the Sierra Nevada, where "not the law, but the land sets the limits." The desert world was both inspiring and beautiful, but its extreme climate and furtive creatures kept the wanderer at bay. Writers like Austin showed that America's wastelands could be wonderlands, but they abandoned the sense of connectedness Thoreau and Burroughs found in their northeastern woods. In his 1910 *Henry Thoreau and Other Children of the Open Air,* Theodore Watts-Dunton emphasized the way Thoreau imbedded himself into the world around him: "A squirrel or raccoon or woodchuck, bolder than the rest, would approach the motionless man silently and warily, and ready to make retreat at the smallest movement of an arm.... The raccoons approached nearer. The squirrels did the same, til at last they positively touched him.... An intimacy soon sprang up between him and them." Most late-century wilderness writing centered on the adventure of confronting a remote and alien natural world; America still awaited someone who could imagine these exotic places on terms as familiar and inviting as Thoreau's Concord or Burroughs's Hudson Highlands.[53]

John Muir

Western nature writing reached its apogee in John Muir, who found in the Sierra Nevada a wilderness far different from that described by Thoreau or Burroughs.[54] This was scenery at its most sublime, and Muir churned this experience into a froth of ecstatic and religious references that profoundly altered the way America thought about nature. And like Thoreau, he embedded himself in this craggy landscape, achieving an intimacy every bit as familiar as the natural world of Thoreau and Burroughs. Muir was born in Scotland, and when he was young his family moved to Wisconsin. During a boyhood shadowed by his father's stern sense of duty and equally grim theological rigor, he learned to view nature as a life-affirming refuge. Where Thoreau's move to Walden was a philosophical decision, Muir's escape to the Sierra Nevada was driven by his experience with crushing toil, nay-saying religion, and overbearing patriarchal authority.

In 1864 Muir left the farm for Canada to avoid the military draft. He returned in 1866, worked briefly in a foundry, and after recovering from a serious eye injury decided on a walking tour of South America, only to be struck down by fever in Florida. He boarded a steamer and sailed to San Francisco, where he immediately "inquired for the nearest way out of town."[55] He first spied the Sierra crest from the western rim of the San Joachin Valley. "At my feet lay the Great Central Valley of California, level and flowery, like a lake of pure sunshine, forty or fifty miles wide . . . and from the eastern boundary of this vast golden flowerbed rose the mighty Sierra, miles in height, and so gloriously colored and so radiant, it seemed not clothed with light, but wholly composed of it, like a wall of some celestial city." Muir spent his first summer in the Sierra in 1868 as a sheepherder, and in a spiritual sense, he never left.[56]

As a natural scientist, Muir was far more engaged than Thoreau. He discovered living glaciers in the Sierra and successfully defended his geological theories against those who saw catastrophic earthquakes as the primary source of mountain building. Because he thought in geological time, his nature was dynamic and immensely powerful, and his understanding of these great earth events gave his writing a unique aura of primal energy. Burroughs, who visited Yosemite Valley in 1909, regarded the towering walls and tumbling waters as he regarded his eastern woods: "You at once feel the spell of the brooding calm and sheltered seclusion," he wrote. Where Burroughs and Thoreau both emphasized the "home instinct," Muir's essays suggested wanderlust. "To read Muir is to be in the presence not of a tranquil, chatty companion like Burroughs. It is rather to be with a tempestuous soul whose units are storms and mountain ranges and mighty glacial moraines, who strides excitedly along the bare tops of ragged peaks and rejoices in their vastness and awfulness, who cries, 'Come with me along the glaciers and see God making landscapes!'"[57]

One of the few nature writers of his day to appreciate the evolutionary aspects of landscape formation, Muir was fascinated by the power of glaciers, earthquakes, floods, avalanches, fires, and storms. Watching a forest fire boil up out of the Kaweah Basin, he was transfixed by the sheer elemental force of this "master scourge and controller of the distribution of trees." It raced up the chaparral slopes "in a broad cataract of flames, now bending down low to feed on the green bushes, devouring acres of them at a breath, now towering high in the air as if looking abroad to choose a way, then stooping to feed again." During a mountain storm he climbed a tall tree and while swaying like a "supple goldenrod" absorbed a lesson in tree perseverance. "Consider what centuries of storms have fallen upon them since they were first planted—hail, to break the tender seedlings; lightning, to scorch and shatter; snow, winds, and avalanches, to crush and overwhelm—while the manifest result of all this wild storm-culture is the glorious perfection we behold." Glaciers required aeons to shape mountains, but fires, earthquakes, and storms could change the face of the region in an instant—"simply by giving the mountains a shake." However terrifying, these forces were "only harmonious notes in the song of creation, varied expressions of God's love." Here indeed was a feeling of transcendence.[58]

Muir was familiar with Thoreau's writing, and there were similarities in the way the two men approached nature. Both were solitary explorers, both saw religious significance in nature, and both viewed nature holistically. More significantly, both immersed themselves in their environment: Muir bathed in the beatific glow of a High Sierra summer, and Thoreau hunkered down beside a turtle laying eggs. Muir's descriptions were more whimsical, but his kinship with the creatures he encountered was as genuine as Thoreau's. Water ouzels, at home amid the cascades and cliffs, were especially dear: "Every breath he draws is part of a song, and he gets his first music lessons before he is born; for the eggs vibrate in time with the tones of the waterfalls." Like Muir, the ouzel was equally ebullient in any weather: "He *must* sing, though the heavens fall." If indeed the purpose of nature writing was to touch the heart, Muir was the genre's master.[59]

There were differences as well, and as with Burroughs, these help explain the resilience that carried Thoreau beyond the turn-of-the-century nature-study movement. Some could be attributed to the vastly different landscapes the two men explored. Concord's closed-in forests and pinched farmlands inspired austere and pensive commentary on nature's wildness, while Muir's sweeping canyons and lush sun-soaked meadows gave rise to buoyant orations on nature's divinity. Muir cherished the uninhabitable world of ice and stone above the timberline, while Thoreau, like Emerson, believed that nature was meaningful only when it was the object of human thought or activity.⁶⁰ Scrambling up a barren talus slope would have appalled Thoreau, who had no perceptual means of connecting to a wilderness this profound, while sauntering through a second-growth New England forest would have similarly annoyed Muir. On his trip to Maine in 1846, Thoreau climbed Mount Katahdin, and this, aside from his treks along the beaches of Cape Cod, was his only experience with the monumental landscapes Muir saw everywhere in the Sierra. Shrouded in low-hanging clouds and braced against a damp wind, Thoreau lingered only for a few minutes on the high tableland before he retreated, uttering agoraphobic pronouncements against a landscape that offered too much space and too little life. When Muir stood in similar circumstances atop North Dome, some two thousand feet above the Yosemite Valley floor, he was ecstatic. The vast, barren landscape and great stretches of space and time put him in direct contact with the infinite. Thoreau, like most nature writers of his day, was satisfied with the subtle wildness of a cultivated field or cutover woodlot; Muir required high, remote canyons and towering sequoias to frame his relation to nature.⁶¹

There were other differences that put Thoreau in the class of great literature and Muir, like Burroughs, in the camp of the turn-of-the-century nature writer. Muir was an unstoppable talker, but his writing was labored, and when he did write, he composed in a style one critic described as "adjectivorous"; he made his point by overworking terms like *glorious* and *radiant*. Thoreau was a measured, classical writer who took immense pride in the perfect sentence or metaphor; Muir was an eyewitness to ecstasy.⁶² Muir's writing was also guided by his nature advocacy. While Thoreau made a few eloquent gestures toward preserving his native town, Muir threw himself passionately into the effort to save the Sierra's delicate meadows, towering sequoias, and pristine valleys from grazers, loggers, and dam builders. "Any fool can destroy trees," he famously wrote. "They cannot run away; and if they could, they would still be destroyed—chased and hunted down as long as fun or a dollar could be got out of their bark hides . . . or magnificent bold backbones." He spoke to readers on the highest moral plane, but his preservationist zeal overshadowed his aspirations as a writer. More impassioned than Thoreau, he epitomized the turn-of-the-century nature writer's focus on conservation and recreation as opposed to lasting literary legacy.⁶³

Here again, philosophical differences separated the two men. Concord's familiar landscapes seemed wild to Thoreau because wildness was a philosophical construct born of his wish to understand the primal self and glimpse the unknowable essence behind the veil of nature. As a poet and philosopher, he could find metaphors and allegories in even the most common scene. Muir's wildness was simpler, born of his awestruck fascination with a vast, monumental, and sublime physical presence. His vision was panoramic, but as a scholar wrote, "he seems not able to get beyond the thought of reproducing the scene." To writers in Muir's age, nature was truly transcendent only where it was dramatic, remote, exotic, or monumental; elsewhere, as Burroughs intimated, it was simply a walk in the woods.[64]

Muir, like Burroughs, demonstrates the way Thoreau's use of nature differed from that of the turn-of-the-century writer. The Sierra peak, the Hudson Highlands, and the Concord woods all offered an opportunity to connect emotionally with nature, but the meaning of this connection changed in the decades after 1862. For Thoreau, nature was the quest for a metaphor; for Burroughs, a search for grand stories encapsulated in small events; and for Muir, an immersion in the sublime. Thoreau found transcendence, if not sublimity, in his familiar surroundings. He was a "literary *Genius loci*," bent on knowing and connecting with every rock and rill of his familiar world. He discovered "more on a few acres than many human beings do on square miles" and gave these few acres personality, flavor, appeal—and a sense of wildness.[65] Muir reveled in the monumental and paid less attention to the spiritual nuance in the ground under his feet. He represented a new view of nature—boundless and majestic but otherwise simply corporeal.

Nature Study and Nature Fiction

America's fascination with nature had been fueled by a nostalgic mood among first- or second-generation urban migrants, but by the beginning of the new century the simple walk-in-the-woods narrative, stripped of transcendent meaning, was losing its appeal. Some writers, like Muir, responded by discovering the sublime in remote and monumental places. Others added a more compelling story line to their description of nearby nature. Collecting observations that were sufficiently interesting to serve these narratives required time in the field, great patience, a lively imagination, and no small amount of luck. Thoreau met this challenge by devoting his entire life to field study and by giving even the most mundane event metaphorical significance. Latter-day nature writers, having set aside both hard science and high philosophy, were forced to find literary merit in the facts as they found them.

Their success depended on giving these discoveries, as Peter Schmitt writes, "all the conventions of dramatic action."[66]

All nature writers were to some degree torn between their obligation to the fact and their commitment to the story, but just where they positioned themselves along the boundary between fact and fantasy was a matter of individual taste. Some were "gushy," as Kirkham put it, tempted by the naïveté of the urban reader to invest their topics with more sentiment and less science. Other writers hewed to the facts, observing nature with a "cold and calculating eye." While the former risked their credibility, the latter imparted too little zest to their stories. The balance depended on whether the author saw nature writing as fiction or nonfiction. "It is not the eye that sees, but the man behind the eye," Bradford Torrey explained. But how much license should be given to the man behind the eye? Wrestling with the same question, Dallas Sharp cautioned that "if my chippy sings, it must sing a chippy's simple song, not some gloria that only 'the careless angels know.' It must not do any extraordinary thing for me; but it may lead me to do an extraordinary thing—to have an extraordinary thought, or suggestion, or emotion." Yet, as Sharp observed, no matter how factual, nature writing was, by definition, a "more or less . . . fraud." Imagining the self in nature required at least some literary license, and this pushed the entire genre to the brink: when the reader's faith was "threatened by obvious insincerity or by the laughter of its critics, the whole mythical structure might crumble."[67]

This faith was shaken when the pressure to popularize nature encouraged a new form of literature known as animal fiction. The genre was pioneered by nature writer Ernest Thompson Seton, whose *Wild Animals I Have Known* ran through ten editions in the first few years after its publication in 1898. Born in England, Seton emigrated to the Canadian West in 1866, and while hunting on the prairie he learned to sketch wildlife, read animal tracks, and "recreate the story of their lives" through observation, deduction, and narrative imagination. He later moved to New Mexico, where he wrote stories about individual animals that revealed curious or compelling details about their species behavior. Young readers sympathized with his creatures, marveled at his Indian lore, and learned about nature through nature's eyes. Encouraged by this eager young audience, he sometimes gave his animals more sentience and moral bearing than science might allow.[68] Although immensely popular, his stories troubled those who linked their writing more closely to facts from the field.

The Reverend William J. Long wrote in a similar vein for *Youth's Companion* and later in children's books, among them *Ways of the Wood Folk, Fowls of the Air,* and *School of the Woods*. His stories conveyed the impression that woodland behavior was not much different from the behavior of his young readers. Typically, he opened with a few well-established facts to buttress his credibility and then narrated a personal experience with a particular group of animals. Each episode revealed personality traits—curiosity, pride, perseverance, spirit, playfulness, or humor—that characterized both the species and his animal hero. Like Seton, Long insisted that his material came from actual observation—his own or those of the hunters and woodsmen with whom he traveled—and as a graduate of Harvard College, Andover Theological Seminary, and Heidelberg University, he verified his accounts by simply announcing that he was "accustomed to being believed when I speak."[69] While his stories generally stayed within the bounds of credibility, he occasionally crossed the threshold. In a 1903 *Outlook* article, for instance, he described a woodcock making a cast of mud and sticks for its broken leg.

Stories like these, as Sharp said, threw a shadow across the entire genre. Nature writing depended on the presumption of scientific truth, no matter how thin. To establish this, the author began, as Sharp put it, with a "solemn, pious preface, wherein he declares that the following observations are exactly as he personally saw them; that they are true altogether; that he has the affidavits to prove it; and the Indians and the Eskimos to swear the affidavits prove it." But as he pointed out, this protestation raised suspicions that all other accounts were less than true. Sensitive to the damage that Seton, Long, and others might do to the field, John Burroughs wrote a long article in the *Atlantic Monthly* in May 1903 titled "Real and Sham Natural History." He began by listing those whom he considered genuine naturalists and then flayed Seton and Long for taking "liberties . . . with the facts." In reply Long insisted that animal behavior was individualistic and thus not subject to scrutiny based on generalizations about species behavior. At this point, Theodore Roosevelt, himself a noted outdoorsman, stepped into the fray with his own criticism of the so-called nature fakirs. Long replied again with an open letter chastising the president for using his office to seize the high ground. Roosevelt might have understood these animal stories better, Long insisted, had he not been so preoccupied with "killing everything in sight." The only time he got near the heart of an animal, he put a "bullet through it."[70]

To bring the debate to a close, Roosevelt arranged a symposium in the September 1907 *Everybody's* magazine that included testimony from the most respected field naturalists in his acquaintance. He also wrote to Seton, urging him to confine his stories to the facts. Taking Roosevelt's advice to heart, Seton abandoned animal fiction and produced several authoritative works on wildlife, including *Lives of Game Animals* which, ironically, won the John Burroughs Medal from the American Museum of Natural History for its excellence as a work of natural history. Roosevelt's symposium and other forms of public exposure reined in the nature fakirs, and in a few years the debate was all but forgotten.[71] Still, the flurry of accusations and counteraccusations touched even the most respected figures in the field and challenged the credibility of virtually everything written about nature. And if the nature writer's primary appeal was sentiment, reining in the emotional narrative had a significant constraining effect on the entire genre. For this and other reasons, nature writing faded in the years following World War I. Burroughs, Muir, Torrey, and a few others managed through sheer literary talent to retain readers without overtaxing the instinct to empathize with animals, but those with less stylistic acumen fell by the wayside.

Was Thoreau a Nature Fakir?

Thoreau's journal, published in 1906, was caught up in the nature-fakir debate. The literary critic Norman Foerster maintained that he "had no excuse, scientifically speaking, for many of the blunders he committed" and insisted that "any schoolboy with the same advantages—spyglass, books, and a love of nature—could in five years equal, nay excel, Thoreau's total knowledge of birds." In his preface to the journal, Bradford Torrey admitted that Thoreau could identify only a small portion of the common birds of Massachusetts, "wonderful as his knowledge seemed to those who, like Emerson, knew practically nothing." Field equipment was primitive in Thoreau's day, Torrey continued, but these errors were still mystifying: "How could an ornithological observer . . . be in the field daily for ten or fifteen years before setting eyes upon his first rose-breasted grosbeak?"[72] Reviewers were quick to take advantage of this skepticism. "Mr. Torrey has by no means a high opinion of Thoreau as a naturalist," one observed, then concluded that Thoreau was "essentially an amateur."[73] Burroughs, like Torrey, was puzzled: "Considering that Thoreau spent half of each day for upward of twenty years in the open air, bent upon spying out nature's ways and doings . . . it is remarkable that he made so few real observations." Fannie Hardy Eckstorm, a Maine naturalist and folklorist who knew the woods of her state more intimately than any writer of her time, challenged the "popular notion that Thoreau was a great woodsman." *The Maine Woods* was replete with errors, and his bird list made it clear that he was not an ornithologist. Still, she found compensation in his literary skill: "He had the art . . . to see the human values of natural objects, to perceive the ideal elements of unreasoning nature and the service of those ideals to the soul of man."[74]

Responding to a complaint that Thoreau described a "spot" on a nighthawk's wing rather than a "bar," Francis Allen argued that he was not offering a scientific description but simply "recording an *impression* of the bird as seen in flight." Allen's interpretation, although it probably failed to convince dedicated bird-watchers, expressed the lasting merit in Thoreau's work: the impression of nature was more important than nature itself. Most defenders, however, insisted on the quality of his physical observations—his discovery, for instance, of new species of fish, mice, plants, and tortoises. To these loyalists, Thoreau was still a nature narrator first and a philosopher of nature only incidentally. "As we read, we feel at times a wish that he would sooner reach his conclusions on philosophical or political questions, because we are sure they will be followed by some bright reference to a bird or beast, simply phrased, yet so cunningly that the creature stands before us," Charles Abbott mused. It was Thoreau's genius, Charles Richardson declared in his 1891 literary history, that he got near to "Nature's heart" and described it in "simple, true, poetic, eloquent words."[75]

Writing in the same year as Richardson, the literary critic Joshua Caldwell marveled that a man so obscure in his own lifetime could be so widely recognized at the end of the century. Was the antebellum reader at fault for not recognizing Thoreau's genius, or were the turn-of-the-century nature lovers to be blamed for trumpeting the virtues of a minor literary figure? Caldwell suspected the latter. He found much to admire in Thoreau's idealism and his unbending moral fiber, but these characteristics were not in themselves a foundation for literary fame. *Yankee in Canada, The Maine Woods,* and *Cape Cod* would remain of interest only among those living in these places, and "Civil Disobedience," "Slavery in Massachusetts," "Life without Principle," and "John Brown" would be read only while these issues remained timely. Otherwise, Caldwell found a certain "incompleteness and want of harmony" in the entire corpus. His reputation, Caldwell thought, had been artificially advanced first by his Concord friends, then by publishers who issued "books so handsomely bound and so highly indorsed [they] could not have failed to sell," and finally by those caught up in the enthusiasm for outdoor life.

Paul More agreed. Thoreau was too little interested in people to be a great writer; there was none of the fiery spirit that caused Lord Byron to mingle compassion for humanity with his devotion to the Alpine solitudes.[76]

Where Eckstorm felt Thoreau would be better read as a poet than as a naturalist, Caldwell saw natural history as his only true genius. Had he confined himself to nature writing, "the foundations of his fame would have been much more firmly laid." But, of course, standing him on this particular pedestal was problematic; it reduced his books and essays to a simple exercise in description no different from the hundreds of volumes that crowded the booksellers' shelves in Caldwell's day. Caldwell himself recognized the consequences: there was "no reason for concluding that Thoreau can maintain his present prominence among American writers, or that his place in literature, if permanent at all, will be a high one."[77] Caldwell overlooked a great deal in his assessment of Thoreau's writing, but his commentary suggests the ambiguous effect nature writing had on the meaning and message of his work.

Transcendence

Like Caldwell, historians of literary canon have been puzzled by Thoreau's sudden rise to fame among scholars such as Foerster and popularizers such as Lincoln Adams. The literary historian Lawrence Buell, like Caldwell, attributes this to Thoreau's friends and publishers, but he notes that "Thoreau's advocates could not have succeeded if history weren't already running their way"—a reference to the cultural shift in the perception of nature at the turn of the century. Still, Buell admits that "just what it was that put Thoreau in a different category from his successors was never precisely identified." Indeed, there are continuities enough to suggest that he was simply a forerunner to a literary movement that disappeared with the American entry into World War I. Most turn-of-the-century writers, like Thoreau, were interested primarily in nearby nature, and they shared Thoreau's interest in what Charles Abbott called "philosophical zoology"—animal behavior understood from the animal's point of view.[78] Thoreau's attempt to commune with woodchucks, foxes, frogs, and other creatures provided grounding for the animal stories that gained such popularity at the turn of the century.

Other features, however, set him apart from this genre and assured him a lasting place in the literary pantheon. First was his total and unconditional dedication to the natural world. As one critic pointed out, the sixty-eight hundred printed pages of his journal, "wrought for no eyes save his own," attested to a life given over completely to nature.[79] The results of this single-mindedness were evident in his lofty, indeed spiritual, regard for nature and in the exquisite balance he struck between fact, symbol, and imagination.

Second, unlike later writers, he used nature as a vehicle for self-discovery. Others wrote to make their readers aware of nature; Thoreau wrote to make them aware of themselves. Nature was a mere starting point for the spiritual awakening that would transfix their lives, as it transfixed his. He saw nature, as Norman Foerster said, "through the refracting medium of his personality," but he also used it as a means of understanding his personality. His classical background taught him that transformation was the mission of all great literature, and his own writing was no exception. As he explored the world around him, he became better acquainted with his own consciousness and more determined to make his life "equal [in] simplicity . . . with the earth herself." He offered redemption rather than escape: a chance to "thrum with the excitement of the universe," as Carl Van Doren put it, but also to put himself in harmony with these vibrations.[80] The heady combination of inspection and introspection gave his writing a sense of high purpose that was lacking in later writers, who vacillated between blustering masculine self-assertion, like Maurice Thompson, and passive observation, like John Burroughs.

Third, he wrote with an unshakable conviction that nature's operations mirrored divine law. As a dedicated transcendentalist surrounded by others who shared his faith in higher truths, he crowned nature with a symbolic superstructure that would have been impossible to construct in any other time or place. He aimed at high truth, while later nature writers aspired to factual truth. Foerster put this succinctly: "Thoreau's view of life was genuinely imaginative, sincerely idealistic, whereas the view of life that one finds in the typical nature-writing of the twentieth century is absurdly shallow and sentimental."[81] Turn-of-the-century readers may have found this idealism distracting, but it lent his words an incredible power that sustained him when outdoor enthusiasm succumbed to urban cultural influences after World War I.

Finally, Thoreau coupled his spiritual interpretation of nature to his reform ideals. The connection was obscure, but the two sides of his legacy were in subtle ways mutually reinforcing. On the centennial of his birth in 1917, Houghton Mifflin reissued Edward Emerson's *Henry Thoreau: As*

Remembered by a Young Friend, which had been dedicated to rescuing Thoreau's reputation from his nineteenth-century critics. "I saw this man," Emerson wrote, "always spoken of with affection and respect by my parents and other near friends; knew him [to be] strongly, but not noisily, interested on the side of Freedom in the great struggle that then stirred the country." Emerson's Lincolnesque tribute struck home: no other writer had been able to connect nature to the idea of human freedom as resoundingly as Thoreau. The centennial came amid the anxieties of European war, and this, too, reinforced the popular impression that Thoreau wrote about nature with a sense of social purpose. A *Cleveland Plain Dealer* editor remembered him as "an odd man" who preferred the friendship of birds, bugs, and beasts to humans, but he considered Thoreau a model for sane living in an insane world. The philosophic truths in *Walden*—simplicity, individualism, spiritual sensitivity—stood out against the banality of commerce and the trauma of war and gave his writing a universality missing in contemporary books on nature.[82] This side of Thoreau—his critique of society against the backdrop of nature—would sustain him through the decades between the two world wars.

The connection between Thoreau and the nature-study movement was problematic, but it was an important turning point in the trajectory of his reputation. "I went to the woods because I wished to live deliberately, to front only the essential facts of life, and see if I could not learn what it had to teach, and not, when I came to die, discover that I had not lived," Thoreau said in the opening lines of *Walden*. The nature writers who went to the woods at the turn of the century learned something far less inspirational, but in their zeal they managed to convey a deep-seated passion for the outdoors to an American public still ambivalent about the idea of nature. They gave the woods and fields emotional significance, if not transcendent value. Nostalgia, therapeutic composure, masculine affirmation, and in Muir's case sheer ecstasy made nature accessible to a broader class of people than those reached by the transcendentalists, and in a nation overwhelmed by the multiple complications of urban-industrial life, the natural world once again made sense. And this, after all, was the message Thoreau struggled to convey to the American people.[83]

CHAPTER 4

THOREAU FOR THE AGES, THOREAU FOR THE TIMES, 1920-1960

Speaking to the Wellesley College graduating class of 1930, the essayist and social reformer Raymond Fosdick recalled that eighty-five years earlier, "a picturesque and somewhat fantastic Yankee" had marched off, ax in hand, to build a cabin in the Walden woods. The act resulted in one of the great works of modern literature, well known to those in his audience, but Fosdick reminded them that the world had changed since that day. America's productive capacity had expanded beyond the dreams of Thoreau's contemporaries, challenging the nation's capacity to consume and "bringing forth modern publicity methods, sales quotas, a wholly new economic theory, [and] a grinding competition of man against man, business against business, industry against industry." *Walden* was clearly a classic, but Fosdick wondered about its meaning for the modern age: "What possible message for us can a man have," he asked, "who during eight months spent $8.74 for food and was so afraid of the tyranny of possessions that he threw away the only ornaments that his cabin boasted—three pieces of limestone that he had picked up on the shore?" Was Thoreau still relevant in the age of mass production and mass consumption?[1]

Others raised similar concerns. In his 1936 *History of American Letters*, Walter Taylor praised Thoreau's social criticism but admitted his solutions made sense only to the "society of independent farmers, artisans, and small

85

merchants in which he lived." Two years later naturalist Donald Peattie described the huge chasm that had opened between Thoreau's world and his own. When *Walden* was published, Peattie wrote, America was buoyant and confident, its belief system predicated on the omnipotence of God and the essential goodness of humanity. Peattie's generation could muster no such optimism. Inexplicable economic gyrations—overproduction in the 1920s and underproduction in the 1930s—made the *Walden* chapter on economics seem simplistic, and in the lengthening shadow of the machine, individualism seemed all but irrelevant. Looking out across this altered landscape, Peattie recommended reading Thoreau for his timeless nature images rather than his dated social commentary.[2]

In the late nineteenth century Thoreau's friends rebuilt his reputation on the strength of the nature-study movement, but in the decades after World War I interest in nature waned, as Americans once again embraced a burgeoning industrial economy promising an endless train of modern consumer marvels—automobiles, radios, movies, washing machines, refrigerators, frozen foods. Many a writer acclaimed at the heyday of the nature-study movement lapsed into obscurity in the decades that followed. Thoreau might well have shared their fate, but in fact his reputation became more firmly lodged in both the literary canon and popular symbolism. As Robert Sattelmeyer points out, *Walden* was excerpted in *Reader's Digest* in the 1930s, and "however bowdlerized and distorted, . . . such excerpts marked a sort of 'arrival' . . . in a popular medium not associated with either the academy or highbrow culture." During these years Thoreau's popularity was sustained by a set of cultural forces more closely attuned to "Civil Disobedience" than to *Walden*, while the latter, according to Sattelmeyer, was itself incorporated into an "oppositional canon" as a "reformist document."[3]

Given this transformation, Fosdick's concern about Thoreau's relevance seems misplaced. The momentous events of the interwar decades—mass consumerism, economic collapse, European totalitarianism—sparked a nationwide discussion of the fundamental social values Thoreau championed nearly a century earlier, and the result was a surprisingly modern symbology of the man and his works. Americans distanced themselves from nature in the machine age, but they found Thoreau more timely than ever. In his *Essays in Freedom and Rebellion,* Henry Nevison painted a picture of the Concord proselytizer "standing alone, illuminated by the fire of a holy indignation, deserted by his . . . friends [and] violently opposed even by that

'Abolition Committee' which was founded . . . with the express object of maintaining the cause for which Thoreau fought." It was this Thoreau—the tax resister, the champion of John Brown, the defender of civil liberties—who appealed in the interwar years. Earlier scholars had considered *Walden* a book of "beautiful nature writing curiously introduced by a hundred pages . . . of ill-advised and ill-tempered diatribe against society," but as the literary critic Charles Walcutt cautioned in 1940, overlooking these comments on personal freedom left readers easy prey for demagogues at a time when individualism was besieged on all sides. Thoreau, Russell Blankenship insisted, was "first of all a critic of human institutions, and only incidentally a student of nature." He was a rebel and a heretic, modern not because he believed in nature but because he refused to believe in the state. "If ever we needed Thoreau," Thomas Lyle Collins wrote in the *Sewanee Review*, "we need him now."[4]

During the interwar years Thoreau's reputation was clouded by a tension between those who considered his nature writing timeless and those who believed his social commentary to be timely. Literary biographers and scholarly critics chafed at the practice of using Thoreau to buttress contemporary political viewpoints and found him timeless because his writing spoke across the ages to those yearning for a deeper connection to nature. Popular writers and journalists saw him as timely because he assured Americans that their core values would survive the traumas of global war and economic collapse. At the end of this stormy period, scholars and popularizers turned once again to the timeless Thoreau—the Concord naturalist who led them through woods and fields on an adventure of discovery and self-discovery. But by this time the idea of nature had changed once again, and America's favorite nature writer returned with a far different message.

Machines and Materialism in the 1920s

Thoreau's reappearance as a social critic reflected the widespread sense of disillusion that fell on the nation in the wake of World War I. Writing for an audience increasingly doubtful about the autonomy of the individual in the industrial age, novelists such as Theodore Dreiser, Edith Wharton, Sinclair Lewis, Sherwood Anderson, John Dos Passos, and Willa Cather built their stories around characters trapped by forces well beyond their control.

For these writers, the decade's brilliant surge in industrial output did little more than erode the individual's standing in society. Fosdick explained this modern dilemma:

> We cannot have clothes without a cotton mill; we cannot have a cotton mill without machinery; we cannot have machinery without steel.... Civilization has, in fact, become a great machine, the wheels of which must be kept turning or the people will starve ... and with it all has come ... the spirit of hurry and worry such as our grandfathers with all their lack of conveniences never dreamed of.... Life has become more and more a standardized process, in which there is little of serenity or of leisure.[5]

When the machines ran, America prospered; when they stopped, the economy faltered; and when they ran too fast, production exceeded the capacity to consume, forcing society to generate more demand by stimulating new desires, which in turn forced individuals to work even harder. As the philosopher James McKaye pointed out, the modern economy achieved its greatest efficiency "when men are cogs in a machine," and under these circumstances individualism—refusing to join the other cogs—was an affront to the American economy. This was the national paradox: machines should have prepared the way for a new American enlightenment, yet they seemed to suppress rather than foster culture. It was still possible, Brooks Atkinson thought, that the nation could harness the power of the machine to reward Americans with both goods and contemplative leisure, but this would take a revolution in values—indeed, a reassessment of what it meant to be an American.[6]

Questions like these led critics on a search for the modern Thoreau. According to the novelist Cornelia Cannon, his work was a corrective for the nation's obsession with pointless productivity. Even at the beginning of the Industrial Revolution, he understood that new technologies could be complications as much as conveniences, and his years at Walden proved that life was better without them. Thoreau biographer Henry Canby mused that in the fullness of time, Americans might grow tired of the bacchanalia of things and transform their industrial technologies into engines of liberation. "What if I do not want varied food, extravagant clothes, excessive transportation, nervous excitement? You must want them, says industrialism, or you will not produce. Right, replies Thoreau, then I will cut the dilemma by reducing my material wants, and thus provide easily for my intellectual and esthetic being. My solution is Walden; what is yours?"[7]

In the 1920s personal freedom was on the minds of many intellectuals who saw the advance of industrial capitalism as a threat to the social values

Thoreau held dear. For the historians Charles Beard and Mary Beard, who published *The Rise of American Civilization* in 1927, the Civil War brought the question of personal liberty to the fore. Although slavery had divided the nation, the industrial technologies that emerged after the war—the telegraph, the transcontinental railroad, the electric motor, Linotype, the telephone, the automobile, the assembly line—tightened the bonds of national interdependency under the aegis of the corporation, an agency "rash to the point of peril, [and] defiant of all petty material limitations." Awed by the power of these economic giants, publishers, teachers, ministers, and professors transferred their moral authority to the business system, and this abdication bound the nation intellectually as well as economically to the corporation. Although Beard and Beard offered no thoughts on how personal freedom might fare in this tightly interwoven society, they provided a brilliant analysis of the historical trends that made it so precarious in the modern age.[8]

The social critic Lewis Mumford's *Golden Day*, published in 1926, and its 1931 sequel, *The Brown Decades*, revealed a similar story of diminished personal autonomy. Mumford opened his history of American belles lettres with the westward movement in the 1790s. Down the Ohio River and out onto the Great Plains, he wrote, scrambled a land-hungry people whose dispersion marked one of the greatest exercises in personal liberty in world history. But like Beard and Beard, he saw these disintegrating forces checked by an expanding commercial and industrial system, and, also like them, he saw the danger in this concentration of power.[9] Out of these contesting impulses emerged the brilliant prose and verses of Emerson, Thoreau, Whitman, Hawthorne, Melville, and others whose celebration of freedom produced a cultural baseline from which the nation descended, after the Civil War, into a "debauch of materialism." In the pastoral inclinations of this "golden day," Mumford found a solid foundation for American culture, and it was here that Thoreau's renunciation of the "reckless waste of life . . . which followed the introduction of the machine" became relevant to the modern era. Despite the weave of industrial interdependency, Thoreau offered a way to preserve personal liberty; he simply asked, "Shall we always study to obtain more of these things, and not sometimes be content with less?" Instead of looking on Thoreau as a writer from another era, Mumford suggested that it was "perhaps more accurate to think of [him] . . . as the forerunner . . . of a fresh line of effort and action."[10]

In his 1927 *Main Currents in American Thought,* Vernon Parrington joined Beard and Beard as well as Mumford in tracing the social and cultural implications of the machine age, and, like Mumford, he saw Thoreau's social commentary as a benchmark in the individualist challenge to this tightly integrated economic system. One of the first literary scholars to recognize Thoreau's potential as a social theorist, Parrington "set the tone" for the coming decade of Thoreau scholarship, as Robert Sattelmeyer says. According to Parrington, Thoreau "did not understand why Americans should boast of [an industrial] . . . system that provided vulgar leisure for the masters at the cost of serfdom for the workers." Thoreau saw only three options for those seeking to protect their personal liberty: they could exploit themselves to accumulate wealth, they could exploit others to the same end, or they could reduce their material needs and liberate themselves from the demands of the industrial system. The agrarian society in which Thoreau envisioned these choices was lost to history, but, according to Parrington, his "transcendental declaration of independence" was still relevant to the modern age.[11]

Thoreau in the Thirties: Conflicting Interpretations

Public intellectuals like Fosdick, Beard and Beard, Mumford, and Parrington saw the modern Thoreau as a timely social critic. Literary biographers, still dedicated to the idea that Thoreau was ageless, portrayed him as America's consummate nature writer. *Henry Thoreau: Bachelor of Nature,* published in 1925 by the French literary critic Léon Bazalgette and translated into English by Van Wyck Brooks, touched on Thoreau's social philosophy but gave it a flavor of the woods by comparing him to the French naturalist philosopher Jean-Jacques Rousseau. Bazalgette's main concern was presenting Thoreau as the American outdoorsman, particularly in the passages gleaned from *The Maine Woods.*[12] Bazalgette's biography was distinctive for its flamboyant style, crafted to introduce this American primitive to French readers. A poet himself, he imagined Thoreau, as one reviewer put it, sweeping through the Concord scene "as in a picaresque novel." The technique, according to another critic, had all the mannerisms of a bad novel: "the use of the present tense in a wild struggle for vividness, the direct address with the wearisome epithet, the question flung at a hypothetical audience." A bit more kindly, Norman Foerster characterized the book as "vivacious."[13] Despite literary approach, Bazalgette brought Thoreau to life: "As you seem him pass, with his rough clothes, . . . with the long, swinging step of a man who is used to walking great distances, hands behind his back and fists clenched, often with his eyes on the ground, the impression of physical resistance this thin little fellow gives is in flat contradiction to the meagre frame. When he lifts his eyes and looks at you it is if a jet of implacable sincerity and perspicacity has struck you; the whole man is revealed in those eyes."[14]

Three years after publication of *Bachelor of Nature*, the Trinity College English professor Odell Shepard presented a more scholarly tribute to Thoreau's skills as a nature writer in his *Heart of Thoreau's Journals*, which distilled the intimidating two million words in the journals into a single volume favoring nature descriptions in the choice of entries. In a brief introduction, Shepard drew attention to Thoreau's genius in that genre. Theater critic Brooks Atkinson's *Henry Thoreau: The Cosmic Yankee*, also published in 1927, likewise downplayed Thoreau's social philosophy. His antislavery activity, Atkinson wrote, revealed a "less worthy side" of Thoreau's character. "Was he not pusillanimous, vindictive, and feline in his attack? Alas! Most of his public appearances . . . were unworthy of the poet who sang of Nature in *Walden* and recorded the mysteries of the Concord and Merrimack Rivers in chryselephantine style."[15]

In 1939 Henry Canby, editor of the *Saturday Review of Literature*, published the major Thoreau biography of the decade, simply titled *Thoreau*. Curiously, in the magazine articles that led up to in the biography, Canby had emphasized Thoreau's social thought—the "danger of becoming a machine thinking like a machine"—but in the biography he argued that Thoreau was neither a committed abolitionist nor a consistent critic of the state; nature was the single constant in his life.[16] Reaction to this interpretation was mixed. Howard Zahniser, later to become executive secretary of the Wilderness Society, found the nature theme too subdued in Canby's biography, but the literary critics Charles Walcutt and Clifton Fadiman complained that Canby virtually ignored Thoreau's social criticism. According to Walcutt, he "handl[ed] . . . the bombshells of his most explosive ideas as if they were roses."[17]

Focused largely on the nature themes in Thoreau's work, the interwar biographies failed to address the question Fosdick had raised about his relevance: He was indeed timeless as a nature writer, but how timely was he? If scholars like Shepard and Canby skirted this question, newspaper and magazine critics found him perfectly attuned to the Depression decade. *Reader's Digest* published a series of *Walden* excerpts, introducing them as a "record of an experiment in serene living, a venture in simplicity and discipline as timely today as it was nearly 100 years ago." In a 1937 article titled "One

Man Revolution," novelist Sinclair Lewis summarized Thoreau's timeliness in an era of scarcity: "Devoting a shrewd Yankee brain to the accurate measuring of his own wants, he saw just how few things he needed to wear and eat and own in order to be comfortable." Lewis hoped that "100,000 copies [of *Walden*] will be given as Christmas presents . . . to all young persons who are, and very reasonably, worrying about their economic futures, all married couples envious of their friends' automobiles, all Communists, all reactionaries." Thoreau's asceticism had been, to say the least, unfashionable during the 1920s, but in the Depression its logic became clear. He showed readers how to avoid the dilemma of the machine age, and when the machines stopped, his frugality appeared all the more sensible—perhaps even liberating.[18]

Reflecting on this and other commentary at the end of the Depression, Randall Stewart found three reasons to consider Thoreau modern. First, as literary scholars pointed out, his genius at expressing the idea of nature appealed to all readers in all ages. Second, as public intellectuals, newspaper editors, and social commentators insisted, his social essays spoke specifically to the modern age. He pondered the relation between self and society and composed thousands of journal pages to resolve this issue to his own satisfaction. Being sure of himself, he stood firm on the principle of personal freedom, and this display of resolve spoke to a generation no longer secure in its own moral footing. And third, Thoreau was timely, Stewart thought, because he foresaw the "modern aggrandizement of the state." With the rise of dictatorships in Europe and Japan, this side of Thoreau had "never been more crucial." Despite the eclipse of nature study, Thoreau's message remained both timeless and timely. In these difficult times, America needed a social critic as much as it needed a poet of nature.[19]

Thoreau among the Radicals

During the Depression, as historian Gary Scharnhorst noted, Americans abandoned "the courtly debate over Thoreau's [personal] virtues" and turned instead to his bearing as a radical social thinker—a theme British scholars had taken for granted for decades. If public intellectuals such as Fosdick and Lewis refashioned Thoreau to address the social concerns of the era, Marxists had an equally pressing reason for revising his legacy. Since at least the turn of the century they had been searching for an indigenous strain of radicalism to validate the socialist critique of American society, and Thoreau seemed appropriate to this project. In his 1908 *Spirit of American Literature,* John Macy presented him as a bitter foe of capitalism. As a socialist Macy was, in Lawrence Buell's words, "the first American to put Thoreau's . . . 'Civil Disobedience' on the same plane of importance as *Walden*." John Edwards, writing a few years later in the *Socialist Review,* pared away the descriptions of nature to reveal "the marrow of Thoreau's teaching": his insistence that much of the world's work was wasted on producing profits for the idle rich. For Macy, Edwards, and other radicals, Thoreau represented an "unbroken tradition that went back politically to Thomas Jefferson."[20]

The Marxist literary critic V. F. Calverton described Thoreau in his 1932 *Liberation of American Literature* as "the clearest voice for social ethics that ever spoke out in America." Calverton reasoned that writers such as Emerson, Whitman, and Thoreau had been entranced by the dynamic classless society emerging on the western frontier and cast their poems and essays as a tribute to the personal freedom this society represented. Thus, they forged an enduring petit bourgeois ideology for America, and this was the basis for Thoreau's radicalism. Horrified by the oppression of enslaved people in the plantation South and the industrial Northeast, he penned essays that were "quick with the dynamite of revolt," but his dissent was circumscribed by the bourgeois individualism out of which it emerged. He "hated the state because it taxed him, and . . . hated society because . . . it thwarted his freedom of enterprise and advance." His social commentary was only partially modern, suited to his own liberation but not to the liberation of the world.[21]

Granville Hicks's *Great Tradition,* published in 1933, was less steeped in class analysis, but he, too, saw Thoreau representing both the strengths and the weaknesses of American radicalism. He found industrial capitalism a threat to his egalitarian sensibilities and counseled his neighbors to live more meaningfully by renouncing the fruits of factory production. This plea went unheeded, Hicks felt, because Americans needed a philosophy that humanized rather than rejected the machine. "And with that problem Thoreau had no concern." He could have used his understanding of social injustice to engineer a revolution, but, as Emerson said, he instead chose to captain a huckleberry party.[22] Radicals like Macy, Calverton, and Hicks found Thoreau relevant because he understood the oppressive nature of American capitalism but outdated because he responded to this oppression with a message of individualism rather than collective action.

Personal Freedom in the Totalitarian Era

Thoreau's individualism became timely in a different way in the late 1930s. When the specter of totalitarianism appeared in Europe in the mid-1930s, American writers and artists embraced populist themes as a way of affirming the nation's commitment to democracy. The New Deal Federal Writers and Federal Art Projects and Resettlement Administration, along with regionalist artists like Thomas Hart Benton, Grant Wood, and John Steuart Curry and left-leaning writers like John Dos Passos and John Steinbeck, celebrated the commonsense democracy of the American folk, and in the same vein critics highlighted Thoreau's descriptions of those Concordians he called "natural men": woodcutters, farmers, trappers, and fishers who embodied the New England pioneering spirit. According to the Harvard English professor F. O. Matthiessen, Thoreau "had a relish for old sayings and for rural slang, and set down many fragments of conversation with his friends the woodchoppers and the farmers." In 1936 Francis Allen and the artist N. C. Wyeth published *Men of Concord and Some Others as Portrayed in the Journal of Henry David Thoreau,* featuring gossipy journal selections in which Thoreau described his traditionalist neighbors. Thoreau's commentary on these sturdy and independent folk was reassuring: America at its core was resistant to mass politics and totalitarian solutions.[23]

Populist themes suggested a resistance to dictatorship in America, but in the mid-1930s radical assaults on the American political system were appearing frequently in the media and democracy was faring poorly abroad. In his *Fountainheads of Freedom,* published just before America entered World War II, Irwin Edman reminded readers "how long is the history of tyranny" and how short the history of democracy. As the nation prepared to defend its freedoms, Edman thought it was important to examine the values upon which they rested, and Thoreau, not surprisingly, figured prominently in the pages of his book, not as a bachelor of nature but as a critic of state authority. Thoreau's essay on civil disobedience, Edman wrote, was one of the nation's most important bulwarks against tyranny—a true fountainhead of freedom. Thomas Collins described the same essay as "supercharged political dynamite," a magnificent proclamation in defense of democracy.[24]

By the 1940s Thoreau stood among the nation's most popular writers, both timeless and timely, and when America entered World War II, the government printed 155,000 copies of *Walden* in a special edition for soldiers. The destructive force of the world war, the most mechanized in human history, drove home Thoreau's misgivings about the machine age and highlighted the prescience of his social essays. "Civil Disobedience," Walter Harding wrote in early 1945, had animated the struggle for self-determination in Great Britain, India, South Africa, Central America, and occupied Europe, and these same ideas would guide Americans through the difficult days ahead.[25] In June 1945, shortly before the end of the war, the *New York Times* reflected on Thoreau's opposition to the Mexican War and concluded that "since eleven million of our young men have had to drop whatever they were doing and defend our liberties, and since more than 250,000 of them have already been killed in defense of America on foreign soil, it would be easy to conclude that Thoreau was right and society is wrong, and that everyone should turn artisan, farmer, poet, and philosopher." Yet, as the correspondent pointed out, the global war preserved what Thoreau valued most in life: "freedom to speak, freedom to worship, freedom from want, freedom from fear."[26] Ambivalence notwithstanding, the *Times* editorial demonstrated the need to invoke Thoreau in moments of national crisis.

Throughout the interwar years nature had not been a prominent theme in American writing, yet by the end of the era *Walden* was internationally known, one of only twenty volumes in American literature to appear on the UNESCO world classics list. The year 1945 marked the centenary of Thoreau's move to Walden Pond and 1954 the centenary of *Walden*'s publication. Between these two dates Americans celebrated Thoreau as never before. The tributes were directed at his brilliant depiction of nature, but they also reflected his fit with the progressive temper in the years immediately following the nation's brush with totalitarianism.[27] Morris Longstreth attributed *Walden*'s popularity in part to "the terrible scare we have just had" and compared his abolitionist speeches to the campaigns against Nazism and fascism. In separate articles, C. R. B. Combellack and R. N. Stromberg compared Thoreau's impact on the world to that of Karl Marx. The latter was the more inclusive thinker, but Thoreau was more relevant to modern America. He wrote with style, unlike the pontifical author of the *Communist Manifesto,* but, more important, he insisted that individual will was more enduring than collective will, and in the aftermath of a war against totalitarianism, this was a timely insight indeed. According to Jacques Ducharme, *Walden* remained "the clearest expression possible of what it means to be an American."[28]

In the face of postwar uncertainty, commentators turned to Thoreau. As early as 1928 scientists delving into the structure of matter had discovered an incomparably powerful store of energy sequestered in the atom, but as Raymond Fosdick commented at the time, atomic power could either liberate the world or blow it "into oblivion." He pondered the wisdom of leaving this new technology in the hands of those who studied means but not ends.[29] Two decades later the naturalist and social critic Joseph Wood Krutch described the bomb as a symbolic watershed. Humanity in the past, he pointed out, had been "saved as much by its helplessness" in the face of natural forces as by its own farsightedness. The bomb marked the beginning of a new age: "the first time . . . in a specific instance, we may have more to fear than to hope from a sudden acquisition of power."[30] The destruction of Nagasaki and Hiroshima showed the nation to be "more bewildered, more despairing than . . . ever," Henry Miller wrote in the introduction to a new edition of Thoreau's political essays. Herbert West added that "in a time of greater and greater regimentation . . . honest and rugged individualism . . . is the only thing that will save us from becoming the victims not only of machines, . . . but also of power-loving authoritarian and totalitarian governments." Pondering the timeliness of Thoreau's principles, John Haynes Holmes observed that "we must build anew the rights of man."[31]

A World without Critics

Thoreau's reputation was sustained through the interwar years by his social commentary: his pronouncements on the machine age in the 1920s, his emphasis on simple living in the 1930s, and his living example of principled individualism in the 1940s. The Cold War brought another turn in American political culture when in April 1954 Senator Joseph McCarthy began holding hearings in the Senate Subcommittee on Investigations. McCarthy launched a sustained prosecution of American nonconformists and radicals that altered the nation's political climate—and the tenor of commentary on Thoreau's political writings. McCarthyism affected American literature as well as its politics. The magazine publisher Richard Boyer fell victim to the committee by simply quoting Thoreau and Emerson. Sensitive to pressures such as these, Wendell Glick took pains to show that Thoreau's political essays offered nothing to "those anarchists and extremists . . . who were seeking to sweep away completely all political institutions." The novelist and critic Waldo Frank observed that at the very moment *Walden* became a classic, its ideals became obsolete. "Today, anyone who insisted 'on walking out of step because he heard a different drummer,' would be inconspicuously trampled on by the American march." But others found Thoreau all the more relevant in the Cold War era. Distressed by the conformist mood, the Thoreau Society recommended "Civil Disobedience," "Slavery in Massachusetts," and "Plea for John Brown" to those who saw him only as the author of *Walden*.[32]

The tense atmosphere created by the McCarthy hearings scattered Thoreau scholarship in a number of directions. Shortly after the war Nick Ford published an article challenging Henry Canby's assertion that Thoreau was not a committed abolitionist. Ford found ample evidence of antislavery activity in Thoreau's journal and essays and concluded that he was "an active champion of all kinds of freedom." Seven years later G. M. Ostrander argued in the *Mississippi Valley Historical Review* that Thoreau was indeed an abolitionist, but not in fact a champion of freedom. He and Emerson, in Ostrander's view, had been duped by John Brown, a convicted embezzler who led his band of outlaws in the "cold-blooded midnight murders of five proslavery men at Pottawatomie Creek." By portraying Brown as a martyred saint, the two transcendentalists created a dangerous myth that rationalized "hideous acts" committed by equally gullible partisans. Ostrander offered this as a cautionary tale at a time when communist conspiracies might seem equally appealing to naive liberals. As Samuel Middlebrook pointed out in G. R. Mason's 1956 *Great American Liberals,* Thoreau fitted somewhere among the champions of freedom, "but what kind of liberal he was, what specific freedoms he sought for himself and others, what dangers he warned against, and how useful his ideas still are—all these are questions worthy of examination."[33]

The timeliness of Thoreau's social commentary was hotly debated in the Cold War years. In the widely read magazine *Commonweal*, C. C. Hollis argued that Thoreau's insistence on individual conscience denied the fundamental Lockean principle that "man needs the state . . . for his own social welfare," and in the more scholarly journal *Ethics* Vincent Buranelli claimed that elevating the individual over the state violated the Kantian categorical imperative: if everyone acted only on inner impulses, social life would come to a standstill. "To a political scientist, who must deal with the tangibles of life," Robert LaForte asserted, "Henry David Thoreau seems highly absurd." Others, like the Christian anarchist Robert Ludlow and the Unitarian pacifist John Haynes Holmes, cautioned that subordinating individual conscience to the state would court totalitarianism—the threat that made "the revival of Thoreau's essay so timely."[34]

The postwar years saw a confusion of voices seeking to balance Thoreau's timelessness as a nature writer against his role as a timely social critic. "The potent seeds of *Walden* have sometimes fallen into unexpected places," Alexandra Krastin wrote on the centenary of the book's publication. It inspired dissenters, encouraged individualists, enthralled nature lovers, and "because of Thoreau's habit of daily bathing in the pond, a nudist magazine has claimed him as one of their own." Krastin dispelled this confusion by reducing Thoreau's besieged philosophy to a single theme: "If life seems too complex, he urges simplifying." Arguing similarly, Alfred Kazin wrote that Thoreau displayed his genius by "stripping life down to fundamentals and essentials." Popular writers such as Krastin and Kazin were probably closer to the reigning impression of Thoreau than scholars who scrutinized the finer details of his political thought, but the polarized commentary in the press made one thing clear: Thoreau's literary legacy had changed. Like *Walden*, the political essays were becoming a staple of American literature, even in a world without critics.[35]

Thoreau Becomes a Literary Stylist

In an influential essay written at the end of the Cold War era, the critical theorist Stanley Hyman recounted the many scholarly misjudgments that obscured Thoreau's reputation since his canonization in the early twentieth century. Among others, John Macy saw him as a radical, Léon Bazalgette as a savage, V. F. Calverton as a bourgeois individualist, and Henry Canby as a hermit. None of these portraits suited Thoreau, in Hyman's view; he was first and foremost a writer, a master of metaphor and symbol. To be sure, he had been "a nut reformer" in his own time and, as such, merely "one of the hordes in his period." But this "comic little figure" was also, ironically, "the most ringing and magnificent polemicist American has ever produced." This suggested to Hyman that his lasting legacy would be his writing style, not his politics. As a critique of industrial society, *Walden* was no longer timely, but as an elaborate symbolic tale of withdrawal, purification, and rebirth, it was timeless. As the historian Gary Scharnhorst pointed out, Hyman's emphasis on the transcendence of language allowed him to "divert . . . critical attention away from [Thoreau's] 'absurd' political defiance." Hyman plucked Thoreau from the radical tradition and repositioned him among mainstream writers such as Hawthorne and Melville, undistinguished by any timely political message. Hyman's assessment never reached a popular audience, but it forecast a scholarly perspective that would have lasting implications.[36]

The Cold War atmosphere fragmented the commentary on Thoreau's writing, and in the midst of this controversy some critics, like Hyman, found a safe haven in linguistics. During these years Francis O. Matthiessen, a Harvard historian who published biographies of several well-known nineteenth- and twentieth-century authors, pioneered a New Critical methodology concentrated almost exclusively on stylistic inflection and thematic organization. The American canon had been established for a half century, he reasoned; it was time to consider seriously the stylistic foundations of these classics. In his 1941 *American Renaissance: Art and Expression in the Age of Emerson and Whitman,* he reminded readers that the political content in Thoreau's work was a product of the times and therefore of little consequence to modern criticism. By contrast, Thoreau's use of language, image, metaphor, and symbol was timeless—the "unchanging stuff of humanity."[37]

The New Criticism abandoned what Howard Mumford Jones called "the persistent effort of academic criticism to find a usable past." There was, of course, much to be discovered in reading *Walden* purely as a work of art, and in doing so Matthiessen elevated Thoreau as a consummate American stylist. But the focus on close textual analysis was also a means of diminishing his importance as a social critic, and the techniques Matthiessen pioneered were used by more conservative scholars to deflect attention from the Thoreau who spoke to the political issues of the day. Lyndon Shanley's *The Making of "Walden,"* published in 1957, epitomized this technique by dwelling almost exclusively on form, structure, word choice, symbol, and order of presentation. In *Shores of America,* published in 1958, Sherman Paul insisted that viewing Thoreau as a social critic was "one of the most persistent errors . . . that has never been sufficiently dispelled." *Walden* was not a tribute to personal freedom but a message about redemption, described metaphorically in the transition from winter to spring at Walden Pond. Earlier scholars, according to Robert Cobb, saw the man as a reflection of his times, but with the ascendancy of the New Criticism, "we are all sufficiently influenced or intimidated . . . to minimize the biographical aspects of literature lest we be charged with moralizing or with ignoring the texts themselves."[38] Thoreau was not modern; he was merely timeless.

Once Again the Nature Writer

The shift away from Thoreau's political philosophy in the 1950s coincided with an upsurge in outdoor recreation and renewed interest in his nature writing. Auto camping became an important form of recreation during the

1930s, and in the 1940s this and other types of outdoor recreation provided release from the pent-up anxieties and frustrations left from a decade of depression and war.[39] In summer, according to *Time* magazine, millions of Americans "packed their children into sedans and station wagons and hit the road. For the moment, at least, summertime rites seemed more important than civil rights; personal clouds were fluffier than the far-away blossom of the latest atomic shot; disarmament was something for Harold Stassen to worry about; and international problems from Arabs to Zhukov, all belonged to Ike."[40] More directly, the postwar boom in outdoor recreation reflected trends in a shorter workweek, rising discretionary income, longer vacations, and an emphasis on active as opposed to passive leisure. Improved roads, highways, and campgrounds expanded the reach of the postwar recreationist.

Taking inspiration from Thoreau's passion for the local environment, John Kieran, author of *Footnotes on Nature,* applauded the "modest adventures" available even in his readers' own backyards. Edwin Way Teale wrote a fascinating natural history of Times Square, and William Beebe's *Unseen Life of New York,* published in 1953, showed that New York City was full of wildlife small enough, common enough, or stealthy enough to elude the human instinct to "exterminate every species not his own." Having traveled to the ends of the earth and the depths of the ocean under the auspices of the Bronx Zoo, Beebe discovered an equally exotic natural world in his own city environs. Turkeys roamed the outskirts, beavers plied the nearby wetlands, wildcats cried in the night, coyotes prowled the downtown parks, and opossums wandered the neighborhoods. Gulls, turtles, garter snakes, bullfrogs, and peepers made the Bronx River their home. Even New Yorkers, he felt, could make an acquaintance with nature just as Thoreau had done in the Concord woods.[41]

Joseph Wood Krutch, professor of literature at Columbia University and drama critic for the *Nation* magazine, rose to the fore as America's most beloved contemporary nature writer, and his trajectory through the mid-twentieth century shows how Thoreau became once again relevant as a nature writer. In the 1920s Krutch wrote several articles criticizing modern consumer culture, and in a score of essays culminating in his 1929 *Modern Temper,* he voiced his preference for a more organic and less technological way of life. "We are disillusioned with the laboratory, not because we have lost faith in the truth of its findings, but because we have lost faith in the power of those findings to help us." After reading *Walden* in 1930, he used

Thoreau to express these misgivings about modernism. Like the Concord author, he saw material acquisitiveness as a form of slavery, but where Thoreau blamed individual consumers for their desperation, Krutch saw them trapped by the imperatives of modern society. "A whole new science of exploitation by persuasion has grown up and the practice of it has become the profession of thousands." Krutch's 1948 biography, *Henry David Thoreau*, provided a formula for breaking free of these compulsions. "What Thoreau had always sought in his intercourse with living things and even with the very hills and fields themselves was that warm and sympathetic sense of oneness, that escape from the self into the All." Krutch saw Thoreau as a rebel against materialism, but he tailored his antimaterialist message to the postwar yearning for social reconciliation. Thoreau proposed, as Krutch put it, "passive resistance to society, the refusal of the individual to engage in activities and competitions which he does not want to engage in.... He can, as a solitary individual, lay down the burden. If enough men do the same, society will be transformed; but if all but you and I insist upon carrying it, then at least you and I will have saved our souls." Krutch himself laid down his burden in 1952 and left the city for Arizona, completing his trajectory from social pessimist to nature writer—from *Modern Temper* to *Desert Year*. Thoreau was timely, in Krutch's estimation, in presenting nature as a release from decades of depression and war.[42]

Aside from Krutch, the most influential advocate for Thoreau's nature writing was Pulitzer Prize–winning naturalist and photographer Edwin Way Teale. Like Krutch, Teale defined Thoreau principally as a naturalist. Those who overlooked this aspect of his writing, he thought, separated Thoreau from the "very fountainhead of his inspiration." And like Krutch, Teale read into Thoreau the mood of withdrawal and reconciliation prevalent in postwar America. In his *North with the Spring*, published in 1951, Teale narrated a pilgrimage from the Carolinas to Walden Pond as he followed the spring sweeping northward at an average rate of about fifteen miles a day. "Behind us,... city pallor was increasing. Tempers were growing short in the dead air of underventilated offices. That quiet desperation, which Thoreau says characterizes the mass of men, was taking on new intensity." Adding to Krutch's interpretation of *Walden* as withdrawal, Teale embraced the message of renewal. Journeying northward, he left behind a sweltering civilization in quest of perpetual springtime. In his eyes, Thoreau's nature offered both refuge and hope: a place where the reader could stand once again on solid footing and gain assurance that whatever the devastation, nature possessed the seeds of springtime rebirth. For those whose lives had been shattered by the events of the century's middle decades, this message was perhaps social commentary enough.[43]

The Thoreauvian Choice in the Cold War Era

Withdrawal from the city was again in vogue in the postwar years, generating a rich record of country living that helped shape Thoreau's message for the postwar world. Back-to-the-land books had all but disappeared in the 1920s as the focus of American cultural life shifted to the metropolis, but the anxieties of the nuclear age breathed new life into the genre. *Walden*'s introductory phrases once again rang through the press, as in countless iterations authors took up the challenge of explaining their own withdrawal to the woods. Thoreau's choice was not a difficult leap of the imagination, since the war had loosened Americans from their moorings and sharpened the urge to abandon society. "During the past winter I have observed more than one fellow veteran look longingly for a Walden," Carl Bode wrote in 1946.[44]

Postwar country-life books followed a familiar motif in which the urban-based professional writer abandoned the city for a simpler life. Each struck a somewhat different balance between nostalgia, science, and poetic imagination, but they shared certain themes in common. Like Thoreau, they addressed a deep desire to return to a simpler and settled place. After years of war, depression, and dislocation, they fed a huge market among readers yearning for the familiar and the durable—a place like Walden Pond. Henry Beston began his widely read *Northern Farm* with a mantra-like account of his return to the Maine coast. "I watched the city withdraw to the south," he wrote. "Home. Going home." The global trauma of the 1930s and 1940s left him heartsick and uprooted—"Home. Going home." City life had been so artificial that he could scarcely determine day from night, and he anticipated that the cycle of seasons in Maine would reconnect him to the land.[45] Walden Pond, among all its other symbolic representations, was a known place—an earth dwelling.

These books gave postwar Americans a new and very concrete interpretation of Thoreau's Walden experiment, but they were also, like Krutch's Thoreau, subtly judgmental. Like *Walden*, they documented a return to a timeless nature, but also like *Walden*, they conveyed a timely appraisal of their own society. Inspired by Thoreau, country-life authors saw themselves as models of individualist resistance to federalizing forces, mass media, metropolitan culture, and the modern obsession with machine-made things. Lewis Gannett's *Cream Hill: Discoveries of a Week-End Countryman* described the satisfactions of reducing needs and meeting nature on equal terms, but like Thoreau, Gannett made simple living an implicit indictment of society.[46] The turn to nature was a quest for rootedness but also, as with Thoreau, a stand against the machine.

A large number of these back-to-the-landers counted themselves among the decentralist movement, which set as its task the dismantling of various state-encouraged monopolies over landholding, housing, resource ownership, labor, production, and credit. Because cities were hopelessly hierarchical, decentralists typically relocated in rural areas where life was more democratic and egalitarian. In 1945 Benson Landis published an article in *Christian Century* titled "Decentralist at Walden Pond," pointing to *Walden* as a blueprint for the movement. The chapter "Economy," he instructed, offered a surprisingly modern guide to the decentralized way of life.[47] Landis was somewhat unusual in taking *Walden* this literally, but his interest in Thoreau as a principled homesteader was telling.

Ralph Borsodi, among the most prominent of these country-life authors, typifies the distrust of centralized authority that ran through the back-to-the-land literature. Borsodi's father had been involved in land-reform movements in Hungary, but Borsodi himself took up a career in advertising. Increasingly dissatisfied with work and city life, he read Henry George and began pondering the relation between modern economics, nature, freedom, and democracy. In the early 1920s he moved his family to a seven-acre homestead in New York, where he wrote several books criticizing the advertising industry and narrating his homesteading experiences. Among them was his popular *Flight from the City*, published in 1933.[48] Along with Borsodi, Hal Borland, a Columbia University School of Journalism professor, helped shape the back-to-the-land genre. With his wife, also a writer, Borland moved to a farm in Salisbury, Connecticut, where he wrote a weekly column for the *New York Times*, made regular contributions to the *Berkshire Eagle* and the *Progressive*, and published around twenty books. In the lives of his rural neighbors he discovered an elemental egalitarianism that confirmed the decentralist suspicion of urban social hierarchies. Americans, he thought, were "safe from regimentation" as long as Thoreau's choice was, at least theoretically, available to them. Henry Beston's *Northern Farm*, Margaret Snyder's *The Chosen Valley*, and Howard Hush's *Eastwick, U.S.A*, all published in 1948, drew similarly upon the decentralist idyll of withdrawal and simplicity and, like *Walden,* offered this as a critique of modern society.⁴⁹

Along with their escapist theme and critique of modernism, the back-to-the-land books shared with *Walden* a keen sensitivity to nature's dynamics. J. A. Baker's *The Hill of Summer,* according to a reviewer, was written by a poet but appealed because it showed "almost equal respect for predator and prey, [and] for the balance that is nature herself." As social thinkers who shared Thoreau's ecologically sensitive interest in nature, the back-to-the-land writers pioneered a conservation message for the postwar world. In *This Hill, This Valley,* Borland drew attention to the vulnerability of America's unspoiled natural areas, which were disappearing with "incredible rapidly." The machine age threatened American individualism, but it was no less a threat to nature: "the loss of rivers by pollution, the destruction of villages by the concrete viaducts of six-lane highways, the sacrifice of roadside beauty for refreshment booths and filling stations, and the disfiguration of wide stretches of the landscape by poorly designed houses in badly arranged settings." As a spiritual and practical guide for the back-to-the-land movement, Thoreau stood on the threshold of modernity in yet another way. Landscapes, he had insisted, reflected the moral posture of those who inhabited them, and thus the ravaged countryside, as Borland described it, was a powerful indictment of modern consumer society.⁵⁰

Nature and Renewal

The search for refuge in nature was a compelling theme in postwar Thoreau commentary, but as Edwin Way Teale hinted in *North with the Spring,* Thoreau's emphasis on renewal was equally appealing. Thoreau closed his famous book with a metaphor of springtime renewal and wrote elsewhere of human redemption and organic rebirth. Sensitive to the symbolic power of this message, Hal Borland wrote in awed terms of the regenerative process on his own farm: "If I go away for a month and leave my clearing untended, I shall return to find how tenuous my foothold really is. Though I use them often, the paths through my woods have to be cleared several times each Summer. I cut a tree and neglect to grub out the roots, and the next time I look at the stump it is hidden in a thicket of second-growth shoots as high as my head." The springtime renewal of nature was also a dominant motif in Sherman Paul's 1958 literary biography, *Shores of America.* While living at the pond, Thoreau experienced the "stages of autumnal consciousness," Paul wrote, and he arrived at the "promise of ecstatic rebirth in the spring." After two decades of depression and war, Americans could not have missed this message.[51]

In his *Almanac for Moderns,* Donald Culross Peattie looked at the same quest for renewal with a naturalist's eye. The first croaking of the frog in spring, Peattie wrote, "speaks of the return of life to the earth. It tells of all that is most unutterable in evolution—the terrible continuity and fluidity of protoplasm, the irrepressible forces of reproduction—not mystical human love, but the cold batrachian jelly by which we vertebrates are linked to the things that creep and writhe and are blind yet breed and have being." Paul interpreted Thoreau's springtime as an ethereal symbol of hope; Peattie infused this metaphor with a primal sense of oneness in nature that foreshadowed the values of the environmental movement. "The earth, the soil itself, has a dreaming quality about it," he wrote. "It is warm now to the touch; it has come alive; it hides secrets that in a moment, in a little while, it will tell. Some of them are bursting out already—the first leaves of wildflowers uncurling, the spears of mottled adder's tongue leaves and the furled up flags of bloodroot. Old earth is great with her children, the bulb and the grub, and the sleepy mammal and the seed."[52]

Peattie blended Thoreau's mystical vision of renewal with a new ecological understanding tinted by the fading images of wartime carnage. Nature was a battle between death and life, but it was more than that: a "sort of terrible mating of substances, dissolving and fusing from one species into another." Like Thoreau, he enjoyed the sensuousness of wading into ponds, where he came in contact with the "very medium of life itself"—water alive with sponges, shards of crayfish, strands of algae, and the mud "out of which small nameless things come kicking and twisting." But Peattie understood these interactions in ways no nineteenth-century naturalist could have. Thoreau's pond was a transcendental metaphor for regeneration; Peattie's pond was the base of a biological pyramid, a "spawning factory" upon which layer upon layer of grazers and predators drew sustenance.[53] It was a complex machine, like the interconnected machines that fueled the consumer economy, but it was also something quite different—something more primal and organic: something even more redemptive than Walden Pond.

Peattie's nature—interconnected, interwoven, and thoroughly wild at this primordial level—served as a bridge between the Thoreau's Concord world and the interconnected ecology that would become so attractive to the environmental era. Thoreau observed inward; he studied nature to understand himself. Peattie observed outward; he studied nature to understand its connection to humanity. Thus, he understood, as did Thoreau intuitively, the consequences of disrupting this delicate set of relationships, and this put him in touch with the decentralist critique articulated in Borland's *This Hill, This Valley*. When the birds that frequented his pond were slain, the hunter "lets loose their prey, and his worst enemy, the insects," Peattie wrote, and from this ecological lesson he moved on to a broader cycle of abuses and consequences unleashed by the machines of mass production. Man "wastes his forests faster than he replaces them, and slaughters the mink and the beaver and the seal. Man devours his limited coal supply even faster; he fouls the rivers, invents poison gases and turns his destruction even on his own kind. And in the end he may present the spectacle of some Brobdingnagian spoiled baby, gulping down his cake and howling for it too." Thoreau had anticipated these disastrous events by joining together his timely suspicion of consumerism and his timeless understanding of nature. As Peattie said, he was "knotty, tough, difficult of access, solid grain from root to twig, that no dull hatchet can split." But his writing "prods us awake."[54] The ecological Thoreau, the chastising poet-naturalist, was indeed a Thoreau for the times.

For some, the modern Thoreau—the timely Thoreau—was an escapist who liberated himself from the tyranny of the machine simply by "sitting in his sun-filled doorway from sunrise to noon, as naturally as a woodchuck outside his burrow." Others saw him as a key to renewing democracy and freedom in a disillusioned postwar world. Still others considered him a prophet of America's new relation to nature, in "complete and sympathetic intimacy with . . . [the] environment." But for most, he was the man who renounced the machine and its productions in order to find simpler satisfactions in exploring nature and his own soul. It was in all these incarnations that Peattie found inspiration as he waded through the fermenting primal muck of the frog pond. This same inspiring message would launch the environmental movement, once the materialist debauch of the postwar years had run its course.[55]

CHAPTER 5

THOREAU IN A CHANGING POLITICAL WORLD, 1960-1970

On the centenary of *Walden*'s publication in 1954, Duke University professor Lewis Leary wrote in the *Nation* magazine that it seemed "almost a miracle" a book as "potentially incendiary" as Thoreau's could have survived over the previous hundred years. Leary was by no means unusual in expressing surprise at Thoreau's fame; nor was he unusual, on the eve of the civil rights movement, in casting Thoreau as incendiary. Despite Thoreau's insistence on distancing himself from all partisan causes in his own day, he had been enjoined in virtually every political movement since, with the possible exception of women's suffrage. Still, there was something unique in Leary's tone. At no previous point in history had Thoreau been so universally embraced for his political views, and at no previous point in history had he been embraced so passionately. In the decade after Leary's pronouncement, Thoreau became a true American icon—not only as the nation's best-loved poet-naturalist but also as its most notorious civil disobedient. When Leary made his pronouncement in 1954, Thoreau was still relatively unknown outside of academe; by the end of the next decade, he was America's most widely recognized author. How did that happen?[1]

The answer lies partly in his malleability. By the time Leary wrote his tribute in 1954, Thoreau had been identified as a poet, a naturalist, a moralist, a political theorist, a philosopher, a literary craftsman, an exemplar of simple living, an advocate of freedom, a friend to the oppressed, and a protector of small animals. And, of course, each of these images could be substantiated in his writing. In 1956 Louis Salomon published an article in *College English* describing the mistakes his students commonly made in their essays on *Walden*. To preempt this misreading, he handed them a list of the "commonest delusions about Thoreau." He was *not* a hermit, Salomon pointed out, nor was he opposed to government. He was neither antithetical to material comfort nor lazy. He appreciated the benefits of modern commerce and technology, and he was well acquainted with the practical side of life. Salomon offered ample quotes from *Walden* to justify each of these caveats, but a few months later Wade Thompson published a rebuttal using an equally long list of quotes to prove that Salomon's students were in fact correct in each of these assertions. Thoreau quite clearly believed that "trade curses everything it handles," he was "completely opposed to organized society and government," and he railed against the corrosive influence of material comforts. The difficulty with Salomon's method, Thompson concluded, was that "no author has ever contradicted himself . . . more frequently and with gayer abandon than Thoreau." He was "practical or impractical, prophet or blind man, naturalist or supernaturalist, 'a clammy prig' or a warm genial companion—depending almost totally on how one chooses to look at him."[2] For the scholar hoping to make sense of Thoreau, these contradictory pronouncements were exasperating, but they help explain why this odd transcendentalist philosopher could become so universally appealing in the 1960s. Each partisan group chose to look at him in its own way, and this multiplicity of claims broadcast his illusive thoughts across the political landscape.

Thoreau scholars overcame this inherent ambiguity by tightening their focus on Thoreau's literary style. "The academic professionalization of the 1950s," the literary historian Lawrence Buell writes, was a "harbinger of the more intensively specialized industry of Thoreau textual studies that has followed." The 1950s thus saw a widening gap between the arcane criticism that marked Thoreau scholarship in the college classroom and the popular perception of the man on the streets. What was surprising, however, was the degree to which scholarship shadowed the popular Thoreau in the decade that followed. Despite the turn to the New Criticism, academics participated in the radicalization of Thoreau, through either positive or negative commentary.[3]

If the academic Thoreau was increasingly obscure, the popular Thoreau was increasingly vibrant. In part, this was because he was a master at what one biographer called the "brief gnomic sentence" that packed "much thought into little room." His brilliant stylistic flourishes, terse and often ironic, were as enigmatic as they were inspiring; the same phrase could be appropriated for a commercial advertisement or a political rally. He could enter into the political discourse at almost any point, speaking on behalf of such diverse causes as antimilitarism, nature appreciation, homeopathy, and organic gardening. The nudist journal *Sunshine and Health* pointed out that he was known to explore the Assabet River wearing nothing but a hat, and the British *Vegetarian Messenger* quoted his declaration that "it is part of the destiny of the human race in its gradual improvement to leave off eating animals, as surely as the savage tribes left off eating each other."[4] He could inspire any number of causes—or serve as lightning rod for those who opposed them. In either case, his writing propelled him to the forefront of popular political consciousness, for some a champion of social justice and for others an enemy of the state.

This literary legacy was particularly suited to the political culture of the 1960s. When Leary wrote his tribute to *Walden* in 1954, the nation was entering a complex and contentious era of transition, shifting from Cold War consensus to cultural and political rebellion, and Thoreau's writing mirrored the complexities of this changing political milieu. He reveled in the paradoxes of his own day and spoke unabashedly on both sides of the great debate over the coming industrial order. This illusiveness, so confusing to critics in his own century, contributed to his popularity in the next, as partisans adapted his various facades to the great political questions of the day. Readers could admire an author fascinated with technology yet willing to question its impact on human freedom, a celibate who reveled in the sensual touch of nature, a pioneering ecological thinker who reigned as America's greatest nature-poet, a committed abolitionist who denounced all political causes, an enemy of the state who urged the government to take greater responsibility for protecting the environment. Americans in the 1960s, in short, could well appreciate an author who seemed to exemplify the complexity of their own society.[5]

Thoreau Resurgent

To be sure, Thoreau's popular image had been on the rise since World War II. This was evident in his nomination to the Hall of Fame for Great Americans at New York University in 1960. A 630-foot-long colonnade designed by architect Stanford White, the Hall of Fame was founded in 1900, and new inductees were added every five years based on selections made by a board of university officials, prominent individuals, and state senators. In the initial ballot in 1900, Thoreau received only three votes of the sixty-one required for election. Emerson, Longfellow, and Irving were among the eleven whose busts were installed in the hall. James Russell Lowell was inducted in 1905, and Thoreau was not among the candidates again until 1920, when he received six votes. His name garnered only thirty-eight votes in 1930, just above Stonewall Jackson and below John Singleton Copley. In 1940 only Stephen Foster was added, with Thoreau and three others close behind.

His candidacy gained support when the Thoreau Society was formed in 1941 in Concord and took on the campaign to install him in the Hall of Fame. Thoreau enthusiasts had been meeting in Concord since the beginning of the century, but the force behind the modern Thoreau Society was the English professor Walter Harding, then teaching in western Massachusetts.[6] To a reading group that met occasionally in Concord, Harding proposed an annual pilgrimage to the pond. Nearly two hundred showed up in July 1941 and chose University of North Carolina professor Raymond Adams as its first president. The following year Harding, as secretary-treasurer, issued the first *Thoreau Society Bulletin*—two mimeographed sheets circulating to around 160 readers.[7]

The new society worked steadily on the Hall of Fame campaign. Thoreau received thirty-six votes in 1945, thirty-three in 1950, and fifty-four in 1955. With backing from the society and from Ohio investment banker Theodore Bailey, who spent twenty years lobbying for this outcome, Thoreau was elected in 1960 along with Thomas Edison. This saddled the Thoreau Society with the task of raising $10,774 to create a bust and fund an induction ceremony. Recalling that Thoreau built his Walden hut for $28, some argued that the niche should be left empty as a tribute to his doctrine of simplicity. Others complained about the public acclaim: "Never has a man of such implacable privacy become a prophet on such a public scale," the New York theater critic Brooks Atkinson wrote ironically. The Hall of Fame director observed that he had "never before encountered so much uncivil disobedience." The issue was resolved, and in 1962, on the centenary of Thoreau's death, the bust was unveiled. In a final irony, the practice of adding inductees to the Hall of Fame was soon after abandoned, and the hall fell into disrepair.[8]

The centenary of Thoreau's death also occasioned a major biography written by society founder Walter Harding. As a professor of English at the State University of New York at Geneseo, Harding published around twenty-five books and anthologies on his favorite topic, and chief among these was *Days of Henry Thoreau*. The book was considered definitive—a tribute to Harding's "single-minded devotion"—and unlike many earlier biographies, it was written for popular consumption, avoiding ponderous exegesis and focusing, as the title suggests, on Thoreau's day-to-day experience. Harding's close rendering revealed the complete man—neither cynic nor idler but rather a hardworking surveyor, lecturer, inventor, writer, and most endearingly a friend to the animals of the forest. Harding humanized his subject without appearing defensive, but as University of Maryland professor Carl Bode pointed out, he looked "somehow . . . smaller in these pages than we thought he was." Harvard's Howard Mumford Jones described the biography as somewhat "pedestrian" and novelist Sterling North a "trifle tedious." Both, however, agreed that what *Days* lacked in drama, it made up for in factual authority. *Days* became the standard reference for Thoreau's life, if not his literary achievement.[9]

The Aura of Activism

Throughout the century leading up to Leary's 1954 pronouncement, critics had been confounded by a certain dualism in Thoreau's legacy. Some saw him as a nature writer, as he seemed to be in *Walden,* and others a social critic, as reflected in "Civil Disobedience." In the 1960s it was the latter that gave him visibility. "He was only incidentally a naturalist," Boston College professor John J. McAleer insisted. "His first commitments were to philosophy and reform." In "Winter Walk" he emphasized the whiteness of the snow-blanketed woods merely to draw attention to society's impurities, and in "Autumnal Tints" the brilliant fall colors seemed less important than the fact that farmers failed to notice them. "Just as we settle with him into the joys of Nature he thwacks us with some unpleasant truth about Society." Writing in the *English Journal* in 1962, Leo Bressler encouraged teachers to present him not as a "nineteenth century Nature Boy" but as an embodiment of youthful rebellion. Responding to this turn in Thoreau's image, the *New York Times* in 1967 offered up a full-page "Baker's Dozen of Writers Comment on 'Civil Disobedience,'" with opinions ranging from William F. Buckley Jr. on the Right to Noam Chomsky on the Left.[10]

The rediscovery of "Civil Disobedience" reflected the changes in political temper in the 1960s. In the 1950s students expressed admiration for

Thoreau's writing but considered his social message outdated, but by the middle of that decade academic life was changing. GI Bill college graduates began joining college and university faculties. Less elite in their background, they were less inclined to support the establishment, and their tenuring coincided with the end of the McCarthy era. This younger faculty reconfigured disciplines like history, sociology, and political science to stress ordinary people, class analysis, and collective protest. They were prepared, as a group, to see Thoreau less as a literary project and more as a source of political inspiration. At the same time, students and young people in general were becoming socially sensitized by memories of Hiroshima, Nagasaki, and the Nuremberg Trials. Postwar prosperity released many from the pressing concerns of job security and at the same time left them disillusioned with the materialist orientation that accompanied this prosperity. John F. Kennedy's appeal to moral responsibility sent many down the path to protest, but clearly the most important sources of youth rebellion were opposition to the Vietnam War, the rediscovery of poverty in America, the nationalist revolutions in the colonial world, and the surge in black civil rights activism at home. Released from the Cold War fixation on ideological conformity, freed from the illusion of a classless society, and inspired by the moral commitment of black civil rights workers, college-age youth moved into the political arena.[11]

Protests over Vietnam accelerated with passage of the Gulf of Tonkin Resolution in 1964, which implied congressional consent for the war, and demonstrations in support of civil rights, free speech, the environment, and women's rights added to the political turmoil. This popular dissent raised concerns among conservative Americans who feared, as Supreme Court justice Abe Fortas put it, that "widespread mass civil disobedience ... put severe strains on our constitutional system." In Fortas's eyes, young people were sincere in their concern for civil rights, poverty, campus democracy, and the war, but the combined assault on traditional social norms and political procedures produced a whole generation of discontents—hippies, psychedelic drug users, flower children, activists, and militants—whose influence was far more dangerous that the challenge to any specific government policy.[12]

This changing political mood affected the way both scholars and popularizers looked at Thoreau. Writing in the *Emerson Society Quarterly* in 1966, Louisiana State University English professor Lewis Simpson denounced the comfortable, banal Thoreauviana featured in words-to-live-by columns and asked how Thoreau might be rescued from such "well-meaning yet essentially corrupting treatment." The Thoreau Society's Charles White likewise urged fellow members to rethink their ways of celebrating the man. Nature walks, slide shows, and photography contests were harmless enough, but "Thoreau and what he stood for should not be co-opted into boosterism for the Concord Chamber of Commerce." The novelist and social activist Truman Nelson announced a new Thoreau—a "great captain of liberty," inspiring not because of his nature studies but because of his "emblematic actions." Looking back on the decade in 1976, Northwestern University professor Lyndon Shanley quipped that most people in the 1960s thought Thoreau "spent half of his life in jail, and the other half living at Walden Pond."[13]

The Concord jail and Walden Pond were symbolic because they answered a fundamental question that troubled American youth in the 1960s: how to live a moral life as a member of an immoral society. Willard Uphaus faced this dilemma head-on during the McCarthy hearings in the late 1950s when as director of the World Fellowship Center in New Hampshire he refused to turn over the center's guest list to the committee and was imprisoned. Although he lost his appeal before the U.S. Supreme Court, he felt personally vindicated. "As Americans, Thoreau and I leaned on the same tradition," he wrote. "I felt . . . that Thoreau would have supported me in my full noncooperation with what I believed to be bad law, even if it meant prison."[14]

This was the dilemma that Thoreau addressed in "Civil Disobedience." The essay expressed a profound cynicism about society, but it also embodied Thoreau's faith in the perfectibility of the same society. This apparent contradiction captured the mood of the 1960s protest movement, which despite profound disillusion was founded on a faith that bringing attention to a problem could help resolve it. Other aspects of Thoreau's commentary—nonconformity, passive resistance, antimaterialism—were inspiring as well. Shirley Cochell, writing in the *Senior Scholastic,* recommended teaching Thoreau as "the hero of the hippies, the inspiration of the protest marchers, the model of a man who had the courage to stand apart from his society to analyze it." Max Lerner listed the many forms of social injustice that earned his enmity: "the factory system, the corporations, business enterprise, acquisitiveness, the vandalism of natural resources, the vested commercial and intellectual interests, the cry for expansion, the clannishness and theocratic smugness of New England society, the herd-mindedness of the people, [the] unthinking civic allegiance they paid to an opportunist and imperialist government." Social discontents indeed had much to choose from.[15]

As Robert Downs pointed out in his *Books That Changed the World,* a young Hindu lawyer living in South Africa in 1907 considered the conundrum of living morally in an immoral society, and from Gandhi's India Thoreau's call for passive resistance and civil disobedience spread across Asia, Africa, and South America. The Reverend Martin Luther King Jr. read the essay in college and read it several times again as he considered strategies for the Southern Christian Leadership Conference following the 1955 Montgomery bus boycott. King had been disturbed by the fact that the Montgomery protest had been compared to boycott methods used by segregationist White Citizens Councils. "Up to this time I had uncritically accepted that method as our course of action. Now certain doubts began to bother me. . . . A boycott suggests an economic squeeze, leaving one bogged down in a negative. But we were concerned with positive." King saw a connection between Thoreau's essay and the marches, sit-ins, and demonstrations that characterized the civil rights movement in the early 1960s: "We were simply saying to the white community, 'we can no longer lend our cooperation to an evil system.'" Like Uphaus, King learned from Thoreau that to accept evil without protest was to cooperate with it, and from this realization he went on to perfect a strategy for asserting moral authority in an immoral society. "It goes without saying," he wrote in 1962, "that the teachings of Thoreau are alive today, indeed, they are more alive today than ever before."[16]

Sensing Thoreau's popularity, in 1970 the playwrights Jerome Lawrence and Robert E. Lee, creators of *Inherit the Wind* and *Auntie Mame,* launched *The Night Thoreau Spent in Jail,* a two-act "soap box," as one critic called it, in which the hero reflects on his incarceration and the events that led to it. Following the premier performance at Ohio State University, the campus newspaper commented that the play "lures the spectator's conscience into the open, then socks it . . . hard enough to draw blood." Between its premier in 1970 and 1974, it was performed some two thousand times, mostly on American college campuses but also in Australia, England, Holland, Ireland, Yugoslavia, Austria, Germany, and even the Soviet Union. This led *Literary Cavalcade* to conclude that Thoreau belonged "more to the 1970s than to the age in which he lived."[17]

The play demonstrated just how adaptable Thoreau was in the 1960s. Strident, self-confident, and fully engaged, he became, according to the *Chicago Sun-Times* theater critic Barry Kritzberg, "a hero of our time," but only because the "Now Generation" had attached its own meaning to his rather innocuous life. "Henry did his own thing, to be sure," Kritzberg continued, "but sit-ins, demonstrations, and political meetings were simply not his bag." In the *Midwest Quarterly* Charles Clerc complained that "Henry is less a character [in the play] than he is a walking *Reader's Digest* Condensed Version of The Good Life by Thoreau." The secret of the playwrights' success, Clerc suggested, was casting Thoreau as a youthful rebel and his mentor, Emerson, as a stodgy, older intellectual. "It does not escape notice that Henry is under thirty."[18]

Was Thoreau an Anarchist?

The "Now Thoreau," as the *Ohio State Lantern* put it, was not always so self-evident. In his *American Mind in the Mid-Nineteenth Century*, Irving Bartlett assured readers that "when loyalty to state collided with loyalty to the higher law, Thoreau knew what his duty was." In fact, Thoreau never made clear what he meant by duty or, for that matter, how he defined the state. Thoreau scholars Sherman Paul and Lyndon Shanley insisted that he saw government, in the main, as a useful instrument, but Townsend Scudder saw him as a biblical David, "armed and ready to fight . . . [a] government [that] threatens to become a tyrant Goliath." Like Scudder, Truman Nelson thought in more radical terms. "How Thoreau pours scorn on this liberalism," he marveled. "I could never understand how writing as full of revolutionary incitements as 'Civil Disobedience' can be fed like pap to students without, until recently, causing any noticeable upheavals."[19]

In his landmark *Intellectual Origins of American Radicalism*, published in 1968, Stoughton Lynd gave a good deal of thought to Thoreau's interpretation of higher duty and the state.[20] The question of the day, according to Lynd, was "what does Henry Thoreau think?" But again, it was not clear what Henry *did* think. He was often considered a pacifist, having inspired Mahatma Gandhi, but as Lynd pointed out, he also defended John Brown's desperate raid on Harpers Ferry. "Why shrink from violence when for once it is employed in a righteous cause?" Thoreau wrote. Was he an anarchist? Thoreau began his essay on civil disobedience with a decidedly anarchical pronouncement: "I heartily accept the motto, 'That government is best which governs least'; and . . . it finally amounts to this, which also I believe,—'That government is best which governs not at all.'" But again Lynd qualified, since Thoreau asked a great deal indeed from the same government in the near term. If he was neither pacifist nor anarchist, was he a revolutionary? He was, Lynd concluded, because he pioneered the three elements that defined a truly American form of radicalism: direct action, civil disobedience, and nonviolence. This, Lynd announced, was the "essential quality of the new radicalism" that was sweeping across America—a radicalism unaligned with any particular ideology but beholden to higher law and revolutionary in its focus on specific injustice. Thoreau had become, in short, the perfect New Left protester.[21]

Inasmuch as Lynd, like Nelson, was a public intellectual, his book helped position Thoreau in popular thought as an American rebel, but Lynd also touched off a heated debate about where he fitted into this radical tradition. Robert Dickens considered Thoreau a prescient critic of the industrial system, but where Lynd saw his individualism as a new form of radicalism, Dickens saw it as "the greatest cop-out of all, because it fails to recognize that man is . . . part of a social/natural environment by necessity." Nelson, whose radical lineage went back to the 1930s, agreed with Dickens: "If you declare your liberation from all institutions . . . you are really un-free, an aimless wanderer on a darkling plain." This was Thoreau's fatal contradiction: "In one vein he wants to . . . help settle the great struggle of his time, by force if necessary, and in the other he proclaims himself an avowed recluse, unable to share a common opinion with anyone." As an Old Left radical, Nelson saw this as the dilemma of Lynd's New Left as well.[22]

Others claimed Thoreau for the anarchist camp. As early as 1931 Eunice Schuster had lumped him with divine-light enthusiasts, antinomians, and Quakers in her study of native anarchism, and Joseph Blau's 1952 *Men and Movements in American Philosophy* listed him as a Christian anarchist. During the 1960s several others underscored his anarchist pronouncements. Saul Padover's popular *The Genius of America,* published at the beginning of the decade, identified high-profile figures representing various strands in American political philosophy: Adams as America's aristocrat, Jefferson its democrat, Hamilton its conservative, Madison its republican, and Thoreau its anarchist. Betty Schechter's 1963 *Peaceable Revolution* described him likewise as an anarchist because he refused to pay taxes, and novelist and essayist Dachine Rainer declared that true anarchists were so rare in America that she was "reluctant to accept Stoughton Lynd's removal of Thoreau from their number."[23] Others argued that Thoreau defied *all* ideological categories. Charles Anderson pointed out that all modern political philosophies, left or right, were judged on their capacity to increase or redistribute material wealth; Thoreau, of course, rejected materialism as a criterion for success.[24] Thoreau's duty remained as illusive as ever, but the impassioned debate over his identity kept him in the public eye.

Was Henry a Hippie?

If political protesters were attuned to "Civil Disobedience," *Walden* earned Thoreau equal recognition among cultural dissidents. In the 1960s the multiple controversies tearing at the fabric of American society set in motion a reaction in which young idealists simply divorced themselves, like Thoreau at Walden Pond, from mainstream culture. As one scholar explained, the use of napalm against the people of Vietnam was "enough to make young people opt out," and the strategy of nuclear deterrence through mutual assured destruction added another surreal element to American foreign policy. These developments deepened the disillusionment brought on by years of seemingly fruitless attempts to end war, poverty, and racism. Young Americans searched for moral footing in a society demoralized by unresponsive politics, uncreative work, and unrewarding consumption. To outsiders, the counterculture revolt seemed inchoate, but ultimately, as another observer pointed out, "there is no form of protest so profound as simply saying 'No.'"[25] The statement had a subtly Thoreauvian ring to it.

There were precedents for the 1960s counterculture. The dissipation of Victorian-age values in the 1890s gave rise to bohemian art and fashion, and the "Lost Generation" emerged out of the moral exhaustion caused by World War I. The Depression and World War II set the scene for the Beat Generation, and the rich literary achievement of this movement provided intellectual grounding for 1960s dropouts. Each of these cultural developments responded in some fashion to the "quiet desperation" Thoreau brought to light in the 1850s, and each included a ritualized nonconformity as outré as Thoreau's. From bohemian to beatnik, the literature of the counterculture emphasized the moral necessity of abandoning social convention and living completely in the present. "The mad ones," as Jack Kerouac famously called the beat poets in his novel *On the Road*, "never yawn or say commonplace thing, but burn, burn, burn like fabulous yellow roman candles exploding like spiders across the stars." Works by Kerouac, Allen Ginsberg, Lawrence Ferlinghetti, William S. Burroughs, Alan Watts, Gary Snyder, and others included numerous references to Thoreau. As the historian Rod Phillips wrote, beat authors "played an important role in this shift in American attitudes toward nature," and this shift carried the heavy imprint of Henry David Thoreau.[26]

The higher laws embodied in "Civil Disobedience" were less important to the counterculture, which was predicated on moral relativism. It was *Walden*, with its emphasis on individualism, withdrawal, and antimaterialism, that became the bible of the hippie movement. Like "Civil Disobedience," *Walden* offered guidance to a generation questioning their cooperation with an immoral society, but in this case its message was withdrawal, not confrontation. In a 1969 article titled "Flower Power: A Student's Guide to Pre-Hippie Transcendentalism," Paul Wild argued that Thoreau's retreat to Walden is "not significantly different from the hippie's dropping out," and Wild's article was followed by scores of others comparing *Walden* to the counterculture. Like hippies, Thoreau sought alternatives to the "stultifying demands of conventional life," and like hippies, he abandoned society, seeking greater self-consciousness. In his *Hippies in Our Midst,* Delbert Earisman described him in distinctly counterculture terms: he lived "simply and organically" and followed the "code of the hippies—let each person find his own thing and do it, and don't try to put your thing on any body else." The *Chicago Tribune*'s John McCutcheon quoted Thoreau—"beware of all enterprises that require new clothes"—and in the journal *Existentialism and Ethical Humanism,* Kenneth Smith argued that "reading Thoreau today is an exercise in 'blowing your mind.'" Thoreau, Smith wrote, dealt squarely with one of the most pressing dilemmas facing the 1960s generation: "how to live in, but not of, an immoral society"—essentially the same message political dissenters gleaned from his essay on civil disobedience. As Smith's article suggests, the hippie persona found its way into the academic press.[27]

In 1962, when Thoreau was inducted into the Hall of Fame, Malvina Hoffman, who sculpted the bust for the hall, unveiled a commemorative medallion showing him as a clean-shaven young man. Five years later Leonard Baskin, another well-known artist, crafted a commemorative stamp for the U.S. Postal Service on the sesquicentennial of Thoreau's birth. This time the image was fully bearded, expressing a complex personality, "slightly battered by life," and maybe harboring some "unresolved psychological issues." Along with the beard, Baskin gave Thoreau long, ruffled hair and a glazed, almost drug-induced expression.[28] The stark differences between the medallion and the stamp highlight the change in Thoreau's image over these few years.

To say the least, the stamp drew attention to Thoreau. The Concord Center Post Office received 1.5 million copies in anticipation of the day-of-issue rush, and in Greenwich Village the *East Village Other* featured a full-page, front-cover reproduction, pronouncing Thoreau "one of America's first hippies." According to the *Times,* "lower East Side hippies" were lined up outside the Peter Stuyvesant Post Office waiting to buy the stamp.[29] Across the country, newspapers ran editorials claiming that Thoreau was "taking a licking" or would have showed a strong "stamp of disapproval." A less amused *Columbus (OH) Dispatch* editor grumbled that "such a distinguished American deserves better." Concord's Mary Sherwood described the stamp as fitting for a "thug, Bolshevik communist, . . . [or] FBI-Wanted Criminal." At the annual meeting of the Thoreau Society, Raymond Adams, the group's president, couched his criticism carefully. "If one looks long and hard enough at it, one can detect a certain basic humanity groping through the smudges. In full color sympathetically done, it might very well be a haunting portrait. But in black-and-white the size of a postage stamp, it is more likely the humanity . . . will be lost and the smudges . . . will remain." A Postal Service representative reminded critics that Thoreau's neighbors "often ridiculed him because he . . . was . . . unkempt," and Baskin himself disparaged those who preferred "an inoffensive . . . innocuous stamp . . . minimizing the real qualities of his character and life."[30]

There were other flash points in the cultural struggle over Thoreau's identity. In a 1976 article in the *Thoreau Society Bulletin,* Michael Johnson reported that in 1851, Thoreau had been given ether as a painkiller during a tooth extraction, and in his journal he described this "ethereal experience" as a pleasant, dreamy interval "between one life and another." He not only enjoyed the ether but recommended it to others: "You expand like a seed in the ground. You exist in your roots, like a tree in the winter. If you have an inclination to travel, take the ether; you go beyond the furthest star." The article, like Baskin's image, echoed through the counterculture press. Lee Burress imagined him, like Jefferson Airplane's Grace Slick, advising friends to "feed your head," and a *Boston Herald* editor praised "Henry the Hippie" for his life of joyful bliss. "Some would say he was crazy; we think he was merely turned on."[31] Again conservatives were dismayed at this new turn in Thoreau's identity. William Bottorff and David Hoch insisted that Thoreau never again mentioned ether, and the *San Francisco Examiner*'s Guy Wright pointed out that in real life, Thoreau was a square: he avoided alcohol or tobacco, "and so far as anyone knows he died a virgin."[32]

The controversy over Henry the Hippie seems petty in the overall legacy of Thoreau criticism, but it highlights the acute public sensitivity to his image in the 1960s. For generations he had been accepted as the incarnation of what it meant to be an American, and the attention given his long hair, beard, and escape to Walden challenged the mainstream values he represented so brilliantly in his writing. With commentary on Thoreau appearing in newspapers across the nation, Joseph Wood Krutch, America's best-known authority on his work, felt compelled to offer perspective. After touring Haight-Ashbury in 1967, Krutch reported that "hippies in increasing numbers are exercising a human right to come as near as our society permits to freedom from . . . the obligation to be socially useful." He recalled Thoreau's fierce sense of commitment and his dedication to society and suggested that those who abandoned these sturdy virtues were polar opposites rather than kindred spirits. Having similarly pronounced judgment on 1960s activists, Krutch concluded that T. S. Eliot might well be wrong: society would end with "both a bang and a whimper—the bang being the violence, private, revolutionary and international, now everywhere so prevalent; the whimper, the hippie's nervous 'I love you, so please love me.'"[33]

Second Thoughts

Writing in the *Emerson Society Quarterly* in 1960, Alexander Kern observed that "students have of late . . . shocked some of their professors by claiming that [Thoreau] is better than Emerson." In part, this was because his "intransigent individualism" resonated with the rebellious spirit of the age, but according to Kern this distressed many in the literary establishment, and the response was "likely to be violent." To be sure, some scholars reacted simply by downplaying his radicalism. Catholic theologian William Herr suggested that he was far more temperate than radicals assumed. It was true that his allegiance to the state was contingent, but he had no reservations about endorsing specific state functions such as maintaining roads, parks, public forests, ferries, horse troughs, and police and fire companies. His definition of civil disobedience, Herr pointed out, did not include the riots, pickets, boycotts, hunger strikes, freedom rides, marches, sit-ins, and the other media events that defined 1960s protest, and because he had no faith in majority rule, he saw no peculiar desire to sway popular opinion by bringing attention to himself. His night in the Concord jail was simply a "solitary act of an individual concerned about his own moral health."[34]

Other scholars, as Kern predicted, reacted more violently. In an article titled "Can Dissenters Really Claim Thoreau?" the political philosopher Hannah Arendt denounced the doctrine of civil disobedience as a threat to the legitimacy of the state, and Stanford University political scientist Heinz Eulau pointed out that after John Brown's raid at Harpers Ferry, Thoreau abandoned nonviolent protest and excoriated all those who adhered to quietist approaches. The lesson was clear: his individualistic philosophy was "inherently deficient for political purposes" and certainly not a model for modern protest. Lewis Van Dusen denounced him in the *American Bar Association Journal:* "Civil disobedience is a counsel of despair and defeat, so undemocratic that it could bring about an authoritarian state." Writers in popular publications echoed these sentiments. In an *Atlantic Monthly* article, essayist Richard Revere argued that Thoreau's moral absolutism drove him to violent solutions. "The alienated feel that the evidence is already in, that we have compromised ourselves fatally, and that the role of the individual is either to destroy the society or drop out of it." Frederick Sanders wrote in the conservative *National Review* that Thoreau was "concerned solely with preserving the purity of his moral position" and was thus disposed to accept any means of achieving it, including "the most destructive consequences imaginable for himself as well as other people." He was a "totalist," an "apocalyptic," and an "authoritarian." Absolutists like Thoreau insisted on a morally absolute end, while the state insisted just as adamantly on maintaining order. "Finally, this formula leads to totalitarian dictatorship."[35] Solicitor General Erwin Griswold devoted an entire article in the *Christian Science Monitor* to the dangers of civil disobedience, urging Thoreau's followers to consider the doctrine more carefully "if true freedom—not frenetic license—is to endure."[36] Arguments like these showed how polarized the commentary had become. Where scholars such as Leary and Lynd saw him as a champion of freedom, others such as Eulau and Revere cast him as a harbinger of totalitarianism. Thoreau's essay was clearly at the center of political discourse in the 1960s.

Critics like these raised an issue that threaded through the controversy over Thoreau's relevance: Was individual conscience an appropriate guide to political behavior in a world that no longer recognized moral absolutes? As several commentators pointed out, Thoreau heeded an inner voice he believed to be divine in origin and universal in scope. Slavery was morally wrong, and Thoreau assumed that all morally upright New Englanders would perceive it that way. Since Thoreau's time, pragmatist philosophers such as Charles Pearce, William James, and John Dewey had argued for a more relative and mutable concept of truth, and at some level most modern academics accepted their judgments. Was civil disobedience justifiable in a society where the voice of conscience was fragmented and indeterminate? Perhaps, Winfield Scott argued, certain moral values were "applicable to any age," but still there was reason to doubt that the doctrine of principled individualism could guide an ideologically heterogeneous nation.[37]

Mad Henry

As Alexander Kern suggested, the reaction to Thoreau was indeed violent. But in a sense, it was also predictable. For generations his writing had unsettled conventional thinkers, who responded by highlighting his unorthodox personality as a way of discrediting him. In the twentieth century these critics gained a new tool at the hands of Sigmund Freud. Biographers began using psychoanalysis as early as 1928, when Gorham Munson pointed out that "in the face of the modern deterministic trend of psychology one cannot picture Thoreau as a free moral agent." Munson balanced this thought against Thoreau's wisdom and learning and concluded that although he may have been compelled to behave as he did, he took care "to inflect his actions with the logic of experimentation."[38]

By the 1930s the craft of biography included an almost obligatory psychological profile. Ludwig Lewisholm's pretentious and dismissive *Expression in America*, for instance, described Thoreau as "hopelessly inhibited, probably to the point of psychical impotence." In his 1939 biography Henry Canby insisted that after his brief romance with Ellen Sewall, Thoreau sublimated his emotional impulses. This fueled his passion for nature, which he vented in lyrical descriptions of trees, ponds, plants, and animals. The response to Canby was mixed. Irwin Edman faulted him for failing to follow through on the "trace of latent sexual inversion," but F. O. Matthiessen found his "diluted Freudianism" unrewarding, while Clifton Fadiman dismissed it altogether: "It's true enough that Thoreau could extract more satisfaction from five minutes with a chickadee than most men could from five millennia with Cleopatra. But this hardly proves that he chose the chickadee because he couldn't cuddle Cleopatra." Thomas Collins, another reviewer, observed that Canby seemed mindful of the pitfalls in Freudian analysis, but Collins feared that the "careless reader" might come to a conclusion "already . . . too often held: namely, that Thoreau was a freak and a misanthrope."[39]

Collins's fears were not unfounded. During the Cold War, distrust of Thoreau's political principles combined with the vogue for Freudian psychoanalysis to inspire a great deal of probing into the life behind his life. Conditioned by the McCarthyite turn against nonconformity, the literary scholar

Tyrus Hillway affected astonishment that Concord people had tolerated an eccentric like Thoreau in their midst, and the literary critic Stanley Hyman insisted that the Walden experiment was not a social message but rather a psycholiterary event: "The saint withdraws to Walden Pond, which of course is no real pond, but himself in the glory of infancy prior to his initiation into consciousness; and he experiences the thrill of repossessing a disinherited part of himself."[40] The most intensive psychobiography of the time was written by University of Minnesota psychology student David Kalman, whose paper was digested in the *Thoreau Society Bulletin* in 1948. Kalman argued that Thoreau was tortured by a harsh superego and by feelings of guilt for "not living up to society's ideals." His "rapturous lines on nature," according to Kalman, were an attempt to sublimate his frustrated sex drive, his sense of inferiority, and his latent homosexuality. A decade later New York University PhD student Raymond Gozzi again combed through Thoreau's journals and found passages that explained not only his nature fixation but also his rigid political doctrines. Like Kalman, Gozzi assumed that Thoreau's childhood insecurities left him vulnerable to an "unresolved Oedipus complex," a hypothesis he supported by exhibiting a picture of Thoreau's father with a "hard set to his mouth and jaw." This posture—common actually to midcentury portraiture—suggested that Thoreau equated his father with Jehovah. Descriptions of Thoreau's own military-like bearing convinced Gozzi that he was compulsive, obsessional, and rigid in ethical matters, all a result of his "unconscious libidinal regression to the anal-sadistic, pre-genital level." John Brown's raid at Harpers Ferry was a vicarious release of his "seething unconscious aggression," and it was significant, Gozzi thought, that Thoreau's "final illness" began a year to the day after he learned of Brown's death. From this, Gozzi concluded that Thoreau's fatal tuberculosis was psychosomatic, representing "the retaliation of his superego for the aggression he had expressed against all his judges."[41]

Although the studies by Kalman and Gozzi were never published in full, they found their way into the conservative critique of Thoreau and his politics. The most widely read application of the Kalman-Gozzi approach came in 1956 when the last of Thoreau's forty-seven journal volumes, covering the years 1840–41, was located in the hands of a private collector and purchased by the Pierpont Morgan Library. The volume was published separately in 1958 as *Consciousness in Concord,* along with commentary by the Harvard historian Perry Miller.[42]

Thoreau had never been an easy fit in Miller's scholarly agenda, which included framing the transcendental movement as a philosophical as opposed to a political event. In an earlier anthology of transcendental thought, Miller culled the political discourses by Orestes Brownson and Theodore Parker because, he insisted, they were irrelevant to American history.[43] Thoreau suffered an even worse fate. In his preface to *Consciousness in Concord,* Miller pointed out that it would be "trite to say that the *Journal* is in any sense a 'sublimation' of inhibited loves or a 'compensation' for a ghastly sense of inferiority," but trite or not, he threw himself into the task of unmasking what he called Thoreau's "delirium of self-consciousness."[44] Drawing attention to Thoreau's obsession with particular natural phenomena, Miller concluded that these fixations were sexually charged, and following the lead of Kalman and Gozzi, he built a case for Thoreau's homoeroticism. He minimized the Ellen Sewall affair and then dismissed it by resorting to circumlocution: "It may at least be posed as a question whether Henry Thoreau . . . had the slightest inclination to offer himself as husband."[45]

Miller mined the volume for expressions of an erotic obsession with nature. Again parroting Gozzi, he analyzed Thoreau's celebration of springtime at the end of *Walden*—the well-known passage on thawing sand and clay in the railroad cut by Walden Pond. Reducing one of the most compelling spiritual passages in the book to a horribly misapplied Freudian image, Miller described the scene as an "afterbirth of mud and clay . . . filthy because it precedes (and must precede) the flowery spring of youth and music." In Miller's telling, the passage was simply an expression of contorted libido, but once again he refused to take responsibility for his insinuations. "The pages by which Henry Thoreau—deliberately, we may be sure!—brings his book . . . to its climax in a slime of sand demand more analysis than they have received. Once more, every reader is on his own. But none can blink the fact that in this return of fertility the scene is predestined to sterility." Miller went on to describe an incident in which Thoreau and a companion accidentally set fire to the woods. In his journal Thoreau wrote that the fire was contained within a hundred acres, but Miller insisted it threatened the entire town, and because this "master of woodcraft" was too competent to carelessly ignite a forest fire, Miller surmised that it was set deliberately. In a particularly ungraceful turn of phrase, he noted that six years after the fire incident Thoreau was "internally compelled to vomit forth the cancer of his guilt" by writing about it in his journal. With this incident as proof, he dismissed Thoreau's political essays—inspiration for civil rights leaders around the world—as written by a tortured soul raging against society.[46]

The introduction to *Consciousness in Concord* was, to say the least, not Perry Miller at his best. Whether this was simply another example of rendering transcendentalism ideologically harmless, a resurfacing of the old Cambridge-Concord tension, or an expression of concurrence with Harvard's equally sanctimonious James Russell Lowell, his scholarship was far from dispassionate. Gary Scharnhorst explained the outburst as a rivalry among Harvard critical schools, Miller representing American studies and F. O. Matthiessen the New Criticism. In a broader sense, Miller's animus fitted a pattern in the Cold War–era Thoreau criticism in being, as the historian Lance Newman put it, "closely related to the anticommunist crusades of the 1950s." In any case, the reaction to Miller was telling. "To committed disciples of Henry Thoreau this must be dispiriting," Henry Pochmann wrote in the journal *American Literature.* "It took nearly a century to lay the ghost that Lowell raised in his critical appraisal of 1865; and now . . . the Thoreauvians may be expected to rise in wrath against Mr. Miller for what they will regard as an unseasonable effort to 'do in' their idol all over again."[47]

Given Miller's immense academic stature and the conformist mood in 1958, Thoreau scholars were slow to rise in wrath, but the uneasy stir in academe was noticeable. In a veiled aside, Cornell English professor Stephen Whicher pointed out that Thoreau's masterful prose stood "in silent reproach" next to Miller's own recondite and cumbersome wording. Among those with at least one foot outside the halls of the academy—the public intellectuals—reaction was more pointed. Walter Harding, author of *The Days of Henry David Thoreau* and Thoreau's most persistent champion, challenged Miller's dismissal of the Ellen Sewall affair by locating several of Sewall's grandchildren and poring over letters, diaries, and other documents that proved the romance was genuine and in every respect normal.[48] Wayne State University professor Leo Stoller pointed out that the "vague comments about Thoreau's homosexuality" were lifted from a "footnote reference to a summarized doctoral dissertation by a teacher of literature turned amateur psychoanalyst and to the digest of a psychology student's term paper that was later disowned by the professor on whose book it is based."[49]

Newspaper reviews were mixed. The *New York Times* considered *Consciousness in Concord* the best book on Thoreau since Brooks Atkinson's *Cosmic Yankee,* and the *Berkshire Eagle* saw it as "the most important discussion of Thoreau since Emerson's valedictory essay of 1862." Others were circumspect. The *Boston Herald*'s Robert Taylor deemed it thorough but deceptive: "Professor Miller warns the reader that 'psychologizing by laymen is dangerous'... and thereupon progresses... through a psychiatric description of Thoreau's artistry... based on a flimsy set of suppositions." Closer to home, the *Concord Journal* censured Miller's "contempt for Concord" and his "preconceived sense of superiority over Thoreau himself."[50]

Miller's most vigorous critic was Odell Shepard, a Pulitzer Prize–winning emeritus English professor from Trinity College in Connecticut, whose 1927 *Heart of Thoreau's Journals* helped define Thoreau as a literary stylist. Incensed by Miller's misreading of the journal, Shepard published overlapping reviews in the *Nation* and the *Emerson Society Quarterly*. As he pointed out, Miller's introduction was three times as long as the document it introduced, and it was made to seem longer still by "frequent inaccuracies of statement, by assertions unproved and unprovable, by confusions and inconsistencies of thought, by the dragging-in of matters wholly adventitious, and by the use and abuse of violent language in a prose style habitually feeble, fumbling, slovenly and dull." When the reader finally arrived at the journal itself, the feeling of relief was short-lived; Miller continued his commentary in a "barrage" of 428 footnotes and another 300 textual notes, all of them brimming with intellectual indignation. "Meanwhile... [the reader] has an uneasy feeling that this editor does not really know what he is talking about." The amateurish use of Freudian jargon, Shepard insisted, simply masked Miller's complete bafflement at Thoreau's use of metaphor and symbol. At this point, Shepard related, the reader "ceases to take any interest in Professor Miller's opinions as such, and begins to watch his aberrations from common sense with an amusement often rising to hilarity." Shepard recommended that the reader take up *Consciousness in Concord* but ignore the editorial interruptions. "The Commentator has made it a little difficult for us to do that, but not impossible. He may, in time, attempt it himself."[51]

Despite its limitations, Miller's editorializing set the tone for the conservative reaction to Thoreau in the early 1960s. Brooks Atkinson, who admired Thoreau's literary output, noted the emotional price he paid for his "belligerent renunciations" of society, and the literary critic Quentin Anderson labeled him a "complex and tortured man, who surely invites... sympathy." How, Anderson wondered, could Americans "make a national cult" out of a figure this irrational? In 1962 Stanley Hyman, who earlier described the Walden experiment as a return to the womb, highlighted Thoreau's admission that he was "a diseased bundle of nerves" and suggested the retreat to the pond was not only a mother fixation but also a desperate attempt at therapy. That same year, incredibly, University of Maryland professor Carl Bode announced that Thoreau's "unconscious life" had not yet received the attention it deserved. For starters, Bode speculated that an "incipient homosexuality" lay behind Thoreau's attachment to Emerson and John Brown, and in a bizarre retelling of Gozzi's psychosomatic interpretation, he insisted that although Thoreau died of tuberculosis, "at the unconscious level [he] . . . ended his life of his own accord. . . . He had to expiate his intolerably increasing load of guilt." Using Miller-like circumlocution, Princeton University Press director Herbert Bailey insisted once again that the forest fire was Thoreau's revenge on the town: "Could as good a woodsman as Thoreau have started it accidentally, or was this a Freudian manifestation of his hatred of society?"[52]

Leon Edel's *Henry D. Thoreau,* a short literary biography published in the University of Minnesota writers series, drew together these psychobiographical strands for an end-of-the-decade assessment of the unmasked Thoreau. After a shallow summary of Thoreau's writing taken largely from F. O. Matthiessen, Edel described the author as a "dependent, insecure, mother-attached" figure hunkered in the woods, where he compensated for his emotional constraints by avoiding women and lavishing his affections on plants and animals. Edel used this framework to describe his own contribution to Thoreau scholarship. In a subsequent article, he proposed to "unscramble the Thoreauvian myth in the light of *Walden*'s history as a classic, in the light cast by the absence of wilderness and the presence of technology, and in the light of the art of biography, that is, the writing of the lives of men whose creation is self-assertion or aggression—a personal myth cast upon the world." To those who managed to follow this logic, he posed a question: Why "*really* did Thoreau go to Walden Pond?" Edel began with the forest fire as an expression of Thoreau's "inner rage" at society. Obviously not an outdoorsman, Edel insisted that Thoreau must have known that "fires may not be lit out-of-doors." Edel then claimed that the move to the pond was a ploy to arouse sympathy among those in Concord who ostracized him for setting the woods on fire. Likewise, Thoreau's famous essay on civil disobedience was a product of hysteria and "hatred of authority." Responding to Edel in the *American Scholar,* John Shirigian asked why it was so difficult to believe that Thoreau went to Walden "for the reason he gives." Did the fact that he borrowed an ax to build the hut invalidate his claim to simplicity and independence? "Why do we insist on this kind of absolutism in the case of Thoreau and no one else?" What, Elaine Cogswell asked, was the point in reducing the "twenty-seven year-old Thoreau to an egocentric, narcissistic, mother-attached fellow securing his freedom at the expense of others?"[53]

As Shirigian and Cogswell implied, academics like Miller and Edel were heaping on the author of "Civil Disobedience" all the perceived sins of the 1960s radicals, especially those that threatened the decorum of the campus environment. And predictably, when campus politics returned to normal, the tenor of literary assessment did so as well. Mark Moller's "Thoreau, Womankind, and Sexuality," published in the *Emerson Society Quarterly* in 1974, made no mention of sexual repression and instead pointed to "a number of affectionate friendships" among his Concord acquaintances. When Thoreau's father died he was indeed left in a household of females—sister, mother, aunts, boarders—but this did no more than explain his long absences in the countryside. The journal contained a number of misogynist remarks, Moller pointed out, but Thoreau aimed his criticism not so much at women as at "the assumption that the first business of any . . . woman is to be as pretty and charming as possible . . . in order to attract the admiration of men."[54]

That same year saw the appearance of English professor James McIntosh's *Thoreau as Romantic Naturalist: His Shifting Stance toward Nature*. The book was sensitive in tone, but given McIntosh's focus on the conflicted idea of nature in Thoreau's writing, the rash of psychobiographies was difficult to ignore. McIntosh agreed that sexual feelings ran "like submerged streams through his experience of . . . nature." Thoreau was "fascinated but troubled by natural, primitive men," and even by his own body, which he sometimes loved and sometimes loathed. "He relishes the fertile swamps and bogs of Concord extravagantly, but is . . . appalled to find phallic fungi growing there." Unlike Miller, McIntosh was sympathetic to Thoreau, and he was far more conversant with Thoreau's life and writing. But his psychoanalytical reductionism stripped away much of the transcendental mystery that so inspired the environmentalists just then emerging as Thoreau's most enthusiastic believers. McIntosh's *Romantic Naturalist* was published in 1974, and from that point on the intense psychoanalysis appeared in Thoreau scholarship only sporadically. The making of Mad Henry had little lasting impact on Thoreau's academic reputation and probably none on his popular image, but it did once again underscore the degree to which he was embedded—for better or worse—in the discourse of 1960s.[55]

Simplicity in the Age of Mass Consumption

Late in the 1960s *Walden* reached a new audience with a somewhat less controversial message, and it was here that Thoreau became truly iconic. America emerged from World War II almost alone among industrial nations with its economy intact, and this, coupled with the release of consumer demand held back by decades of depression and war, brought an era of unprecedented economic prosperity. In response, corporate leaders, union representatives, and federal policymakers negotiated an entente that pegged wages to inflation and used rising levels of consumption to sustain this economic growth. The Harvard economist John Kenneth Galbraith, working with the Eisenhower administration, promoted an aggressive Keynesian countercyclical program that used federal spending on military hardware, highways, public services, education, and housing as a means of checking economic downturns. The idea of using federal funds and private consumption as a foundation for social prosperity gained credence, but at the end of the decade Galbraith reconsidered the idea that consumption was synonymous with personal satisfaction. Searching for a new liberal agenda in an age of unprecedented prosperity, he turned to promoting quality of life. Was material comfort a worthy goal for America? Would it not eventually lead to ennui and social restiveness? "Might not one wish for such a revolt?" In 1958 Galbraith published a powerful critique of modern materialism titled *The Affluent Society*, in which he proposed a shift in national priorities from accumulation to better living. He questioned the belief, so deeply imbedded in the American psyche, that all social ills could be cured by increasing production.[56]

Thoreau seemed to anticipate Galbraith's revelation that the emphasis on material goods was misplaced, and this positioned *Walden* as a codicil to *The Affluent Society*. "I also have in mind that seemingly wealthy, but most terribly impoverished class of all," Thoreau wrote, "who have accumulated dross, but know not how to use it, or get rid of it, and thus have forged their own golden or silver fetters." A year after *The Affluent Society* appeared, Joseph Wood Krutch published *Human Nature and the Human Condition*, addressing Galbraith's concerns but adding some of the warnings raised by Thoreau in the 1850s. The accelerating rate of production, Krutch wrote, transformed consumerism into an economic compulsion. "We believe that we cannot stop producing too much without finding ourselves soon incapable of producing enough." This conundrum made plain living in the Thoreauvian mold "a sort of treason—or un-American at the least."⁵⁷

If "Civil Disobedience" was a call to social engagement, *Walden* was the opposite: a call to withdraw from politics to embrace the good life. The book, a newspaper correspondent wrote, "still has much to teach us of peaceful adaptation to a natural environment." The values that rang through its pages—independence, freedom, purity, simplicity—all depended on abandoning the scramble for acquisition and reuniting with the organic world. This was advice that all 1960s Americans could abide, but as Krutch pointed out, in some respects it was also a sort of treason—a subtle echo of the confrontational themes raised in "Civil Disobedience."⁵⁸

Walden offered this vision of simplicity to all manner of readers, but for some, achieving these values required a literal withdrawal to the woods. The back-to-the-land movement, which had captured the American imagination intermittently since the 1890s, resurfaced in the 1970s, as tens of thousands of young enthusiasts turned to farming to reestablish a connection to the land. By 1975 Vermont, the new frontier in small-scale agriculture, was offering Extension Service advice to homesteaders, and Governor Thomas Salmon spoke encouragingly about the coming "revolution in reverse."⁵⁹ Here again, Thoreau moved to the forefront of the modern counterculture crusade.

Helen and Scott Nearing, inspirational figures in this resurgent movement, had settled on a Vermont farm in 1932 and moved to the Maine coast in 1954. They credited their success in part to Thoreau, who proved that determined individuals could lead satisfying lives without engaging the commercial economy. They embraced the Walden Pond homesteader's "tightwad economics [and] his blend of personal optimism and social cynicism," but unlike Thoreau, who spent only two and a half years at the pond, they dedicated their entire lives to self-sufficient living. They sprinkled Thoreau quotes throughout *Living the Good Life* and *Continuing the Good Life,* as Rebecca Gould points out, but their selections "reveal a particular version of Thoreau" that emphasized hard physical labor, simple daily needs, and a vegetarian diet. This, then, was the Thoreau—quietist and removed from society—that back-to-the-landers discovered when they turned the pages of *Living the Good Life* seeking practical advice.⁶⁰

But in this particular Thoreau they found not only a justification for simple living but also a subtle critique of capitalism tempered by Scott Nearing's Marxist background. Read thus, *Walden* was indeed a sort of treason against consumer culture. The impulse behind the new homesteading movement was complex, but whatever the motives, practitioners embraced the idea of separating from the commercial matrix by living simply. The idea of circumventing the corporate economy with wind and solar power, composting toilets, wood heating and cooking stoves, geodesic domes, compost heaps, and intensive food-growing methods inspired a series of "commune books" such as *Mother Earth News, Organic Gardening, The Whole Earth Catalog,* and *The Foxfire Book,* each professing a more organic relation to the land—a "kind of space-age *Walden.*" Like *Walden,* these publications celebrated the satisfactions of living a simple life close to nature, but like "Civil Disobedience," they were vaguely subversive. As the new homesteaders sank roots in rural communities, they fitted into the rural way of life and adopted traditional values such as hard work, neighborhood cooperation, and independence. But they also brought with them a hint of Thoreau's anarchism. "An ancient system of barter is slowly being revived in step with the restoration of the abandoned houses and neglected wellsheds and fallow fields," an observer wrote. Like Thoreau's move to Walden Pond, the homesteaders' emphasis on simple living was a passive rebuke to America's commodity-obsessed culture.[61]

The Civil Disobedient at Walden Pond

In the late 1960s Americans returned to *Walden,* seeking their own separate peace with society and nature. The new homesteading movement—those wishing "to live simply but well on the land, outside the economic institutions that dominate the United States"—epitomized a broader readership that, in the wake of the divisive 1960s protests, found a quiet sense of defiance in Thoreau's classic book. As *Mother Earth News* editor Victor Croley wrote, *Walden* underscored the absurdity of "surround[ing] yourself with possessions" in the nuclear age. What use to "build up a fortune, if in the flash of an eyelid everything—including life itself—can be wiped out?" This was by no means a recipe for revolution; nor was it, as Lewis Leary claimed in 1954, "potentially incendiary." But for new homesteaders and others, it represented a subtle challenge to the capitalist system. "We are bombed around the clock by mass-production, mass-entertainment, mass-suggestion, subtle, insidious, deafening, persistent, all-pervasive," the Reverend Willard Uphaus explained in a speech before the Thoreau Society; it was time to speak out—or move out. The University of Pennsylvania English professor

Leo Bressler praised the book's call for simplification, but he also found in it an echo of "Civil Disobedience"—a ringing protest against "a government that interferes with man's moral choice." *Walden* was not a simple message of withdrawal but rather a "protest magnified into gesture."[62]

The critical tenor in the new homesteading movement, diffuse though it was, brought together the messages in "Civil Disobedience" and *Walden*, and this powerful combination of ideas helps explain Thoreau's universal presence in the discourse of the decade. As a prophet of simple living, he gave voice to America's yearning for nature; as a moralist and political theorist, he resolved the dilemma of living in but not of an unjust society; as a friend to the oppressed, he inspired concern for marginalized people and beleaguered animals; and as the original back-to-the-lander, he exemplified all of these contested cultural currents. Scholars and popularizers were beginning to realize the "important affinities" that united Thoreau's call to protest and his retreat to nature. Together, they were a "total literary achievement."[63]

The emphasis in the 1960s on Thoreau's "Civil Disobedience" tells us little about the idea of nature in modern American society, but it does help us understand how, in the next decade, this ambiguous literary figure was so quickly transformed into an icon of environmentalism. In the 1960s the poet-naturalist and the Concord rebel came together as a single powerful iconic figure. "Civil Disobedience" inspired resistance to the tyranny of the state; *Walden* inspired resistance to the tyranny of things. The former spoke to those troubled by the immorality of a society that endorsed war, racism, sexism, and poverty, and the latter called on them to measure their lives in terms of their own individual freedom and their relation to their natural surroundings. Commenting on yet another new release of *Walden* in 1961, Philip Booth mused that "in this uneasy time, . . . any new reprint of 'Walden' is more than a minor reminder of how much men loose of themselves in conforming to pressures which are, ostensibly, civilized." *Walden* challenged readers, he implied, to rediscover themselves, rediscover nature, and rebuild the civilization they lived in—to tilt at windmills and to live their lives joyously and more naturally while doing so.[64]

CHAPTER 6
AN ENVIRONMENTAL ICON

Writing in the *New York Times* in 1957, economist David Cushman Coyle laid out the case for wilderness preservation in an era of rampant resource exploitation. Once America's remaining pristine places had been mined, drilled, or logged, he pointed out, "it may be impossible to restore [them] by any human agency, or by nature in any foreseeable future." Left intact, they would protect watersheds, prevent soil erosion, provide refuge for plants and animals, and offer a living laboratory of genetics, zoology, botany, and geology. The argument was farsighted in the late 1950s, but Coyle's choice of the *Times* as a vehicle for this message is even more suggestive. Most of New York City's nearly eight million residents would never travel to these remote corners of the continent, and they were likely to benefit more from the material resources these places could yield than from the ecological or recreational rewards they promised. Still, Coyle assumed his readers would "find pleasure and reassurance simply in knowing that such untouched places exist." They were, he thought, more interested in the idea of wilderness than in its potential personal benefit.[1]

That same year wilderness advocate Olaus Murie spoke before a congressional committee that would present to Congress the nation's first wilderness bill in 1958. Murie, like Coyle, made his argument not so much by listing the personal benefits of wilderness preservation as by defending the idea of wilderness, this time by quoting iconic figures such as Ralph Waldo

Emerson, Frederick Law Olmsted, John Muir, Theodore Roosevelt, and Aldo Leopold. He ended his plea with Henry David Thoreau's ringing proclamation, "In Wildness is the preservation of the World." Speaking before the same committee, Representative John Saylor of Pennsylvania again quoted Thoreau and explained that his famous book, *Walden,* was set "in the wild lands around Concord," where Thoreau first discovered the "the tonic of wilderness."[2]

These presentations foreshadowed a subtle tension in the emerging environmental movement. As Coyle and Murie believed, Americans were willing to sacrifice economic resources to protect a nature they would almost surely never experience, but as Saylor suggested, they also wished to experience the tonic of wilderness at a deeply personal level—in a world, perhaps, as familiar as Thoreau's Walden Woods. The environmental activist Ray Mungo faced this tension on a canoe trip commemorating Thoreau's *Week on the Concord and Merrimack Rivers* in 1970. He made the trip because Thoreau used rivers as abstract symbols of free-flowing nature, but Mungo's journey was in fact very concrete; it ended just south of Lowell with his canoe wedged between slimy rocks and abandoned cars and surrounded by "bobbing clumps of feces."[3] How could wildness preserve the world when Thoreau's own backyard was so hopelessly polluted? The tension between abstract nature and concrete nature—between wilderness imagining and environmental living—complicated Thoreau's legacy in the 1970s. He presented a compelling vision of wilderness as a realm of personal freedom but formulated this idea from the vantage of his well-trammeled Walden Woods. Only rarely did scholars, critics, or partisans concern themselves with the ironies of this juxtaposition, but when they did, they discovered a formula that would have pleased Saylor and perhaps even Ray Mungo as he sat in his canoe among the concrete blocks and rusting shopping carts in the lower Merrimack River.

As partisans like Murie and Saylor knew, wilderness preservation was a war of words, and Thoreau's eight resounding words—"In Wildness is the preservation of the World"—were among the most powerful ever written in the defense of nature. By the 1970s *Walden* had been published in 150 editions and translated into every major language; his words had enormous agency, and environmentalists, like the activists of the 1960s, were quick to enlist them. Environmentalists inherited from that stormy earlier decade a Thoreau branded by Left and Right as a protester, reformer, anarchist, individualist, idealist, and counterculturist, and out of these many possibilities they forged a new, more uniform symbol for the environmental age. But fitting Thoreau to the procrustean bed of environmental advocacy took some doing.[4] Just how he became part of the warp and weave of American environmental consciousness is a complicated story.

Thoreau Becomes a Conservationist

By the 1970s Thoreau had been firmly established as America's foremost nature writer, but the decade brought a profound change in how writers and scholars approached the connection between Thoreau and nature. As early as the 1940s they were beginning to perceive him as a nature advocate. Although postwar Americans were not particularly sensitive to environmental issues, the legacy of New Deal water, soil, timber, and recreational conservation lingered, and organizations such as the Sierra Club, National Wildlife Federation, Izaak Walton League, and Audubon Society were beginning to raise concerns not simply about animals, fish, and birds but about their habitats as well. Others voiced fears that the rapidly growing postwar economy would exhaust the world's natural resources. In 1954 Elizabeth Keiper added a somber note to the centennial of *Walden*'s publication in pointing out that the author would have been dismayed at the difficulty of saving even "a bit of forest, a bird sanctuary, a pond or a swamp where the ways and the meaning of the natural world may be learned."[5]

Statements such as this spread through the media, as conservation advocates discovered a trove of supportive ideas in Thoreau's writing. In 1957 Wayne State University professor Leo Stoller published an influential book titled *After Walden: Thoreau's Changing Views on Economic Man* in which he positioned his subject as a founder of the American conservation tradition. After living at Walden Pond, according to Stoller, Thoreau realized that it was impossible to overcome his alienation from nature without addressing his alienation from society. He began recording conversations with farmers and handicraft workers who still followed the old ways, and this taught him that an intimate knowledge of nature's dynamics could be the basis of a new agricultural and industrial order. In Stoller's analysis, Thoreau was less interested in the "untouchable sacred grove" than in the well-managed woodlot, and to this end he filled his journal with thoughts on ways to properly manage Concord's forest resources. He groped his way, as Stoller said, "to the threshold of a fundamentally modern forestry" not by idealizing nature but by showing his neighbors how to work with it. Although he was criticized at the time for his strained interpretations, Stoller effectively presented Thoreau's passion for nature in ways appropriate to the emerging ethic of environmentalism.[6]

This view was popularized in two new biographies in the years surrounding Stoller's book: William Condry's 1954 *Thoreau* and August Derleth's *Concord Rebel,* published in 1962. Both argued that conservation was a major theme in Thoreau's later journal entries, where he recorded, among other things, the devastating effect of human intervention on passenger pigeons, fish, and forests. The decisive turn in Thoreau's reputation came in 1963 with publication of Stewart Udall's *The Quiet Crisis.* In this widely read historical account, itself a benchmark in environmentalist thinking, the interior secretary used the thoughts of explorers, scholars, philosophers, and politicians to piece together a national conservation tradition. Emerson, he wrote, urged scholars to create a national literary tradition by responding "to the rhythms of the . . . earth," and this inspired his Concord neighbor to champion the cause of nature. Like earlier partisans who enlisted Thoreau in their causes, Udall found his intractable individualism a source of frustration. "With his negative feelings about government and politics, he failed to perceive that it would take government action to stop the destruction." Nevertheless, "ideas must precede action, and sometimes the seeds of thought have a long period of germination."[7]

On a more scholarly plane, researchers were beginning to express a greater appreciation for Thoreau's contribution to science. When his journals were first published in 1906, naturalists such as John Burroughs and Bradford Torrey found several misidentifications in his bird and plant species and puzzled over this casual attitude toward scientific detail, but as natural history shifted from taxonomy to habitat and species behavior, commentators overlooked this vagueness in light of Thoreau's contribution to these new fields. Once they began looking, they found that the later journals were crowded with fine-grained descriptions of physical nature. To literary scholars, this was evidence of Thoreau's waning literary creativity. "The last years of the Journal are crammed with tedious and fruitless observations of nature, as if he no longer had creative ideas," Brooks Atkinson complained. But to others, the same entries signaled a rediscovery of nature. Horace Taylor described them as thrumming with "imaginative possibilities in science." The novelist Charles Stewart, writing in the *Atlantic Monthly* in 1935, saw him as "capable of the most painstaking routine of the scientist." He measured snow depths, charted lake bottoms, counted tree rings, inspected birds' nests, and kept careful records of his findings. Those who dismissed these details as minutiae failed to appreciate the scientific implications. "There is no such thing as an unimportant fact," Stewart wrote. "Its significance may depend upon how it fits in with other facts; but you have to get your facts first.... Eventually something will come of them." Thoreau brought together his two passions—science and poetry—into a single powerful vision, not unlike the vision required to see nature as an ecological whole.[8]

Thoreau Becomes an Ecologist

Scholars and popularizers viewed Thoreau in the 1950s as a conservationist, but he was not yet an environmentalist. As Stoller saw it, he "protested vigorously against the deforestation of his native Middlesex County" but argued the point by appealing to his neighbors' economic well-being rather than to the trees' role in the larger scheme of nature.[9] Still, there were some in this era who saw a glimmer of ecological thinking in the balance he struck between poetry and science. Thoreau was first identified as an ecologist in a 1942 *Quarterly Review of Biology* article by Edward S. Deevey Jr., who pointed to his studies of plant seasonality, tree growth, water temperatures, and thermal stratification and concluded that Thoreau was both "scientist and mystic." It was precisely this mix of holistic and particular thinking, Deevey thought, that made him a pioneer in the field of ecology. In 1947 no less an ecologist than Aldo Leopold labeled him "the father of phenology in this country," but the strongest case for Thoreau's ecological understanding was made in a 1951 *Scientific Monthly* article by Philip Whitford and Kathryn Whitford, the former an ecologist and the latter a literary scholar. Taking issue with a host of earlier critics like Burroughs and Torrey, Whitford and Whitford argued that Thoreau developed a scientific method appropriate to the standards of his own times: he observed closely, questioned the accuracy of his own observations, and kept extended records. He studied a single plant repeatedly over several seasons in order to understand its entire life cycle, and by careful observation of stumps and sprout wood he could envision the past composition of a woodlot cut three times over. Charles Metzger, writing in the *Annals of Science*, and Raymond Adams, writing again in *Scientific Monthly*, concluded that Thoreau made important methodological breakthroughs in showing links between plants, animals, soils, and terrain.

He was an ecologist, according to Henry Hayden Clark, "before the name was even invented."[10]

Political Ecology

In a 1954 article titled "Thoreau, Field Naturalist," Alec Lucas reminded readers that Thoreau observed nature by participating in it—by assuming he was part of the world he explored. Henry Schnittkind and Dana Schnittkind similarly pointed to his encounter with a fox in the snowy landscape near Walden Pond. His decision to chase the fox was partly scientific, they observed, but it was also a "contest in speed and cunning between two friends." In this and countless other ways, Thoreau made it clear that animals were brethren and the woods his home—*oikos*.[11]

The idea that humans were part of and thus ethically responsible for the ecologies they inhabited appeared intermittently in the scientific literature since the mid-twentieth century. George Perkins Marsh, writing in 1864, considered the implications of nature's interconnectedness by describing the effects of deforestation on climate, soils, lakes, and streams, and in the following decades a growing number of scientists, including Arthur Tansley in ecosystem analysis, Aldo Leopold and C. Hart Merriam in game management and predator control, Charles Elton in animal relations, Eugene Odum in ecosystem stability, and Henry Cowles in ecological succession, considered the moral implications of their research. In 1935 University of Oklahoma ecologist Paul Sears published a popular study titled *Deserts on the March*, in which he laid out the principles of ecology as they related to human activities such as deforestation. The following year the economist Stuart Chase published *Rich Land Poor Land: A Study of Waste in the Natural Resources of America*, challenging the myth of inexhaustibility. According to the historian Paul Brooks, "Chase was less concerned with the esthetic and spiritual values of nature than he was with the bedrock question: 'Can we find a new ecology which respects nature and still permits technical progress?'"[12]

In the postwar era ecologists were among the first to recognize the effects of rapid population growth on global resources. The understanding that organisms "reproduce far beyond their capacity to survive" was a basic principle of ecology, and humans were no exception. In 1948 Fairfield Osborn, president of the New York Zoological Society and son of the famed naturalist Henry Fairfield Osborn, published a best-selling study titled *Our Plundered*

Planet, arguing that each diminishing resource had to be considered part of a greater "biological scheme." William Vogt, director of the Planned Parenthood Federation of America, expressed similar concerns in his widely read *Road to Survival*. According to Vogt, the "waster's psychology" in postwar America amounted to a form of "lunacy—even criminal lunacy."[13]

The discipline was further politicized in the 1950s as scientists assessed the ecological implications of nuclear fallout and chemical pesticide and herbicide applications. While the discussion of these topics remained largely within scientific circles, a few sounded the alarm, pointing out that both pesticides and radioisotopes diffused rapidly and broadly through air currents, water circulation, and food cycles; both grew in potency as they traveled up the food chain; and both had indeterminate long-term consequences. Neither could be contained after destroying the intended victim, and the indiscriminate use of both was escalating. "We once thought that dilution of man's wastes into the earth's vast currents of air and water was the simple answer to all problems of waste disposal," one group of ecologists wrote. "We know now that these currents are not vast enough to handle safely all the wastes and poisons man is releasing into them."[14] The point was driven home by images of the earth as a solitary planet hanging in the void of space taken during the 1969 moon landing.

Rachel Carson's 1962 *Silent Spring* was a benchmark in politicizing the science of ecology. Given the ivory-tower outlook that characterized science in the early 1960s, it was perhaps necessary that this turn toward advocacy came in the form of a woman entering a predominantly male profession. As biographer Linda Lear argues, Carson's role as a female and outsider in a male-dominated scientific discipline gave her critical perspective, and she used this to apply her scientific understanding to the question of pesticide use and its impact on birds, fish, and, ultimately, humans. According to an earlier biographer, Frank Graham, *Silent Spring* "leaped onto the best-seller lists almost immediately after publication," sparking a controversy that divided the scientific community, spilled out into the popular media, and landed this "improbable revolutionary," as Lear calls her, at the epicenter of an acrimonious debate over the use of chemicals and the health of the environment. Those invested in these chemical applications challenged her conclusions, but as the implications became clear, regulations were tightened, certain pesticides were banned, and a new public attitude toward chemical use took shape. The book, according to Graham, "made large areas of government and the public aware for the first time of the interrelationship of all living things and the dependence of each on a healthy environment for survival."[15]

Silent Spring fused the study of ecology to the cause of environmentalism. Carson's male colleagues, "almost to a man, ... deserted her before the Establishment which controls the funds that keep scientists fat," and with the agricultural and chemical industries, the Department of Agriculture, and most of the scientific community on one side and Carson on the other, it "remained for the amateurs, the naturalists, and the rare scientist of independent temperament" to mount her defense. While her citizen-defenders were forging the principles of ecology into a new militant ideology, a younger generation of scientific ecologists was moving out of the ivory tower and into the public sphere. In a 1969 anthology titled *The Subversive Science: Essays toward an Ecology of Man,* Paul Sears proposed that any ecologist willing to consider humans a part of their ecosystem would be, in the end, an activist.[16]

The debate over *Silent Spring* resonated with the new view of Thoreau as a scientist, and in fact there were similarities that linked him to Rachel Carson. Both pursued natural history as a way of getting closer to fellow living organisms, and both possessed, as biographer Mark Hamilton Lytle says, a "touch of the rebellious spirit." Both were loners and dissenters, and both saw nature as an alternative to materialist encumbrances. And across this great temporal divide, both saw nature as a "web of complex biological relations precious in itself and essential to human survival." Carson's notoriety drew attention to Thoreau's ecological insights, and the similarities between the two, particularly the connection between science and advocacy, underscored Thoreau's relevance as an activist-ecologist.[17]

In the years following publication of *Silent Spring,* Thoreau's multilayered approach to understanding nature—as scientist, seeker, philosopher, and poet—gained greater visibility. Writing in 1965, the University of Illinois English professor Nina Baym emphasized the moral implications in Thoreau's studies: like a good ecologist, he looked for relationships rather than discrete phenomena, and like a good poet, he drew moral and spiritual lessons from these relationships. His insistence on precise measurement, his search for higher meaning, and his yearning for mystic communion all pointed to a deep ethical regard for plants, animals, birds, and fish. In this decade ecology blossomed into a popular concern for the totality of nature and the survival of humanity, and Thoreau's newly discovered ecological sensibilities fitted brilliantly into this new environmentalist outlook. He became, in essence, an ecologically informed advocate for nature—an environmentalist.[18]

This image was sharpened among academics and educated lay readers when the environmental historian Donald Worster published a wide-ranging history of ecological thought titled *Nature's Economy: A History of Ecological Idea* in 1977. Worster situated Thoreau in a larger search for "holistic or integrated perception" of nature that began with Gilbert White's 1787 *Natural History and Antiquities of Selborne.* In a section titled "The Subversive Science," Worster argued that Thoreau's increasingly methodological approach to field study and his self-conscious immersion in the Concord ecosystem led to a proto-environmentalist understanding of nature. It was becoming apparent to Thoreau, according to Worster, that "man had an enormously greater power to disrupt and exterminate than an earlier, more complacent generation had assumed." Like Alec Lucas, Worster saw Thoreau as imbedding himself in the ecologies he explored and emerging with a clear understanding of the importance of all natural creation.[19]

Protecting Nearby Nature

The environmental movement was a response to the revelations in *Silent Spring* and to a series of dramatic pollution events that kept nature in the news for most of the 1960s and 1970s. Pollution first appeared in newspaper headlines in 1948 when a haze of sulfur dioxide emissions from nearby steel plants killed twenty people and hospitalized more than six hundred in Donora, Pennsylvania. In 1953 smog in New York City led to additional deaths, and two years later Congress passed the nation's first air pollution–control act, followed in 1956 with the first meaningful attempt at water-pollution control. In the West, rapid industrialization spurred by federal defense contracts and massive dam-building and irrigation projects changed the complexion of both city and country. These developments brought prosperity and optimism but also fierce resentment, as dams blocked passage for migratory fish and flooded iconic canyons. Uranium and mineral mining scared the landscape, and aboveground nuclear testing spread toxic radioisotopes throughout the Great Basin. The prospect of even more dams on the Colorado, Green, and Yampa Rivers drew nationwide protests.[20]

By the late 1960s environmentalism—political ecology—had become more confrontational. Civil rights and antiwar protest had changed the tenor of American politics, and the strident character of these political activities boosted confidence in grassroots environmental organizing. People across the nation took to the streets in campaigns aimed at protecting the earth, and mainstream conservation organizations became more vocal about dams, oil spills, pollution, offshore drilling, nuclear power generation, solid waste disposal, and unregulated chemical use. These erstwhile protectors of birds, fish, and animals became the backbone of a new, more aggressive environmental crusade.[21]

Beginning with a White House Conference on Natural Beauty in May 1965 and passage of the Wilderness Act that same year, the Johnson administration began taking steps to correct some of the nation's most pressing environmental problems. In 1970 the Environmental Protection Agency was founded, and this touched off a long legislative campaign for air and water standards, more effective solid waste management, and land-use regulation. The federal government addressed the issue of pesticides and toxic contaminants, and under the terms of the earlier Limited Test Ban Treaty restricted aboveground nuclear testing. Dam building, national forest management, and other federal projects were brought under systematic public review.[22]

In keeping with the mood of the nation, Thoreau's popular image as an ecologist assumed confrontational overtones. The local issue that shaped this more aggressive image was a battle over recreational development at Walden Pond. If, as historian Kent Curtis claims, the Walden woods became synonymous with wilderness and love of nature in the environmental decade, it was partly because of a classic environmental battle over the pond between 1957 and 1960.[23] Emerson had purchased the land around the pond in the 1840s, and in subsequent years it served as both a commemorative retreat and a recreational space for the surrounding communities. In 1922 Emerson's daughter Edith arranged for her father's holdings, along with those of the Heywood and Forbes families, to be given to the state as a reserve to memorialize Emerson and Thoreau and to provide recreational access to the pond—as long as no facilities intruded on the pond's woodland character. Over the next two decades the county commissioners added a bathhouse and dock at the south end of the pond. The development raised no vocal protest, but townspeople paused when the city government approved a trailer park, a run of hot-dog stands and filling stations, and a town dump in the neighborhood. In the 1950s recreational use grew ever more intense, with as many as ten thousand visitors picnicking at the pond on hot summer Sundays. *Newsweek* magazine put the dilemma succinctly: locals desperately needed relief from the spreading concrete, yet they found themselves at odds with the "relative few who wish to share the tranquility that Thoreau knew."[24]

Although writers continued to romanticize the pond, its magic was no match for the recreational pressures closing in around it. Thoreau enthusiast Robert Whitcomb made a pilgrimage to the cairn in the woods in 1931 and was shocked by the casual use of this sacred space. "The world has worn a path to [Thoreau's] ... door," he remarked, "—a concrete path." E. B. White likewise visited the pond and composed a mock letter to Thoreau: "I knew I must be nearing your woodland retreat when the Golden Pheasant lunchroom came into view [along with] ... Sealtest ice cream, toasted sandwiches, hot frankfurters, waffles, tonics and lunches." In 1951 naturalist Edwin Way Teale wound his way through a thickening ring of hot-dog stands, restaurants, motor cabins, and parking lots and stood aghast at the weekend litter—"fearful and wonderful evidence of America's high standard of living," as he put it. The complaint about commercialism, a constant murmur since the 1870s, became a clamor in the 1950s.[25]

In response to these recreational pressures, in 1957 the Massachusetts Legislature voted $50,000 to "improve" the pond, and almost immediately county commissioners ordered bulldozers in to scrape clear an acre and a half of slope adjacent to the beach and push tons of topsoil and gravel into the bathing area. Commission chair Thomas Brennan assured the public that the hillside would be revegetated, but even he acknowledged the eyesore. Brennan also suggested a blacktop road to the beach, an expanded bathhouse, an additional parking lot, more picnic tables and benches, creosoted timber bank shoring, and roads through the woods to haul boats to the pond, along with a replica of Thoreau's cabin and removal of the "very unsightly" cairn that marked the original site.[26]

The Thoreau Society met in Concord only a few days after the bulldozers made their way to the beach. Its annual meeting hosted the ambassador from India, who "looked sadly around at the spot which Gandhi had said he wanted to visit above all others." The society formed a Save Walden Committee, retained a lawyer, filed an injunction, and began circularizing newspapers across the United States, Canada, and Great Britain. Within days Concord local politics became international news. One report contrasted the "provincial, narrow minds of the present-day commissioners" with the "universal minds of Emerson and Thoreau," and the *Ottawa Gazette*'s Brian Cahill quoted Thoreau: "A man more right than his neighbors constitutes a majority of one.'" Mail flooded into Concord from all parts of the country, and with the nation watching, the Chamber of Commerce voted to support the Save Walden Committee, claiming that the pond was a "focal point for countless visitors to our town who come here hoping to experience the solitude and nobility of this great American shrine."[27]

Scholars from around the country weighed in. Morris Longstreth, author of *Henry Thoreau: American Rebel*, reminded Americans that they were already stigmatized as a materialistic people willing to sacrifice "natural beauty . . . to utility every time," and Frederic Babcock encouraged lovers of great literature to unite in resisting the effort to "obliterate this seat of American culture." Harvard's Perry Miller dismissed the complaints, arguing that the pond served more people as a recreation area than as a literary sanctuary, but the Michigan State University historian Russell Nye expressed astonishment that "Thoreau's own woods" had been "corrupted by the forces of society which he so brilliantly and acidly denounced." Walden Pond suddenly loomed large as a national treasure, and Thoreau emerged from the controversy a confrontational conservationist.[28]

In May 1960 the Massachusetts Supreme Judicial Court determined that the commission had acted in violation of the original bequest and ordered a halt to the excavation. In July 1965 the reservation was designated a National Historic Landmark, and in 1975 it came under management of the Massachusetts Department of Natural Resources, which proved more sensitive to its unique character. Still, the county refused to repair the hillside, and for the next twenty-two years the damaged slope remained barren and exposed. Concord's Mary Sherwood, who had become America's first certified female forester in 1934, formed the Walden Pond Society in 1978 and renamed it Walden Forever Wild in 1980. With the help of local volunteers and Girl and Boy Scouts, Sherwood, nearly eighty years of age, began filling in gullies, planting trees and native shrubs, and carrying buckets of water to irrigate the seedlings. Maneuvering among beachgoers, Forever Wild volunteers completed the rehabilitation.[29]

The controversy over these few acres of land and water became an important milestone in environmental protection. It proved that even small victories were important in the "ceaseless battle [waged] on a thousand fronts." It gave hope to antiquarian groups that historic and literary sites had legal standing, and it served notice to planners, public officials, and developers that environmental opposition could be quickly mobilized on a national and international scale when precious resources were threatened. Perhaps most important, it showed that nature in familiar, even heavily trafficked, places was indeed precious. As Representative John Saylor intimated in his 1957 speech, it was at this pond, less than two miles from his home, that

Thoreau found the true tonic of wilderness. Toward the end of the Walden dispute, the journalist and conservationist John B. Oakes wrote in the *New York Times* that Americans were "suddenly . . . no longer so wealthy as we had thought in unspoiled natural resources. . . . Even Walden Pond itself was grubbed up and poached upon, until some outraged citizens of Massachusetts finally took up the arms of the law." It would take "desperate measures," he thought, to "save a little scenery, a little forest, a little land in its original state," but Walden—and Thoreau—showed that victory in small battles was both possible and significant.[30]

In Concord planners responded to the Walden dispute by protecting other open spaces. When crews marked trees for road widening or contractors submitted plans for housing projects, citizens besieged the select board with letters, and often the trees or lands were spared. In 1966 public donations allowed Harvard University to purchase six hundred acres of the Estabrook woods in the northwestern section of town, while land trusts acquired another hundred acres as part of the Great Meadows National Wildlife Refuge. Other Thoreau haunts—Fairhaven Hill, Going's Swamp, Owl's Nest Swamp, and the Walden woods—remained accessible to the public. The inspiration for these measures, a local citizen explained, was "all there" in *Walden*.[31]

Conservationists won the battle of Walden, but as Oakes suggested, there were similar threats everywhere, and in the 1970s environmentalists organized across the country to protect nearby nature.[32] Places similar to Walden Pond inspired battles to tighten zoning laws, expand park systems, and create green belts and river and wetland protection zones. Land trusts worked with private owners to acquire woods and forests, schoolchildren planted trees along stream banks, and volunteer organizations helped with landscaping. In each case preservationists invoked the legacy of Thoreau, generally by citing his invocation that "each town should have a park, or rather a primitive forest, of five hundred or a thousand acres, either in one body or several, where a stick should never be cut for fuel, nor for the navy, nor to make wagons, but stand and decay for higher uses—a common possession forever, for instruction and recreation."[33]

Protecting Faraway Nature

Thoreau's words slipped seamlessly into the rhetoric of these local preservationist campaigns, but his credentials as a wilderness advocate were not especially sound. While other naturalists of his time were traversing the uncharted spaces in the Great West, he remained tethered to the hills and hollows of his own hometown, content with wildlands only one or two miles from home. Howard Mumford Jones reminded readers that almost daily he interrupted his "life in the woods" at the pond to return to Concord for meals, odd jobs, or conversation with friends. His first book, *A Week on the Concord and Merrimack Rivers*, was a commentary on humanity rather than a study of wild rivers, and subsequent publications focused on the human drama more than the perils and pleasures of primitive travel. The "wilderness lover," John Hildebridle concluded, was "afraid to leave Concord."[34] In fact, John Muir was far better fitted as an icon of American wilderness values. He not only explored the pathless canyons of the High Sierra but also spearheaded the effort to save them. Although Thoreau longed to protect Concord's woods and fields from avaricious neighbors, he by no means made this his life's work. Why, then, did Thoreau rise to the pinnacle of wilderness iconography alongside Muir?

The movement to protect wilderness began in the 1920s, when district foresters began setting aside primitive areas in the national forests for recreational purposes. In 1951 Howard Zahniser of the Wilderness Society called for congressional legislation to protect undeveloped open spaces in national forests and national parks, and in 1958 Senator Hubert Humphrey of Minnesota and Representative John Saylor of Pennsylvania introduced a wilderness bill in Congress. The movement gained popularity in the 1960s coincident with a backpacking craze brought on by an expansion in leisure time, the emergence of a vigorous outdoor industry specializing in lightweight and portable camping equipment and apparel, and what *New York Times* commentator Oscar Godbout called an "atavistic impulse to live in a tent."[35]

The wilderness movement was accompanied by a new generation of books depicting the experience of nature in rugged and remote regions. Wilderness travelers such as Bob Marshall, William Byron Mowery, and Sigurd Olson described the desolate beauty of undisturbed places where the allure of the land depended in good part on its unforgiving, indeed unwelcoming, character. Given his intense localism, Thoreau was somewhat out of place in this literature, but he was nevertheless quoted widely. Sierra Club director Michael Frome, for instance, used his words frequently but framed them in ways that would have been unfamiliar to the Concord naturalist. In Frome's vision, wilderness was not a source of self-enlightenment or transcendent thought but rather a rare opportunity for self-mastery and mastery over nature. Wilderness was the thrill of the unplanned moment, the expectation of danger, and the apprehension of beauty amid a harsh natural environment.[36]

Thoreau gained popular recognition in this new wilderness literature, but academics also associated him with wilderness, particularly after the publication of *Wilderness and the American Mind* in 1967 by the historian Roderick Nash. In a book surveying wilderness thinking from biblical times on, Nash devoted portions of two chapters to Thoreau's thoughts on the subject, beginning with the proclamation "In Wildness is the preservation of the World." America, Nash explained, "had not heard the like before," and in pioneering the romance of wilderness, Thoreau "came to grips with issues which others had only faintly discerned." The essay "Walking," according to Nash, was a "classic early call for wilderness preservation" in which Thoreau presented primitive nature as a realm of spiritual truths and confessed his unease at the "disappearance of wild country." Used widely as a college text in the 1970s, *Wilderness and the American Mind* placed Thoreau firmly in the tradition of wilderness thinkers.[37]

Katahdin Fears

In light of the rising interest in wilderness, scholars and activists turned to Thoreau's Maine woods experience—his only encounter with a truly wild place—for inspiration. The first of the three essays that made up *The Maine Woods* was based on an 1846 trip up the Penobscot West Branch in the company of an uncle surveying timber prospects. A second trip in 1853 took Thoreau across Moosehead Lake and into the upper West Branch territory, and in 1857 he traveled as far as the headwaters of the north-flowing Allagash River. Published shortly after his death and appearing regularly thereafter in new editions, *The Maine Woods* yielded any number of vivid aphorisms attesting to the spiritual value of wild nature, but as an endorsement of the wilderness experience, it was confusing. To even the casual reader, it was evident that Thoreau was not at home in this vast and dreary place. He acknowledged at the outset that there would be "no sauntering off to see the country," and indeed he stuck mostly to the rivers, trails, and haul roads carved out by north woods lumbermen and river drivers.[38] In his Concord writings he had carefully crafted the illusion that he was part of the nature he explored; in Maine he was an outside observer traveling under the watchful eye of woodsmen and Indian guides and seldom venturing into the forest itself—except to get lost.

Nowhere was this ambiguity more apparent than in his September 1846 ascent of Mount Katahdin. He first saw the mountain "looming almost menacingly in the distance" from the lower West Branch of the Penobscot River. The party camped near the base, and Thoreau set out alone for the peak, working his way up over a thick growth of dwarf spruce. He ascended to the high tableland, and across this immense space he spied the summit, still distant and barely visible through the mist. Standing astride the barren rocks, he realized that wilderness was indeed "stark with menace and mystery." There was nothing metaphorical about this windswept, cloud-raked field of boulders, and this terrifying sense of barrenness yielded, as the literary historian R. D. Richardson wrote, "one of the best statements in American literature about what happens when one comes face to face with the primeval world of matter and force."[39]

Thoreau had climbed the mountain expecting, as always, to use his observations as a foundation for exploring higher truths through analogy and correspondence, but as he stood bracing against the driving mist, struggling to describe the scene, his thoughts turned to classical mythology's nonhumans or prehumans: Cyclops, Prometheus, Caucasus, Aeschylus. The aggregation of loose rocks and stubble on the tableland yielded none of the rich human metaphors and associations that animated his Concord woods. True wilderness, he concluded, was not nature but the primal inorganic material out of which nature was made—"raw materials of a planet dropped from an unseen quarry." Where poets and painters before him had kindled the mountain sublime into soaring inspirational themes, Thoreau felt empty.[40]

On his descent, he passed through a swath of recently burned land, and it was in this dynamic patch of early succession growth, rather than on the barren mountainside, that he reconnected with the regenerative natural forces that he so admired in the cutover forests of Concord. This rather mundane encounter, ironically, inspired the passage most readers associate with his wilderness image: "This was that Earth of which we have heard, made out of Chaos and Old Night. Here was no man's garden, but the unhandselled globe. It was not lawn, nor pasture, nor mead, nor woodland, nor lea, nor arable, nor waste-land. It was the fresh and natural surface of the planet Earth, as it was made forever and ever,—to be the dwelling of man, we say,—so Nature made it, and man may use it if he can." From this mountain sojourn he returned to Concord, convinced that the poet must, "from time to time, . . . drink at some new and more bracing fountain of the Muses, far in the recesses of the wilderness." But needless to say, this was not the wilderness Olaus Murie and John Saylor had in mind when they invoked his name before Congress in 1957.[41]

The Katahdin passages have been subject to more than a century of critical commentary, with no consensus on their full meaning. Thoreau clearly gained a stronger appreciation for nature's elemental energies, and no doubt he crafted this seemingly disordered description as carefully as he did all his writing. As Victor Friesen points out, he borrowed this imagery from Alexander Henry's 1809 *Travels and Adventures in Canada,* in which he found a description of huge rocks scattered randomly as in a "warfare of Titans." Like Henry, Thoreau carefully shaped his wilderness images to appeal to a middle-class readership titillated by Miltonian allusions, but this has not stopped scholars from ferreting out deep personal meanings in the words. According to John Blair and Augustus Trowbridge, Katahdin became "a symbol in Thoreau's mind of the element in nature that defied his understanding," and it troubled his writing for years. Nash claimed that the experience sharpened Thoreau's thinking about the "savage and civilized conditions of man," and as James McIntosh saw it, his "straining attempt to humanize the wilderness" failed as he stood atop the mountain. Leo Stoller claimed that the experience stripped nature of its mystic overtones; it was no longer romantic or mystical but simply a material resource, subject to the conservation ideas he began formulating when he returned to Concord.[42]

Thoreau clearly found the Katahdin wilderness transforming but in ways perhaps too subtle to be understood in the heat of the 1970s preservationist crusades. On Katahdin he realized, for the first time, that true wilderness was completely separate from humanity. Taken aback by the severity and indifference of Katahdin's barren landscape, he came to the conclusion that the "mighty streams, precipitous, icy, savage," that fell from its rock-strewn ravines were like the wild energies that replenished the soul of the poet.[43] But those who massaged these words into a call for preservation missed the point that the panoramic sublime also ruled out any personal contact with nature. Atop Katahdin he learned that wilderness fed the poet's soul, but his deeper sympathies lay with wildness—a subtly different form of inspiration he experienced in his own Concord backyard.

Making Thoreau Wild

In the 1960s Thoreau's adaptability enhanced his reputation as a champion of civil rights; in the 1970s this same quality left preservationists free to mold his powerful phrases, however inconsistent, into modern environmentalist slogans. As Paul Oesher wrote in *Living Wilderness,* he "prized the wilderness and saw in its preservation the hope of the world, yet he took comfort in the warmth of Concord village." His chemistry, Oesher concluded, required "both positive and negative ions."[44] Thus, despite the ambiguities, *The Maine Woods* became a classic in American wilderness literature. For some, the three essays simply affirmed the adventure of backcountry travel. William Condry set the precedent for this in his 1954 biography: "He stayed in settlers' outposts, learned to navigate a batteau in the rapids, made long and strenuous portages round waterfalls, rowed miles along the lakes by moonlight, slept under the stars by log-fires, watched ospreys and bald eagles by day and listened to wolves and owls by night." In Condry's account of the Katahdin ascent, it was Thoreau, compass in hand, who led his party "straight into the woods for many weary miles of thick scrub of oak, birch and spruce almost without halting until they reached the mountain's craggy flank as darkness fell."[45]

For others, *The Maine Woods* offered a more subtle lesson in wilderness appreciation. Thoreau surmised that in desolate places like the Maine woods and the beaches of Cape Cod, we "witness our own limits transgressed," and the phrase intrigued naturalist and critic Joseph Wood Krutch. Here indeed was a power that transcended human existence, and at a time when technology was hurling humanity toward oblivion, Krutch thought, this was a useful reminder: wilderness taught hubris. The book also demonstrated the importance of solitary movement through wild spaces. The journey was "inward" as well as outward, Philip Gura suggested: not only an account of the wild but also an account of "how a man conceives of himself in relation to it." The naturalist John K. Terres saw *The Maine Woods* as a celebration of nature's most easily overlooked achievements: "useless flowers, useless butterflies, useless warblers, and singing birds, useless hawks, useless fossils, useless wilderness."[46] These judgments and others breathed life into the phrase "In Wildness is the preservation of the World."

In a 1964 article in *Appalachia,* Richard Fleck drew three arguments from *The Maine Woods* he thought would be useful to the wilderness movement. First, Thoreau's north woods botanizing showed that wilderness was an invaluable laboratory for understanding natural ecologies. Second, the ebullient phrasing in his account demonstrated the contribution wilderness made to human liberation. And finally, the rich symbolism showed that wilderness could stretch the imagination and broaden outlooks. Fleck's points were shared widely. Reginald Cook devoted much of his 1966 *Passage to Walden* to describing the sense of freedom Thoreau felt in nature, and as president of the Thoreau Society, he helped rebuild Thoreau's reputation around the oft-repeated statement that he wished "to speak a word for Nature, for absolute freedom and wildness, as contrasted with a freedom and culture merely civil."[47]

Thoreau, Alienation, and Nature

Preservationists found food for thought in *The Maine Woods,* but the book's ambiguities pointed to the tensions in a movement that proclaimed wilderness a priceless human resource yet described it as the antipode to human experience. Americans may have missed the full meaning of Thoreau's Katahdin experience, but they well understood the separation and isolation he felt in the driving mist atop the mountain. A sense of alienation pervaded the cultural discourse of the 1970s. The protests of the previous decade had been aimed at clearly identifiable agents of injustice, whether corporations, governments, race supremacists, male chauvinists, or the military-industrial complex. Although the sense of oppression lingered into the 1970s, the source became more diffused and difficult to define. The term *quiet desperation* echoed through the press, interpreted in various ways to mean disassociation from work, society, people, self, or nature. In 1970 the sociologist Philip Slater produced a small but widely read volume titled *The Pursuit of Loneliness,* which captured this anxious mood. According to Slater, in the wake of the various reform movements that gave purpose to public life in the 1960s, society was held together by nothing more than a compulsion for individual aggrandizement, and on this scale individualism was not only immoral but also misguided. Human civilization was an "interconnected whole," he pointed out, and to pretend that each member existed in isolation was socially destructive and personally debilitating. In competition with every other member of society, individuals resorted to chronic calculating behavior, "because they want to look good, impress people, protect themselves from shame and guilt, and avoid confronting people directly." In an organic society they would respond in more community-directed ways—"neither selfish nor unselfish."[48]

Slater's *Pursuit of Loneliness* became a best seller in the 1970s, alerting the nation to the perils of alienation and individualism. A second book, equally as popular, addressed these issues from a different perspective. B. F. Skinner's *Walden II*, originally published in 1948, became a cult book in the 1970s among young people hungering for community and sensitive to their separation from society and nature. A fictional account of life in a communal agrarian village, *Walden II* was a response to Thoreau's claim that the mass of men lived lives of quiet desperation. Skinner, at the time a behavioral psychologist at the University of Minnesota, structured *Walden II* around a series of conflicts in the original *Walden* resulting from Thoreau's individualistic approach to the problem of alienation. Rather than a hermitage, Walden II was a small community founded on rational planning, early behavioral training, and a uniform and collective system of child rearing that left members free to pursue their own interests in music, theater, art, and nature appreciation. The book echoed Thoreau's insistence that inner peace was more important than material goods, and like Thoreau, Skinner prioritized leisure over acquisition. But unlike Thoreau, he believed that quiet desperation was a problem to be resolved at the community level. As he explained, "Thoreau's book is Walden for *one*"; Thoreau "simply didn't go far enough." The behaviorist message that individuals could be conditioned to live the good life remained controversial, but at a more subtle level, Skinner's book launched a broad-based discussion of alienation, individualism, and the meaning of Thoreau's original Walden experiment.[49]

The 1970s debate on alienation, coming as it did in the midst of the environmental movement, highlighted Thoreau's commentary on the separation from nature. In an article titled "A Thoreau for Today," Edwin Smith observed that the "deliberate cultivation of kinship with nature, common enough in Thoreau's day, is notably lacking among us a hundred years later," and John McAleer pointed to the biblical phrase at the conclusion of Thoreau's essay on wild apples: "The apple tree, even all the trees of the field, are withered: because joy is withered away from the sons of men.'" Humanity spurns nature, McAleer concluded, and "courts a new exile." In his book *The Woods: One Man's Escape to Nature,* journalist Charles Seib quoted Henry Beston: "The world today is sick to its thin blood for lack of elemental things, for fire before the hands, for water welling from the earth, for air, for the dear earth itself underfoot."[50]

Some environmentalists saw *The Maine Woods* as a classic encounter with an alien and exotic wilderness, while others used Thoreau's commentary to dramatize humanity's separation from nature. Clearly, Thoreau sensed the thrill of estrangement on Katahdin, but he also demonstrated there and elsewhere just how much an intimate connection to nature meant to him. It was after he withdrew from the tableland that he had his wilderness epiphany: "Rocks, trees, wind on our cheeks! The *solid* earth! The *actual* world! The *common sense! Contact! Contact! Who are we? Where* are we?" Just how much he needed this contact became clear in the descriptions of his Penobscot guide Joe Polis, whose intimacy with nature was everything Thoreau's Katahdin experience was not. Polis, according to Stanley Tag,

> dresses a deer skin, makes campfires, finds dry bark, constructs fir-branch beds, makes a birch-bark bowl, candle, and pipe, splits spruce roots, mixes pitch for repairing his canoe, cleans and cooks fish, spots, shoots, skins, and cooks moose, finds ingredients for and cooks lily [root] soup, follows animal trails and tracks, imitates snakes, owls, and muskrats, knows birds by sight, knows medicinal uses for plants, knows about the lives and behaviour of red squirrels, herons, caribou, and mosquitoes, navigates through woods and waterways, . . . and paddles and portages canoes through rough water and terrain.

The corrective for alienation was not confrontation with primitive nature but a deeper sense of immersion in it.[51]

A few wilderness advocates grasped this more subtle message. In a 1962 article, wilderness guide Sigurd Olson explained that Americans' historic confrontation with western wilderness imprinted them with a "racial consciousness" that rose to the surface in any wilderness setting. But where earlier generations of Americans defined themselves in combat with primitive nature, his backcountry clients, like Joe Polis, defined themselves by connecting to it. Out in the bush, "they laughed more and took pleasure in little things." Pondering the effects of this experience, Olson recalled Thoreau's phrase "In Wildness is the preservation of the World." Like others, he found these words inspiring but also puzzling. Perhaps it was the electrifying touch of this deep racial consciousness that preserved the world or perhaps the rejuvenating energy of the sublime. Or perhaps it was the peace that came in the succor of an all-enveloping nature. However vague his description, Thoreau was describing an experience deeper than a simple mastery over nature, and Olson imagined his clients discovering the same connection as he guided them through the northern lakes and woods.[52]

The campaign for wilderness culminated in the 1964 Wilderness Act. Altogether, the land area of the United States, some 2.3 billion acres, included some 55 million acres of roadless wilderness, mostly in national parks, national forests, and wildlife refuges and on Bureau of Land Management lands or Indian reservations. The Wilderness Act protected 9.1 million acres and provided for a ten-year review of 5.4 million acres of similar primitive areas. According to Interior Secretary Stewart Udall, these lands presented a unique opportunity:

> Elsewhere there are vast tracts of wild land—the Sahara, the Himalayas, the Antarctic—which may always remain inviolate because nature offers terms only the sojourner can accept. But the lands of other temperate countries were long ago pre-empted for specific uses, and only the continental countries with rugged, remote landscapes have a largesse which permits them to weigh the values of a wilderness. . . . And that is why . . . Americans who are convinced that the good life cannot be found in the machine world alone will have their eyes on a document which has been in the hands of Congress since 1958, the Wilderness Bill.

While relatively few Americans would personally reap the rewards of this preservation system, Udall pointed out that "the intensity and rarity" of the wilderness experience gave it a value beyond the idea of the greatest good to the greatest number. Men and women for generations to come, he pointed out, "have a claim that is far larger than our own."[53]

The Wildness of the Common Landscape

The Wilderness Act demonstrated the nation's resolve in protecting untrammeled landscapes most individuals would never see for themselves, but as John Saylor suggested in his 1957 speech, Americans also longed for a wilderness they could experience personally. Thus, it was the Concord essays, rather than *The Maine Woods,* that expressed the clearest vision of Thoreau's connection to the energies that preserved the world. The phrase "In Wildness is the preservation of the World" suggests a subtle difference between wilderness and the term he used in his famous aphorism. The former represented, in his mind, the sparsely settled lands in the American West or on the Canadian Shield. Wildness, by contrast, could be found in more intimate surroundings. As the biologist Daniel Botkin pointed out, it was not the Katahdin heights but the "biologically rich swamp, surrounding him so closely with life that distant vistas were obscured and size became irrelevant, that held the deepest meaning for Thoreau."[54]

The phrase itself came from his essay on "Walking," which was indeed a celebration of the western wilderness, but he explained the term he chose more clearly in an earlier essay titled "Winter Walk," describing the woods of his familiar Concord neighborhood. To the senses, he wrote, the winter landscape appeared cold and dead, but the frigid air left the walker sensitive to subtle sources of warmth—sunlight heating the bare rocks or steam rising from a spring in the woods. And beneath his feet was another source of warmth: a "slumbering subterranean fire in nature which never goes out, and which no cold can chill." It was this latent wildness, the promise of a resurgent springtime nature in the ground beneath his feet, that he saw as the hope of the world. He tasted this wildness in the tang of a wild apple, smelled it in the musky odor of a wet meadow, saw it in the "dazzling and transcendent beauty" of a pond pickerel laid out on the ice, and sensed it in a minnow's instinctive struggle against the current in a small stream. This was the reason he wished to "speak a word for Nature," as he wrote in "Walking," and this was the way the unsettling images of Katahdin diffused into his tribute to the landscapes of home. The Maine woods taught him to appreciate the elemental energies that made nature so resilient, but it was the Concord landscape that connected him to these energies. There, within a mile of home, he experienced nature's wildness by immersion, standing "up to [his] . . . chin in some retired swamp a whole summer day, scenting the wild honeysuckle and bilberry blows, and lulled by the minstrelsy of gnats and mosquitoes."[55] In the Concord woods, to paraphrase Saylor, he first experienced the tonic of wildness, if not wilderness.

Wildness was not a simple concept. In his essays, readers found Thoreau immersing himself in the "organic chaos" of a woods or swamp, only to withdraw again to regard it with the detached eye of a scientist or transcendentalist. As Leo Marx wrote, he embraced wildness as a tonic, but not as an end in itself: "We need it, but not too much of it." This dance of immersion and detachment no doubt confused those seeking a spiritual guide to nature, but it shed light on their struggle to find commonality with a wilderness world they valued principally for its alien and exotic character.[56]

The difference between wilderness and wildness became apparent in a 1962 Sierra Club publication titled *In Wildness Is the Preservation of the World*, featuring the work of well-known nature photographer Eliot Porter. Part of a series of large-format glossy pictorials distributed by the club to promote wilderness preservation, the book contained a selection of seventy-two magnificent high-resolution color photographs linked to Thoreau's comments. *In Wildness* went through two printings of ten thousand copies each in two years and was followed in the series by *The Place No One Knew: Glen Canyon on the Colorado,* which memorialized the wilderness to be flooded by the Glen Canyon Dam.[57]

Porter spent his childhood summers on a family-owned island off the Maine coast, and it was there, "among sweet fern, and bunchberry, bay and twin flower," that he himself first felt "the tonic of wilderness" that Saylor memorialized. Porter taught biochemistry at Harvard before becoming a professional photographer in 1939, and he was already known for his outdoor photography when he was recruited by the Sierra Club. The resulting *In Wildness* was, by one account, "the finest series of photographs ever made to illustrate texts by Thoreau."[58] Adding the power of image to the power of word, it gave final form to Thoreau's reputation as a wilderness icon.

Porter's photographs were clearly inspired by Thoreau's understanding of wildness. Ansel Adams, whose *This Is the American Earth* preceded *In Wildness* in the Sierra Club series, captured the grand sweep of monumental natural features—Yosemite's Half Dome in wintertime, for instance. Where Adams represented the wilderness sublime, Porter concentrated on the intimate details of wild nature: close-ups of running water, iridescent pools, rock textures, lichens, willows, fallen leaves, and patterns in sandstone. In the introduction to *In Wildness,* Joseph Wood Krutch described the uniqueness of Porter's images. "Other writers and other photographers are prone to seek out the unusual, the grandiose, and the far away." They "shock us into awareness," he continued, "by flinging into our faces the obviously stupendous." Porter, like Thoreau, searched for higher truths in the familiar landscape—in "the daily and hourly miracle of the usually unnoticed beauty that is close at hand." His images conveyed a poignant message about the impact of brute-force technologies on delicate features that had taken thousands or millions of years to create, but they also illustrated Thoreau's message: true connection with nature implied an intimacy not readily experienced in the sublime.[59]

Porter's fidelity to detail suggests one of the many ironies in Thoreau's role as wilderness prophet. Typically, advocates applied his eight ambiguous words to the great natural monuments of the West—places far more spectacular than Thoreau could have imagined in the 1850s and in every sense as desolate as Katahdin's tablelands. In his 1957 presidential address to the

Thoreau Society, Wilderness Society executive director Howard Zahniser drew on Thoreau to buttress his message about preserving these iconic landscapes. "Our village life would stagnate if it were not for the unexplored forests and meadows which surround it," Zahniser quoted. "We need . . . to wade sometimes in marshes where the bittern and the meadow-hen lurk, and hear the booming of the snipe." Words describing a two-acre New England swamp became emblematic of the great earth monuments of the American West.[60]

While *The Maine Woods* inspired young Americans to climb towering mountains and explore vast forests, *Walden* offered the tonic of wilderness in nature near at hand. "At a time when few of us can afford to rejuvenating escape to exotic wilderness spaces," Sandra Harbert Petrulionis and Laura Dassow Walls wrote in 2007, "Thoreau gives us instead the 'wild' of backyard places." At Walden Pond, less than two miles from Concord Village, he was able to separate himself from alienating institutions and master the art of "seeing the earth as 'living poetry,'" and in the pages of *Walden* he showed how intensely satisfying this communal relation could be. Here he connected to nature in a way that would have been impossible in the Maine woods—or in the western wilderness. Animals "accepted him as one of their own," biographer Walter Harding wrote. "The rabbits nested beneath his cabin, bumping their foolish heads on the floor as they made their hasty exists. The squirrels explored his furnishings, searching for newer nut supplies. The field mice came to nibble crackers in his fingers." He labored shoeless in the warm soil in his bean field, cultivating a deeply personal relation to the land.[61]

The British poet and naturalist Geoffrey Grigson once observed that American nature writers had been impoverished by their obsession with remote and monumental places. The spectacle of towering peaks and panoramic views distracted them from the endless natural diversity at their feet. For this reason Grigson preferred the more subtle descriptions of nature in British writing. Joseph Wood Krutch agreed that writers like John Muir and Enos Mills had been seduced by grand vistas, but in Thoreau he discovered a credible synthesis of sublime scenery and personal connection. In recording his Katahdin emotions, Thoreau stood with the American romantics who understood the inspirational meaning of great swaths of unpeopled space; in his allegiance to Concord, he was kin to England's Gilbert White, who was at home in Selborne, "fixed and content within the compass of a parish." He ventured along the wilderness trails of Maine and windswept beaches of Cape Cod, but he also discovered an infinitely varied wildness in the

Concord fields and meadows, where the imaginative walker could connect to primitive energies not altogether different from those he witnessed on the slopes of Katahdin. Preservation of the world depended on both wilderness and wildness. For this discovery alone, if for nothing else, Thoreau earned his reputation as an icon of the American wilderness movement.[62]

In the World Is the Preservation of Wildness

In 1982, as the environmental movement went into a new phase devoted to consolidating the legislative victories of the 1970s, the farmer and writer Wendell Berry composed an essay on Thoreau's environmentalist legacy. By this time the rhetoric of wilderness preservation had ossified into a simple message: nature was sacred and civilization profane, and the purpose of the wilderness movement was to keep the two apart. These polarities had to be transcended, Berry thought, by "some kind of peace, even an alliance, between the domestic and the wild." Like Thoreau, he believed in the wildness of all landscapes. "The topsoil, to the extent that it is fertile, is wild; it is a dark wilderness, ultimately unknowable, teeming with wildlife"—a smoldering subterranean fire, as Thoreau had said a century earlier. He agreed that this wildness was redemptive, but he insisted on a corollary to Thoreau's famous aphorism. "So long at least as humans are in the world," Berry insisted, "in human culture is the preservation of wildness." A morally integrated society would cherish and preserve the wild world around and within it. "The good worker loves the board before it becomes a table, loves the tree before it yields to board, loves the forests before it gives up the tree." Alienation threatened both civilization and wilderness; a communal contact between the domestic and the wild preserved both. Lost in the soaring truths environmentalists attached to Thoreau's passage was the understanding that wilderness was redemptive not only in remote and exotic places but also at home, and as Berry realized, a moral appreciation for the wildness of this working and worked-over landscape was the first step in preserving both society and nature. Only a society fully connected to the organic world—everywhere—could be redeemed by nature's wildness.[63]

Thoreau's odyssey from obscure poet to wilderness icon found its final form in the reasoning Berry lent to these eight powerful words. In the decades after World War II, Thoreau added his voice to the great earth-saving movements of the late twentieth century: conservation, political ecology, environmentalism, and finally wilderness preservation. In these various incarnations, his message to America achieved new resonance. As civil dissenter, he understood the necessity of protecting nature from the avarice he so brilliantly underscored in his social essays; as a conservationist, he demonstrated the importance of protecting the resources on which this avaricious civilization depended; as an ecologist, he understood how much the whole of nature depended on stewarding each of these resources; and as a wilderness advocate, he showed that nature's unbounded vitality would preserve the vitality of the world itself. In each of these insights, he drove home the message: society and nature were interdependent. And as he and Berry made clear, neither could be preserved without protecting the relationship between them.

EPILOGUE

THOREAU IN THE MILLENNIAL AGE

In a 2015 *New Yorker* article provocatively titled "Pond Scum," feature writer Kathryn Schulz questioned Thoreau's long-standing position at the apex of the American literary canon. She opened with a scene from his book *Cape Cod*, in which he described the horrific loss of life that resulted when the immigrant ship *St. John*, bound from Galway to Boston, went aground off Cohasset. Thoreau stood on the beach, as she relates, unmoved by the carnage, sympathizing rather with the wind and waves that carried the bodies shoreward. Ignoring the nuances in his description—the numbing effect of death on this scale and the metaphorical indifference of the sea itself—she presented a portrait of Thoreau oddly reminiscent of the post–Civil War critics who disparaged his personality in order to subvert his literary standing. Like so many before her, she determined that he was, "in the fullest sense of the word, self-obsessed: narcissistic, fanatical about self-control, adamant that he required nothing beyond himself to understand and thrive in the world," and so his literary output must be flawed. To confirm this she drew on Robert Louis Stevenson's 1880 critique in *Cornhill Magazine*, which Stevenson later recanted, she neglects to say, and on Vincent Buranelli's "The Case against Thoreau," a tirade on the evils of moral absolutism published in the later years of the McCarthy era. According to Schulz, Thoreau's most distinctive aphorism, "the mass of men lead lives of quiet desperation," was arrogant and assumptive: "It is a mystery to me how a claim so simultaneously insufferable and absurd ever entered the canon of popular quotations." And in like manner, she stripped the literary apparatus—parody, paradox, symbol, metaphor, association—from other Thoreau commentary. Taken out of context, his prose fell leaden at her feet.

Ignoring the possibility that none of the American canon is consumed avidly in modern times, Schulz argued that Thoreau remains popular simply because no one reads him. Adults rely on dim high school impressions that he hated work and challenged the establishment and forget the fact that his writing is "functionally adolescent in tone." She concluded with a thought calculated to raise eyebrows among her liberal *New Yorker* readers: Thoreau's definition of freedom rested on a foundation of misanthropy, and hence he was "far closer in spirit to Ayn Rand" than to the great champions of liberty he supposedly inspired.[1]

Schulz might have thought that she had, at last, laid to rest the ghost of Thoreau, but in fact her interpretation was by no means novel. At least once in every decade since 1862 an author appeared, denouncing his personality in order to highlight the flaws in his writing, and the decades since 1970 were no exception. In 1977 Richard Lebeaux, in his *Young Man Thoreau,* applied Erik Erikson's characterization of adolescent identity crisis to Thoreau and uncovered the psychic struggles that caused him to withdraw into nature. Predicated on an older image of Thoreau family life—a dominating mother and retiring father—Lebeaux's psychobiography added little to the image contrived by McCarthy-era scholars such as Perry Miller and Leon Edel, but in the next decade the Berkeley professor Richard Bridgman pursued the same line of reasoning in his *Dark Thoreau.* Thoreau's self-loathing, according to Bridgman, was "manifested most vividly in his imagery," which included "the mutilated bodies of men, animals, birds, and reptiles, the battered remnants of destroyed life." In the 1990s Robert Milder published *Reimagining Thoreau,* which once again revealed Thoreau's "concern with masculine identity" and coupled this dark psychoanalytic profile with close textual analysis to explain the inconsistencies in various drafts of *Walden.*[2]

A challenge of a different sort came in 2012 with publication of Robert Sullivan's curious *The Thoreau You Don't Know: How Reevaluating the Dean of Green Makes Us Rethink Our World.* Responding to a concern among academics that *Walden* was appearing less frequently on high school English syllabi, Sullivan presented a new, lighter Thoreau whose personality was reminiscent of that created in the 1870s by his friends Harrison Blake, Ellery Channing, and Bronson Alcott. Sullivan's Thoreau was teen friendly; he played in the woods, wrote humorous satire, and was "as practical as he was philosophical, as silly as he was serious." The Thoreau Sullivan crafted was eminently approachable, but he lacked the critical edge and intense symbolism that 1960s radicals and environmentalists found so valuable. According to a reviewer, it was "time to pack the old Thoreau—austere, high-minded, solitary—in mothballs and break out the new . . . , a wisecracking, subversive, entrepreneurial party boy, as likely to dance a jig and break into song as preach at you."[3] Scott Sandage introduced an equally devitalized Thoreau in the opening chapter of his curious *Born Losers*. Taking the famous "quiet desperation" aphorism as text, Sandage pointed out that the promise of American life in fact left many individuals feeling desperately unfulfilled. He offered Thoreau—the man who walked east to Cape Cod rather than follow the dictates of manifest destiny—as comfort for all those who thought their lives fell short of the American Dream. "Let us remember not to strive upwards too long," the original born loser warned. As a reviewer put it, Sullivan presented readers with "an oddball who enjoyed sauntering more than striving, berry picking more than bill counting."[4] The Thoreau imagined by Sullivan and Sandage was far more human than the Thoreau characterized by Schulz, but it had little in common with the righteous and controversial figure that emerged out of the political passions of the 1960s and 1970s.

A more ominous challenge came from the iconoclastic environmentalist Bill McKibben, whose 1989 *New Yorker* article "The End of Nature" centered on Thoreau's 1846 ascent of Mount Katahdin. From the mountaintop, nature seemed wondrous because it was fresh and unspoiled, but almost nothing at this modern juncture could inspire in the same way. Humans, McKibben pointed out, had altered the foundation of all natural systems, even the most remote, and in depriving nature of its independence, they deprived it of its spirituality. Thoreau was important because he saw nature as a portal to divinity; desacralizing nature would render him irrelevant. What would become of a classic like *The Maine Woods* when even the Katahdin wilderness was a human artifact—when "the great pines around its base have been genetically improved"?[5]

Challenges like these were not new, of course. As the columnist Albert Southwick pointed out in the *Boston Globe*, Thoreau had been faulted over the years "for his science, his nature studies, his politics, his economics, his philosophy, his prudery, his dismissive remarks about women and his egoism." Yet for all that, "his disciples multiply." As Southwick suggested, the connection between condemnation and perseverance was more than casual; even as detractors such as Stevenson, Buranelli, Miller, and Edel hammered at his reputation, he steadily gained in prominence—in no small measure because he was indeed controversial.[6] Commenting on this point, Elizabeth Hall Witherell of the Princeton Thoreau Project noted that of all great American writers, Thoreau "provoked the strongest popular reactions, both positive and negative." This, she thought, would ensure his place in the literary pantheon. Indeed, a 1991 Modern Language Association survey found *Walden* still the "single most important work to teach in the country's nineteenth-century literature."[7] What, then, was there about the writer and his personality that sparked such controversy at a time when the passions of the 1960s and 1970s—civil rights, war, and the environment—seemed to have cooled?

Thoreau in the Millennial Age

The academic disciplines that came to maturity at the turn of the century found Thoreau controversial in new ways. In gender studies, for example, some scholars interpreted his writing as an example of masculine hegemony over nature, while others described him as withdrawing from the "masculine world of commerce and industry." Postmodernists saw him as obsessed with "self-fashioning" but quarreled about the selfhood he fashioned: Was he a naturalist, transcendentalist, or simply a nonconformist?[8] Students of literary canon brought to light the complicated process by which he became, by the end of the nineteenth century, "a star of the first magnitude in the firmament of American letters" but differed in attributing his success to his transcendentalist friends, to the market-based decisions of his publishers, or to the intrinsic value of his literary genius.[9] Environmental historians used him as a literary benchmark but offered no new insight into his role in American history. In *Nature's Economy: A History of Ecological Ideas,* Donald Worster positioned him at a critical moment in a succession of ecological thinkers dating back to Gilbert White. William Cronon opened his influential *Changes in the Land: Indians, Colonists, and the Ecology of New England* with Thoreau contemplating the degradation of nature in Concord, and Theodore Steinberg introduced his *Nature Incorporated: Industrialization and the Waters of New England* with Thoreau and his brother boating on the much-diminished waters of the Merrimack River. As Kent Curtis observed, he was less an actor in environmental history than a narrative device.[10]

Political scientists were more receptive to Thoreau's agency but were again divided on his meaning. In her 1994 book, *Thoreau's Nature, Ethics, Politics and the Wild,* Jane Bennett ticked off the various ways his political ideas were still relevant: "claustrophobia, routinization, and the . . . will to mastery are . . . high on Thoreau's list of dangers. . . . He feels oppressed by a distant and centralizing government; he is horrified by the violent destruction of woodlands and the idiotic accumulation of consumption items."[11] His political thought was relevant to modern society, but some critics found it more subdued than those who read him in the turbulent 1960s. In his 1939 biography, Henry Canby had declared Thoreau a reluctant reformer, more interested in nature than politics, and although 1960s scholars rejected this interpretation, it gained appeal in the decades that followed. Michael Bennett argued that Thoreau saw slavery largely in symbolic terms; "inward redemption" was more important than redemption of the South. In *To Set This World Right: The Antislavery Movement in Thoreau's Concord,* Sandra Harbert Petrulionis described his political commitments as intermittent. "He denounced collective reform movements and abolitionist leaders, but on more than one occasion he also acted . . . in concert with the local antislavery societies to which his mother, sisters, and aunts loyally belonged."[12]

Others, however, preferred a more politically impassioned Thoreau. Jay Parnini's *Thirteen Books That Changed America* revived the antimaterialist philosopher of the 1920s and 1930s who challenged the foundations of an acquisitive economy. Others brought back the Thoreau of the 1960s. Brent Powell saw likenesses between the Concord rebel and Martin Luther King Jr., both of them deeply committed to equality, justice, and the call to higher conscience. Labor and environmental historian Chad Montrie framed *Walden* as a foil used to draw attention to the degradation of work in industrial society.[13] In political science as in other disciplines, controversy animated Thoreau scholarship. He was, as Albert Southwick said in his *Boston Globe* article, "misanthropic, prudish, celibate, suspicious of causes, and obsessed with solitude," but at the same time a "friend of animals, lover of nature, mystic, tax-refuser, foe of government, antiwar publicist, advocate of open spaces, partisan of Native Americans, critic of industrial 'progress' and scorner of the consumer ethic." As long as he could simultaneously inspire, enrage, and mystify, he "won't go away."[14]

Thoreau and Nature

Thoreau continued to intrigue academics because he validated deep-seated American values even while he criticized them. To the lay reader, however, he remained popular as the voice of nature, and this, of course, was the foundation of his iconic status. The millennial years brought an outpouring of popular biographies, anthologies, and essays that highlighted Thoreau's nature writing, and among the most significant of these was Bradley Dean's *Faith in a Seed,* which reproduced several popular Thoreau nature essays along with the unpublished and partially completed "Dispersion of Seeds." The anthology was a stunning event—the first new Thoreau manuscript to appear in print in more than a century—but it was also important because it set in motion a debate that crossed over the boundary between academic research and popular reading. In rereading his journals and essays, Dean and others discovered several "new" Thoreaus: he was America's first Darwinian naturalist, its first "deep ecologist," its first authority on humanized ecologies, and its first modern climatologist. These new insights highlight the way Thoreau—and the idea of nature—had changed since the 1970s.[15]

The connection to Darwin was a major advance in Thoreau scholarship, attributable in good part to Max Oelschlaeger's 1991 *Idea of Wilderness from Prehistory to the Age of Ecology.* In his chapter on Thoreau, Oelschlaeger argued that he "clearly . . . grasped the principle of evolution" and saw the cosmos as a "living continuum in which the higher is an elaborated . . . arrangement of the lower." Two years later Gary Paul Nabhan and R. D. Richardson argued in the introduction to *Faith in a Seed* that Thoreau actually anticipated Darwin by using methodologies that "did not become fully articulated in evolutionary ecology until the early 1970s."[16]

The three collaborators on *Faith in a Seed*—Dean, Richardson, and Nabhan—also credited Thoreau as America's first deep ecologist, an attribution that once again embroiled him in controversy. The term had been coined in 1973 by the Norwegian philosopher Arne Næss, an ecocentrist who argued that the human species had no right to reduce the diversity of life on the planet or to judge the worth of other life forms by their contribution to civilization.[17] The most thorough recognition of Thoreau's ecocentrism came with Lawrence Buell's 1995 book, *The Environmental Imagination: Thoreau, Nature Writing, and the Formation of American Culture,* which brought to light a new "green Thoreau" whose view of nature combined transcendental introspection and objective observation. Viewed as a deep-ecology classic, *Walden,* according to Buell, looked "more like a mode of dissent" than an expression of transcendental philosophy.[18] Others agreed. Mark Hamilton Lytle compared him to Rachel Carson in his 2007 biography of the latter, and in the journal *Conservation Biology,* Matthew Child used Thoreau's writing to argue against anthropocentric conservation strategies that judged the worth of each component in a natural system according to its social or economic value. Thoreau, as "an unapologetic . . . freedom fighter for nature," offered an ecocentric alternative that would be immensely useful to twenty-first-century conservation.[19]

In the journal *Between the Species,* Don Mortland cautioned environmentalists like these to read Thoreau a little more carefully; he could be claimed by utilitarians, Mortland argued, just as easily as he was claimed by "New Age" ecologists. In his *Nature Writing: The Pastoral Impulse in America,* Don Scheese likewise imagined Thoreau inhabiting a netherworld between biocentric and anthropocentric approaches, and environmental historian Kent Curtis pictured Thoreau as generally content with the way farmers, fishers, and loggers used nature. Nowhere, according to Curtis, did he suggest "a loss of natural balance at the hands of human society."[20] Despite the lack of consensus, commentators found ways to incorporate Thoreau's thoughts into this newest turn in natural philosophy.

The debate over deep ecology drew attention to a third new interpretation of Thoreau's contribution to ecological thought. Scholars recognized his Concord descriptions as the first attempt in this country to understand nature in a landscape heavily altered by human activity. Daniel Botkin's 2001 *No Man's Garden: Thoreau and a New Vision for Civilization and Nature* drew attention to Thoreau's fondness for what he called a "partially cultivated country." A conservation biologist, Botkin had abandoned the idea of climax ecology—nature essentialized as a static and harmonized balance of forces—for a new ecological paradigm based on a dynamic and somewhat chaotic system of relationships. Thoreau, he pointed out, had no particular faith in the ancient and metaphorical "balance of nature," and this put his widely read book *The Maine Woods* in a new light. While most scholars viewed the book as a celebration of wilderness, Botkin saw it as a record of human activity, with loggers, trappers, hunters, and Native Americans busily at work in the woods. Here, as in the fields and woodlots of Concord, Thoreau pioneered a new approach to understanding the human contribution to a dynamic natural ecology.[21] Eight years later David Foster published *Thoreau's Country: Journey through a Transformed Landscape,* again emphasizing the dynamic qualities in the Concord landscape. Foster combined the rich ecological data in Thoreau's journals with his own expertise as a forester to offer a convincing portrait of New England as a natural landscape in perpetual transition. Like Botkin, he presented Thoreau not as a defender of wilderness but as a naturalist thoroughly at home in the domesticated world and keenly aware of the anthropogenic changes taking place around him. Botkin and Foster were the first scholars since Leo Stoller, in his 1957 *After Walden*, to put this human-nature interface at the center of Thoreau's ecological thinking, and their writing suggests a new understanding of the society-nature relationship in the decades after the environmental era.[22]

Thoreau's close inspection of the Concord landscape yielded another set of insights that put him in the public eye. Over the years, he amassed a record of plant and animal seasonality that proved invaluable to those interested in climate change. His observations on the life cycles of nearly six hundred species drew the attention of the Boston University biologist Richard Primack, who found plants flowering about one week earlier in Concord than in Thoreau's day, due to global climate change and the urban heat-island effect. Primack and his colleagues located several newly arrived plant species, and despite the fact that 35 to 40 percent of Concord's land area had been protected by 2007, some 27 percent of Thoreau's wildflowers had disappeared. The seasonal markers Thoreau used, as Michelle Nijhuis pointed out in *Smithsonian* magazine, were "the pulse of the planet, and everything from agriculture to allergy outbreaks depend on their timing." Unbeknownst to him, Thoreau was documenting the arrival of the Anthropocene.[23]

Newspaper feature writers also used Thoreau as a baseline for documenting ecological change. In 1990, for instance, the wildlife ecologist Anne LaBastille published an article in the *Boston Globe* titled "If Thoreau Could See It Now," tracing the voyage he made with his brother on the Concord and Merrimack Rivers in 1839. Where Thoreau had camped out along the riverbank, modern-day canoeists left the river treading "through a rubble of old carpets, bent bikes, plastic items and building materials," and where Thoreau saw crystal waters as a transcendental metaphor, the canoeing party endured the stench of raw sewage. LaBastille concluded with Thoreau's expression of hope and resignation: "Perchance, after a few thousands of years, if the fishes will be patient, and pass their summers elsewhere . . . the Grass-ground River [will] run clear again."[24]

Thoreau and Wilderness

Like his ecological sensibilities, Thoreau's connection to wilderness remained controversial. In his study of American nature writers, Don Scheese, like

Botkin, reminded readers that Thoreau encountered a great deal of human activity in *The Maine Woods*. Scheese concluded, however, that he was nonetheless content with "reenvisioning a 'virgin' nature"—constructing a wilderness of the mind. James Papa made a similar argument in the *Midwest Quarterly*. Was the Maine woods a true wilderness? The evidence of human activity was everywhere, but Thoreau was nonetheless intent on fashioning "a landscape unconquered by man." According to Papa, the resulting literary images filled a "desperate need in the American psyche."[25]

It was in this way, as a champion of idealized places, that Thoreau was drawn into the major academic debate over the idea of wilderness in the millennial age. In 1996, at a point where the major preservationist battles of the late twentieth century had been won or lost, the environmental historian William Cronon announced that the time had come to rethink the idea of wilderness. His controversial essay "The Trouble with Wilderness" began with a phrase that had inspired preservationist activity since the 1950s—Thoreau's iconic "In Wildness is the preservation of the World." The wildness Thoreau celebrated, Cronon insisted, was a "human creation," an ideal as much as a reality. As such, it was loaded with "some of the deepest core values of the culture that created and idealized it." In the present era this symbol-laden archetype had become a means of escaping a long history of environmental degradation. It preserved the illusion, according to Cronon, that by setting aside a value-laden nature in remote places, "we can somehow wipe clean the slate of our past and return to the tabula rasa that supposedly existed before we began to leave our marks on the world."[26] Fixed on preserving wilderness, we fail to preserve the environment we actually inhabit.

Among the many challenges to Cronon's essay was Donald Worster's "Thoreau and the American Passion for Wilderness," a brief article published in the *Concord Saunterer* in 2002. As Worster related, it had become fashionable by that time, on both the Right and the Left, to attack the wilderness movement as misguided, antihuman, elitist, alienating, or racist, but Worster chose to stick with Thoreau's dictum that wildness would preserve the world. The Wilderness Act, he insisted, was one of America's great legislative accomplishments, and for this he credited Thoreau. "In claiming a career as inspector of the wild, Thoreau is doing more than justifying himself to his readers. He is saying what no one else before him has said so emphatically: that wild nature is worthy of the same respect, devotion, energy, and time that taming the land or other 'trammeling' occupations demand." Thoreau was important because he believed not only in the idea of wilderness but in the wilderness world itself, and he was adamant in associating this wilderness with absolute freedom. Thoreau's wilderness was a place "where one could go to escape from . . . all the faces of unfreedom," and viewed in this way it is a corrective to the abstractions of "freedom" that gave corporations license to exploit nature around the world.[27]

An Icon for the Twenty-First Century

Did the millennial decades sustain Thoreau's status as a popular icon? The answer seemed clear in 1990 during a national controversy over a proposed condominium and office development near Walden Pond. To block the project, rock singer Don Henley staged a benefit concert in Worcester that featured, among other singers and celebrities, Jimmy Buffett, Bonnie Raitt, Bob Seger, Carrie Fisher, Ed Begley Jr., and members of Henley's band, the Eagles. Henley purchased the disputed property and went on to establish the Walden Woods Project to protect more land around the pond. To help fund this he published *Heaven Is Under Our Feet,* a best-selling collection of sixty-eight essays by well-known personalities who attested to Thoreau's legacy and portrayed Walden as a symbol of untainted nature. "With breathtaking foresight," Senator Edward M. Kennedy wrote in his contribution, Thoreau "saw the trend of the nation's increasingly industrialized society . . . and spoke to it in terms that are equally relevant to our own age."[28]

Thoreau remained controversial, as Schulz, Sullivan, Botkin, Cronon, and others remind us, but this was because he, more than any other classic American writer, trained his exquisite prose on matters of deep concern to the nation. Scholars and popularizers alike wove his thoughts into the fundamental social questions of the day: individualism versus community, solitude versus commitment, conscience versus law, particularity versus universality, civilization versus nature. His intense and sustained self-scrutiny had much to offer in an era when selfhood had become dangerously externalized. In an age overwhelmed by digitized information, he stands out, as Robert Sullivan said, as the "secular priest of solitude." Above all, he remained America's "all-purpose symbol of environmentalism," as Jane Bennett put it, feeding the nation's passion "not only for the security of a provident nature, but even more for the wild caprice of an order which transgresses our self-imposed limits." Why read *Walden*? SueEllen Campbell asked rhetorically. "Because it challenges us to live with passion, curiosity, mindfulness. . . . Eyes wide open! Pay attention! . . . Know where we live and what we live for; simplify."²⁹

Thoreau will continue to symbolize nature for America, but just how this symbolism will take shape remains indeterminate. In 1997 Elizabeth Hall Witherell predicted that the "definitive" biography of Thoreau "would never be written" because each era will have to generate a Thoreau of its own. This in itself will guarantee his prominence over the coming generations. As Albert Southwick wrote in his *Boston Globe* article, Thoreau continues to gaze "imperturbably out of those old daguerreotypes just as he did during the Gilded Age, during the giddy '20s, during the Reagan orgy, the same mild hint of disapproval in his eyes." Perhaps, as Kathryn Schulz implied, his words will be less seldom heeded in the overmediated millennial era, but as Southwick wrote, "sometimes, after the aimless whirling of the day, thoughts come in the dead of the night. . . . You do have choices." No wonder, Southwick concluded, "he ranks as the ultimate subversive. No wonder we find him so hard to forget."³⁰

NOTES

Preface

1. Joseph J. Moldenhauer, "The Extra-vagant Maneuver: Paradox in *Walden*," *Graduate Journal* (University of Texas at Austin) 6 (Winter 1964): 97; Saul K. Padover, *The Genius of America: Men Whose Ideas Shaped Our Civilization* (New York: McGraw-Hill, 1960), 198. See also Paul Lauter, "Thoreau's Prophetic Testimony," *Massachusetts Review* 4 (Autumn 1962): 121.

Chapter 1: A Prophet without Honor, 1817-1862

1. *Boston Journal*, July 12, 13, 1917; *Fort Worth (TX) Star-Telegram*, July 12, 1917. See also "Concord Observes Thoreau Centenary," *Boston Advertiser*, October 26, 1917, T. 23, Thoreau Centenary, B, Articles, series III, Walter Harding Collection, Thoreau Institute, Lincoln, MA.
2. Townsend Scudder, "Henry David Thoreau," in *Literary History of the United States*, ed. Robert E. Spiller et al. (New York: Macmillan, 1963–72), 1:388.
3. Wendell Glick quoted in Richard Rutland, "The Search for *Walden*," *Emerson Society Quarterly* 23 (1977): 189; Rutland quoted ibid., 192; Edward O. Wilson quoted in W. Barksdale Maynard, *Walden Pond: A History* (New York: Oxford University Press, 2004), 68. See also Gary Scharnhorst, *Henry David Thoreau: A Case Study in Canonization* (Columbia, SC: Camden House, 1993), 2, 40.
4. *Morning Courier and New-York Enquirer* quoted in Bradley Dean and Gary Scharnhorst, "The Contemporary Reception of *Walden*," *Studies in the American Renaissance* (1990): 316; Lawrence Buell, *The Environmental Imagination: Thoreau, Nature Writing, and the Formation of American Culture* (Cambridge, MA: Harvard University Press, 1995), 24, 115.

5. Walter Harding, *The Days of Henry Thoreau* (New York: Alfred A. Knopf, 1962), xv; V. F. Calverton quoted in Wendell Glick, *The Recognition of Henry David Thoreau: Selected Criticism since 1848* (Ann Arbor: University of Michigan Press, 1969), 14, 338.
6. Mark W. Sullivan, *Picturing Thoreau: Henry David Thoreau in American Visual Culture* (Lanham, MD: Lexington Books, 2015), 3. See also Granville Hicks, "The Complexity of David Thoreau," *New York Times Book Review*, April 3, 1949, 26.
7. Thomas Wentworth Higginson, *Cheerful Yesterdays* (Boston: Houghton Mifflin, 1898), 169; Sandra Harbert Petrulionis, ed., *Thoreau in His Own Time* (Ames: University of Iowa Press, 2012), xiii.
8. Robert D. Richardson Jr., *Henry Thoreau: A Life of the Mind* (Berkeley: University of California Press, 1986), 265; R. L. Duffus, "The Native Character as American Writers Have Interpreted It," *New York Times Book Review*, March 29, 1931, 2; Lewis Mumford, *The Brown Decades* (1931; reprint, New York: Dover, 1966), 59–60.
9. Franklin B. Sanborn, *Henry D. Thoreau* (Boston: Houghton, Mifflin, 1882), 25, 28; Robert A. Gross, "Lonesome in Eden: Dickinson, Thoreau and the Problem of Community in Nineteenth-Century New England," *Canadian Review of American Studies* 14, no. 1 (1983): 3.
10. William M. Condry, *Thoreau* (New York: Philosophical Library, 1954), 14, 24; Harding, *Days of Henry Thoreau*, 157–58, 177; Samuel Arthur Jones, *Thoreau: A Glimpse* (Concord, MA: Albert Lane, 1903), 30–31, 33.
11. Henry Seidel Canby, *Thoreau* (Boston: Houghton Mifflin, 1939), 188; S. A. Jones to Henry Salt, September 16, 1890, in *Toward the Making of Thoreau's Modern Reputation: Selected Correspondence of S. A. Jones, A. W. Hosmer, H. S. Salt, H. G. O. Blake, and D. Ricketson*, ed. Fritz Oehlschlaeger and George Hendrick (Urbana: University of Illinois Press, 1979), 81.
12. Walter Harding, "Henry Thoreau and Ellen Sewall," *South Atlantic Quarterly* 64 (Winter 1965): 102–7; Harding, *Days of Henry Thoreau*, 104; Louise Osgood Koopman, "The Thoreau Romance," *Massachusetts Review* 4 (Autumn 1962): 61–67; Brooks Atkinson, "Daughter Recalls Her Mother's Story of Rejecting Thoreau's Proposal," *New York Times*, March 12, 1963, 5.
13. Scudder, "Henry David Thoreau," 400; Harding, *Days of Henry Thoreau*, 104–7, 112. See also Condry, *Thoreau*, 101; and James Armstrong, "Thoreau as Philosopher of Love," in *Henry David Thoreau: A Profile*, ed. Walter Roy Harding (New York: Hill and Wang, 1971), 223–24.
14. Harriet Mulford Lothrop, *Old Concord: Her Highways and Byways* (Boston: D. Lothrop, 1888), 9–10; Canby, *Thoreau*, 5; Robert A. Gross, "Culture and Cultivation: Agriculture and Society in Thoreau's Concord," *Journal of American History* 69 (June 1982): 43–47; Brian Donahue, *The Great Meadow: Farmers and the Land in Colonial Concord* (New Haven, CT: Yale University Press, 2004).
15. Henry David Thoreau, *The Writings of Henry David Thoreau: Journal*, ed. Bradford Torrey (Boston: Houghton Mifflin, 1906), 3:331, 401, 4:324. See also Melvyn Stokes, introduction to *The Market Revolution in America: Social, Political, and Religious Expressions, 1800–1880*, ed. Melvyn Stokes and Stephen Conway (Charlottesville: University Press of Virginia, 1996), 7; John Lauritz Larson, *The Market Revolution in America: Liberty, Ambition, and the Eclipse of the Common Good* (New York: Cambridge University Press, 2010), 3, 56–64, 76, 87, 89, 98, 103, 108–9; Edward Jarvis, *Traditions and Reminiscences of Concord, Massachusetts, 1779–1878*, ed. Sarah Chapman (Amherst:

University of Massachusetts Press, 1993), 184, 191, 198; and Gross, "Culture and Cultivation," 42, 47–53.
16. Brooks Atkinson, *Henry Thoreau: The Cosmic Yankee* (New York: Alfred A. Knopf, 1927), 13; Anderson Graham, *Nature in Books: Some Studies in Biography* (London: Methuen, 1891), 69.
17. Edward Waldo Emerson, *Emerson in Concord* (Boston: Houghton Mifflin, 1889), 55–56, 58–59, 98, 104; Van Wyck Brooks, *The Flowering of New England* (New York: Dutton, 1940), 198; Julian Hawthorne, *The Memoirs of Julian Hawthorne*, ed. Edith Garrigues Hawthorne (New York: Macmillan, 1938), 10.
18. Scudder, "Henry David Thoreau," 392. See also Philip Van Doren Stern, ed., *The Annotated "Walden"* (New York: C. N. Potter, 1970), 8; Thoreau, *Journal*, 8:146, 9:113–14; and Robert Kuhn McGregor, *A Wider View of the Universe: Henry Thoreau's Study of Nature* (Urbana: University of Illinois Press, 1997), 52.
19. Bronson Alcott, *The Journals of Bronson Alcott*, ed. Odell Shepard (Boston: Little, Brown, 1938), 211, 309 (quotes); Higginson, *Cheerful Yesterdays*, 181–82. See also Mary Elkins Moller, *Thoreau and the Human Community* (Amherst: University of Massachusetts Press, 1980), 52–55; "A. Bronson Alcott's Life," *Kansas City Times*, April 8, 1887; and George F. Hoar, *Autobiography of Seventy Years* (New York: Scribner, 1903), 73.
20. Thoreau, *Journal*, 4:313–14; Moller, *Thoreau and the Human Community*, 102. See also Philip G. Hubert Jr., *Liberty and a Living* (New York: Putnam's, 1889), 194.
21. Margaret Fuller quoted in Scudder, "Henry David Thoreau," 394; Ralph Waldo Emerson quoted in William M. Moss, "'So Many Promising Youths': Emerson's Disappointing Discoveries of New England Poet-Seers," *New England Quarterly* 49 (March 1976): 50.
22. Franklin Sanborn quoted in Henry Williams, "Henry David Thoreau," in *Pertaining to Thoreau: A Gathering of Ten Significant Nineteenth-Century Opinions*, ed. Samuel Arthur Jones (Hartford, CT: Transcendental Books, 1970), 49. See also Henry Stephens Salt, *Life of Henry David Thoreau* (London: W. Scott, 1896), 52; and Edward Waldo Emerson, *Henry Thoreau: As Remembered by a Young Friend* (1917; reprint, Concord, MA: Thoreau Foundation, 1968), 29.
23. Thoreau, *Journal*, 1:434–35. See also Henry David Thoreau to Ralph Waldo Emerson, June 8, 1843, in "The Emerson-Thoreau Correspondence," ed. F. B. Sanborn, *Atlantic Monthly*, May 1892, 588.
24. Isaiah Berlin, *The Roots of Romanticism* (Princeton, NJ: Princeton University Press, 1999), 49, 55; Octavius Brooks Frothingham, *Transcendentalism in New England: A History* (New York: G. Putnam's Sons, 1886), 136.
25. James C. McKusick, *Green Writing: Romanticism and Ecology* (New York: St. Martin's Press, 2000), 1, 41–42, 50, 69, 73 (quote). See also Frothingham, *Transcendentalism in New England*, 76–77, 92, 94–95, 203; and Lance Newman, *Our Common Dwelling: Henry Thoreau, Transcendentalism, and the Class Politics of Nature* (New York: Palgrave Macmillan, 2005), 37, 76–77.
26. Daniel Walker Howe, *What Hath God Wrought: The Transformation of America, 1815–1848* (New York: Oxford University Press, 2007), 616, 627; Ralph Henry Gabriel, "Emerson and Thoreau," in *The Transcendentalist Revolt*, ed. George Frisbie Whicher (Lexington, MA: Heath, 1968), 23–24; Sacvan Bercovitch, *The American Jeremiad* (Madison: University of Wisconsin Press, 1978), 11.

27. Edwin S. Smith, "A Thoreau for Today," pt. 2, *Mainstream* 13 (May 1960): 1–24; Smith, "A Thoreau for Today," pt. 1, *Mainstream* 13 (April 1960): 9–10; Newman, *Our Common Dwelling*, 14, 39, 41; 149; Russell Blankenship, *American Literature as an Expression of the National Mind* (New York: Henry Holt, 1931), 275–86, 298–99; Charles Sellers, *The Market Revolution: Jacksonian America, 1815–1846* (New York: Oxford University Press, 1991), 378–80.
28. Ralph Waldo Emerson quoted in Petrulionis, *Thoreau in His Own Time*, 72. See also Odell Shepard, "Paradox of Thoreau," *Scribner's Magazine*, September 1920, 340; and Alcott to Mrs. A. Bronson Alcott, April 7, 1857, in *The Letters of A. Bronson Alcott*, ed. Richard L. Herrnstadt (Ames: Iowa State University Press, 1968), 240.
29. Clifton Johnson, introduction to *Walden*, by Henry David Thoreau (New York: Thomas Y. Crowell, 1910), viii. See also Maynard, *Walden Pond: A History*, 64, 65, 68, 83; and August William Derleth, *Concord Rebel: A Life of Henry D. Thoreau* (Philadelphia: Chilton, 1962), 53.
30. Richardson, *Henry Thoreau*, 152; Thomas Wentworth Higginson, *Short Studies of American Authors* (Boston: Lee and Shepard, 1888), 25–26.
31. Harding, *Days of Henry Thoreau*, 122–23; Condry, *Thoreau*, 39–40; Thoreau, *Walden*, 107–8, 203; Brooks, *Flowering of New England*, 359.
32. Richardson, *Henry Thoreau*, 154; Thoreau, *Walden*, 118 (first quote); Thoreau, *Journal*, 9:160 (second quote). See also Laura Dassow Walls, *Henry David Thoreau: A Life* (Chicago: University of Chicago Press, 2017), 194.
33. William Condry, "A Hundred Years of *Walden*," *Dublin Magazine* (January–March 1955): 65; McGregor, *Wider View of the Universe*, 75–78, 201 (quote), 202; Thoreau, *Walden*, 426–27. See also Thoreau, *Journal*, 1:361; and Charles A. Madison, "Henry David Thoreau: Transcendental Individualist," *Ethics* 54 (1944): 112.
34. William Howarth, "The Journal of Henry D. Thoreau, 1906–2006," *Princeton University Library Chronicle* 67 (Summer 2006): 639; Townsend Scudder, "Horizons of a Mind," *Saturday Review of Literature* 34 (September 22, 1951): 20–21; Alfred Kazin, "Writing in the Dark," in *Henry David Thoreau: Studies and Commentaries*, ed. Walter Harding, George Brenner, and Paul A. Doyle (Madison, NJ: Fairleigh Dickinson University Press, 1972), 34.
35. Léon Bazalgette, *Henry Thoreau, Bachelor of Nature*, translated by Van Wyck Brooks (London: Jonathan Cape, 1925), 138 (first quote); Celia R. Frease quoted in Walter Harding, ed., *Thoreau as Seen by His Contemporaries* (1960; reprint, New York: Dover, 1989), 208 (second quote); N. C. Wyeth, "Thoreau, His Critics, and the Public," in *Recognition of Thoreau*, by Glick, 231 (third quote); Robert Whitcomb, "The Thoreau 'Country,'" *Bookman* (July 1931): 460 (fourth quote); "Letter from an 'Old Concordian,'" *Bismarck (ND) Daily Tribune*, May 13, 1885 (fifth quote); Ralph Waldo Emerson quoted in Henry David Thoreau, *Thoreau, Philosopher of Freedom: Writings on Liberty by Henry David Thoreau*, ed. James Mackaye (New York: Vanguard Press, 1930), vii (sixth quote). See also *New York Times*, February 17, 1879, 2; William Dean Howells quoted in *New York Times*, July 29, 1894, 22; William Dean Howells, "My First Visit to New England," *Harper's New Monthly Magazine* 89 (August 1894): 447; Priscilla R. Edes, *Some Reminiscences of Old Concord* (Gouverneur, NY: C. A. Livingston, 1903), 31–32; and "Book Storage," *Wilson Library Bulletin* 36 (June 1962): 823.
36. Thoreau, October 24, 1852, *Journal*, 4:397 (first quote); old farmer quoted in Annie Sawyer Downs, "Mr. Hawthorne, Mr. Thoreau, Miss Alcott, Mr. Emerson, and Me," in *American Heritage*, ed. Walter Harding, December 1978, 99 (second quote);

Petrulionis, *Thoreau in His Own Time,* xxvii (third quote). See also Robert M. Thorson, "Thoreau and Asperger's Syndrome?," *Thoreau Society Bulletin* (Spring 2008): 9; Alfred Munroe, "Letter from Concord," *Richmond County Gazette,* in *American Transcendental Quarterly* 36 (Fall 1977): 20; and "Reminiscences of Thoreau: Sic Vita," *Outlook,* December 2, 1899, 815, 820.
37. John Albee, *Remembrances of Emerson* (1901), quoted in *Thoreau in His Own Time,* ed. Petrulionis, 3, 37 (first quote); "Appendix A: Conversation with Horace Hosmer, Action, Mass.," in *Remembrances of Concord and the Thoreaus: Letters of Horace Hosmer to Dr. S. A. Jones,* ed. George Hendrick (Urbana: University of Illinois Press, 1977), 149 (second quote). See also Hoar, *Autobiography of Seventy Years,* 72; Emerson, *Emerson in Concord,* 111; Emerson, *As Remembered by a Young Friend,* 3; and Moller, *Thoreau and the Human Community,* 67, 83.
38. *Portland (ME) Transcript* quoted in John F. Jaques, "An Enthusiastic Newspaper Account of Thoreau's Second Lecture in Portland, Maine, January 15, 1851," *American Literature* 40 (November 1968): 386–88 (both quotes). See also "Frazier Hall Lectures," *Lynn Weekly Reporter,* April 30, 1859, quoted in Harding, *Thoreau as Seen,* 197; *Gloucester (MA) News* quoted in Gary Scharnhorst, *Henry David Thoreau: An Annotated Bibliography of Comment and Criticism before 1900* (New York: Garland, 1992), 8; "Salem Lyceum," *Salem (MA) Observer,* November 25, 1848; and *Gloucester (MA) Telegraph,* December 23, 1848.
39. Moncure Conway quoted in Harding, *Thoreau as Seen,* 111; James Russell Lowell, "A Fable for Critics" (1848), in *Recognition of Thoreau,* by Glick, 3; *Massachusetts Spy* (Worcester), May 9, 1848; Scudder, "Henry David Thoreau," 402. See also "Salem Lyceum," *Salem (MA) Observer,* November 25, 1848.
40. Annie Russell Marble quoted in Henry David Thoreau, *The Maine Woods* (New York: Thomas Y. Crowell, 1906), ix, x.
41. John Hildebidle, "Thoreau at the Edge," *Prose Studies* 15 (December 1992): 355–56; Sherman Paul, "Thoreau, *The Maine Woods,* and the Problem of Ktaadn," in *A Century of Early Ecocriticism,* ed. David Mazel (Athens: University of Georgia Press, 2001), 332; Kelli Olson, "A Cultural Study of Henry D. Thoreau's *The Maine Woods*" (PhD diss., University of Iowa, 2000), 9–11, 37, 39.
42. *Hartford (CT) Daily Courant,* September 1, 1875.
43. Thoreau, *The Writings of Henry David Thoreau,* vol. 1, *A Week on the Concord and Merrimack Rivers* (Boston: Houghton Mifflin, 1893), 11; Walls, *Henry David Thoreau,* 272; Condry, *Thoreau,* 66. See also Scudder, "Henry David Thoreau," 403; *New York Times,* August 31, 1939, 14; and review of *A Week on the Concord and Merrimack Rivers,* by Thoreau, *Liberator* (Boston), June 15, 1849, 96.
44. Sophia Dobson Collet, "Literature of American Individuality," in *Emerson and Thoreau: The Contemporary Reviews,* ed. Joel Myerson (New York: Cambridge University Press, 1992), 359–60; James Russell Lowell, review of *A Week on the Concord and Merrimack Rivers,* ibid., 357; George Ripley, "H. D. Thoreau's Book," in *Pertaining to Thoreau,* ed. Jones, 9–11; Thoreau quoted in Vernon Louis Parrington, *Main Currents in American Thought: An Interpretation of American Literature from the Beginnings to 1920* (1927; reprint, New York: Harcourt, Brace, 1930), 404. See also Derleth, *Concord Rebel,* 86–88; Scudder, "Henry David Thoreau," 402; Salt, *Life of Thoreau,* 107; William Rounseville Alger, review of *A Week on the Concord and Merrimack Rivers,* in *Emerson and Thoreau,* ed. Myerson, 348–49; and *Baltimore Sun,* June 15, 1849.

45. Sanborn, *Henry D. Thoreau,* 299. See also Walls, *Henry David Thoreau,* 266, 268–69; "Book Storage," 823; Hawthorne, *Memoirs,* 109; and Harmon Smith, *My Friend, My Friend: The Story of Thoreau's Relationship with Emerson* (Amherst: University of Massachusetts Press, 1999).
46. Robert Sattelmeyer, "'When He Became My Enemy': Emerson and Thoreau, 1848–49," *New England Quarterly* 62 (June 1989): 188, 190–91, 201 (quote), 203. See also Thoreau, *Journal,* 5:188; and John Brooks More, "Thoreau Rejects Emerson," *American Literature* 4 (November 1932): 241, 252, 254.
47. Fred Lewis Pattee, "Rise of the Nature Writers," in *A History of American Literature since 1870* (New York: Century, 1915), 137; Francis B. Dedmond, "100 Years of *Walden,*" *Concord (MA) Journal,* June 24, 1954, Walden E. Miscellaneous, iii, j. Centenary, series II, Harding Collection; Derleth, *Concord Rebel,* 123.
48. Thoreau, *Walden,* viii, 1, 5 (second quote), 8 (first quote), 13, 87, 91, 119 (third quote), 148. See also McGregor, *Wider View of the Universe,* 200.
49. *Portland (ME) Transcript* quoted in Scharnhorst, *Annotated Bibliography,* 151; *Worcester Palladium* quoted in *Critical Essays on Henry David Thoreau's "Walden,"* ed. Joel Myerson (Boston: G. K. Hall, 1988), 21; *New York Times* quoted in Dean and Scharnhorst, "Contemporary Reception of *Walden,*" 317; review of *Walden,* by Thoreau, in *Recognition of Thoreau,* by Glick, 5; anonymous quote in Downs, "Mr. Hawthorne, Mr. Thoreau, Miss Alcott, Mr. Emerson, and Me," 99. See also *Boston Journal* quoted in Scharnhorst, *Annotated Bibliography,* 26; *New Bedford (MA) Mercury* quoted in Dean and Scharnhorst, "Contemporary Reception of *Walden,*" 302; *Boston Daily Bee,* quoted ibid., 299; "Another Book by Thoreau," in *Circular,* quoted in *Emerson and Thoreau,* ed. Myerson, 371; *Boston Daily Evening Traveller,* quoted ibid., 18; and Walter Harding, "Some Forgotten Reviews of *Walden,*" *Thoreau Society Bulletin* (Winter 1954): 2–3.
50. Review of *Walden,* by Thoreau, in *Emerson and Thoreau,* ed. Myerson, 388 (first quote); letter to the editor, *New York Tribune,* quoted in Harding, *Days of Henry Thoreau,* 240 (second quote). See also *Chambers's Journal, Salem (MA) Register,* and *Providence (RI) Evening Press* all quoted in Dean and Scharnhorst, "Contemporary Reception of *Walden,*" 327–32; Lydia Maria Child (attributed), "Review of *A Week* and *Walden,*" in *Recognition of Thoreau,* by Glick, 9–10, 11; *Boston Daily Atlas,* October 21, 1854; and "Critical Notices," *North American Review* 165 (October 1854): 536.
51. Jesse Clements, *Western Literary Messenger,* quoted in Dean and Scharnhorst, "Contemporary Reception of *Walden,*" 312; *Boston Daily Atlas,* October 21, 1854. See also *Centinel* [sic] *of Freedom* (Newark, NJ), October 20, 1857; *Gloucester (MA) Telegraph,* December 23, 1848; and Edwin Morton, "Thoreau and His Books," *Harvard Magazine,* quoted in Jones, *Pertaining to Thoreau,* 25.
52. *Boston Daily Atlas,* October 21, 1854; "Town and Rural Humbugs," *Knickerbocker Magazine* (1855), quoted in Jones, *Pertaining to Thoreau,* 27–28, 30–31. See also "An American Diogenes," *Chambers's Journal,* quoted in Dean and Scharnhorst, "Contemporary Reception of *Walden,*" 328–32.
53. Dean and Scharnhorst, "Contemporary Reception of *Walden,*" 293 (first quote); *Oneida (NY) Circular* quoted in *Emerson and Thoreau,* ed. Myerson, 413 (second quote); Alcott, *Journals,* 338 (third quote). See also *New York Evening Post* quoted in Gary Scharnhorst, "James T. Fields and Early Notices of *Walden,*" *New England Quarterly* 55 (March 1982): 116; Thomas Starr King quoted in Dean and Scharnhorst, "Contemporary Reception of *Walden,*" 307; and "An Original," *New Orleans Times-Picayune,* April 11, 1849.

54. E. M. Schuster, "Native American Anarchism," *Smith College Studies in History* 17 (October 1931–July 1932): 51–55, 59–64, 66, 69; Alcott, *Journals*, 201, 250; Derleth, *Concord Rebel*, 107; Isabel Paterson, "Henry David Thoreau, Native of Concord," *New York Herald Tribune Weekly Book Review*, October 28, 1945, box 331, "News Clippings, Book Reviews," Thoreau Fellowship Collection, Raymond H. Fogler Library, Special Collections Department, University of Maine, Orono.
55. Alcott, *Journals*, 183–84; George Frisbie Whicher, *Walden Revisited: A Centennial Tribute to Henry David Thoreau* (Chicago: Packard, 1945), 68–72; Carl Bode, "Thoreau the Actor," *American Quarterly* 5 (Autumn 1953): 248.
56. Thoreau quoted in A. Bronson Alcott, *Concord Days* (Boston: Roberts Brothers, 1872), 16–17; "Words That Burn," *National Anti-Slavery Standard*, August 12, 1854. See also *Liberator* (Boston), February 25, 1859; Harding, *Days of Henry Thoreau*, 199–207; and Thoreau, *Journal*, 6:339, 357.
57. *New York Daily Tribune* quoted in Scharnhorst, *Annotated Bibliography*, 55 (quote). See also *Boston Post*, November 7, 1859; Harding, *Days of Henry Thoreau*, 416; Annie Russell Marble, *Thoreau: His Home, Friends and Books* (1902; reprint, New York: AMS Press, 1969), 167, 171; *Liberator* (Boston), November 4, 1859; and *Salem (MA) Register*, November 7, 1859.
58. Thoreau quoted in Charles A. Madison, *Critics and Crusaders: A Century of American Protest* (New York: Henry Holt, 1947), 188 (first quote); Thoreau, *Journal*, 12:325–29, 401, 405, 409, 412 (second quote). See also A. Bronson Alcott to Daniel Ricketson, November 6, 1859, in *Letters of Alcott*, ed. Herrnstadt, 306; Bronson Alcott quoted in Henry Steele Commager, "The Mind of Bronson Alcott," *New York Times*, September 25, 1938, 83; and *New York Evening Post*, December 9, 1859.
59. Walls, *Henry David Thoreau*, 360; William Lyon Phelps, *Henry David Thoreau: A Study* (New York: Macmillan, 1924), 25; Thoreau, *Journal*, 9:151. See also Moller, *Thoreau and the Human Community*, 94; Mary Loomis Todd, "The Thoreau Family Two Generations Ago," in *Thoreau in His Own Time*, ed. Petrulionis, 213; and Canby, *Thoreau*, 343.
60. Edward Sherman Hoar to Edward Sandford Burgess, January 4, 1893, in *Thoreau in His Own Time*, ed. Petrulionis, 142 (first quote); Salt, *Life of Thoreau*, 143 (second quote); Mary Mann to Mrs. Nathaniel Hawthorne, May 1862, in *Thoreau as Seen*, ed. Harding, 114 (third quote).
61. *Boston Daily Advertiser*, May 8, 1862.
62. Ethel Seybold, *Thoreau: The Quest and the Classics* (New Haven, CT: Yale University Press, 1951), 1–2.
63. Daniel Gregory Mason, "The Idealistic Basis of Thoreau's Genius," *Harvard Monthly*, December 1897, 93.

Chapter 2: Thoreau in the Age of Industry, 1862–1890

1. Bronson Alcott to Daniel Ricketson, February 10, 1862, in *The Letters of A. Bronson Alcott*, ed. Richard L. Herrnstadt (Ames: Iowa State University Press, 1968), 326–27. See also H. S. Canby, "Thoreau in History: The Story of a Literary Reputation," *Saturday Review of Literature* 20 (July 15, 1939): 3.
2. Moncure D. Conway, "The Transcendentalists of Concord," *Fraser's Magazine for Town and Country* 70 (August 1864): 256; Joseph Chamberlain, "The Nomad," *Boston Transcript*, October 26, 1921, W6, Walden Pond, l, Walter Harding Collection (hereafter WHC), series III, Thoreau Institute, Lincoln, MA; Charles H. Adams, "Thoreau," *Yale Literary Magazine* 31 (November 1865): 57 (first quote); Joseph

Wood Krutch, "The Steady Fascination of Thoreau," in *The Recognition of Henry David Thoreau: Selected Criticism since 1848*, ed. Wendell Glick (Ann Arbor: University of Michigan Press, 1969), 298 (second quote).

3. A. H. P., "In Winter with Thoreau," *Unitarian Review* (July 1888): 73 (first quote); Thomas Wentworth Higginson, "Henry David Thoreau," in *American Prose*, ed. George Rice Carpenter (New York: Macmillan, 1898), 338 (second quote); *New Haven (CT) Daily Palladium*, October 24, 1863 (third quote). See also "Reviews and Literary Notices: Thoreau's Maine Woods," *Atlantic Monthly*, September 1864, 386; *New York Times*, December 18, 1887, 14; *Boston Daily Atlas*, October 21, 1854; "Notices of New Books: H. D. Thoreau, Cape Cod," *New Englander and Yale Review* (July 1865): 602–3; and Fritz Oehlschlaeger and George Hendrick, eds., *Toward the Making of Thoreau's Modern Reputation: Selected Correspondence of S. A. Jones, A. W. Hosmer, H. S. Salt, H. G. O. Blake, and D. Ricketson* (Urbana: University of Illinois Press, 1979), 12.

4. Henry David Thoreau, *The Writings of Henry David Thoreau*, ed. Bradford Torrey, vol. 2, *Journal* (Boston: Houghton Mifflin, Riverside Press, 1906), 4 (first quote); Ulmus, "Who Is Responsible for New England Pantheism?," *Christian Register* 28 (August 25, 1849): 136 (second quote); *Boston Daily Atlas*, October 21, 1854 (third quote). See also Vernon Louis Parrington, *Main Currents in American Thought: An Interpretation of American Literature from the Beginnings to 1920* (1927; reprint, New York: Harcourt, Brace, 1930), 404; *Baltimore Sun*, June 15, 1849; *New Hampshire Patriot and State Gazette* in Joel Myerson, ed., *Emerson and Thoreau: The Contemporary Reviews* (New York: Cambridge University Press, 1992), 345; "Thoreau's Travels," ibid., 346; Parish Priest, "Henry D. Thoreau," ibid., 432–36; "The Maine Woods," *Universalist Quarterly* 2 (October 1865): 530–31; and Henry Stephens Salt, *Life of Henry David Thoreau* (London: W. Scott, 1896), 107.

5. *New York Times*, November 23, 1863, 2; Alcott to Kenningale Robert Cook, April 9, 1873, in *Letters of Alcott*, ed. Herrnstadt, 589.

6. Canby, "Thoreau in History," 3; Alexandra Krastin, "He Took to the Woods 100 Years Ago," *Saturday Evening Post*, June 30, 1945, 298.

7. Ralph Waldo Emerson to Rufus Wilmot Griswold, September 25, 1841, in *Thoreau in His Own Time*, ed. Sandra Harbert Petrulionis (Ames: University of Iowa Press, 2012), 15 (first quote); Ralph Waldo Emerson, "Biographical Sketch," in *The Writings of Henry David Thoreau*, vol. 1, *A Week on the Concord and Merrimack Rivers*, Riverside Press ed. (Boston: Houghton Mifflin, 1893), xxxiv (second quote).

8. Emerson, "Biographical Sketch," xvii, xvi, xv, xxxv; "The Magazines," *New York Times*, July 28, 1862, 2. See also Leo Marx, "Thoreau's Excursions," *Yale Review* (March 1962): 365; and Gabrielle Fitzgerald, "In Time of War: The Context of Emerson's 'Thoreau,'" *American Transcendental Quarterly* 41 (1979): 5, 8.

9. Franklin B. Sanborn, *Henry D. Thoreau* (Boston: Houghton, Mifflin, 1882), 306 (first quote); *New York Daily Tribune*, July 20, 1865 (second quote); Thomas Wentworth Higginson, "Reviews and Literary Notices," *Atlantic Monthly*, October 1865, 504 (third quote); "Book Notices," *Portland (ME) Transcript*, July 29, 1865, in *Henry David Thoreau: An Annotated Bibliography of Comment and Criticism before 1900*, by Gary Scharnhorst (New York: Garland, 1992), 112 (fourth quote); Henry Seidel Canby, *Thoreau* (Boston: Houghton Mifflin, 1939), 445 (fifth quote). See also Salt, *Life of Thoreau*, 193; and "Reviews and Literary Notices: Thoreau's Letters," *Atlantic Monthly*, October 1865, 504–5.

10. James Russell Lowell, *My Study Windows* (1874; reprint, Boston: Houghton Mifflin,

1889), 197, 200, 109. See also Russell Blankenship, *American Literature as an Expression of the National Mind* (New York: Henry Holt, 1931), 344; Daniel A. Wells, "Thoreau's Reputation in the Major Magazines, 1862-1900: A Summary and Index," *American Periodicals* 4 (1994): 12-13; and Lewis Leary, "Century of *Walden*," *Nation* 179 (August 7, 1954): 114.
11. Lowell, *My Study Windows,* 195, 201, 208.
12. Franklin Benjamin Sanborn, *The Life of Henry David Thoreau* (Boston: Houghton Mifflin, 1917), 372. See also Canby, *Thoreau,* 375.
13. Bernard Smith, *Forces in American Criticism: A Study in the History of American Literary Thought* (New York: Harcourt, Brace, 1939), 23, 25, 27, 235 (quote); Townsend Scudder, "Henry David Thoreau," in *Literary History of the United States,* ed. Robert E. Spiller et al. (New York: Macmillan, 1963-72), 1:410. See also Bronson Alcott, March 6, 1871, in *The Journals of Bronson Alcott,* ed. Odell Shepard (Boston: Little, Brown, 1938), 419; and Oliver Wendell Holmes, *Ralph Waldo Emerson* (Boston: Houghton Mifflin, 1885), 29-33.
14. Richard Rutland, "The Search for *Walden*," *Emerson Society Quarterly* 23 (1977): 191 (first quote); Lowell, *My Study Windows,* 205; Lewis Leary, "Thoreau," in *Eight American Authors,* ed. James Woodress (New York: Modern Language Association, 1956), 144. See also Henry Beetle Hough, *Thoreau of Walden: The Man and His Eventful Life* (New York: Simon and Schuster, 1956), 60-61; B. Smith, *Forces in American Criticism,* 239; and Canby, *Thoreau,* 292.
15. W. R. Alger, "The Literature of Friendship," *North American Review* (July 1856): 110-11, in *A Week on the Concord and Merrimack Rivers,* D, Criticism, iii, series II, WHC; William Rounseville Alger, *The Solitudes of Nature and of Man; or, The Loneliness of Human Life* (Boston: Roberts Brothers, 1866), 329-30, 332, 336. See also Canby, "Thoreau in History," 3.
16. Robert Louis Stevenson, "Henry David Thoreau: His Character and Opinions," in *Recognition of Thoreau,* ed. Glick, 66-68.
17. John Macy, *The Spirit of American Literature* (New York: Boni and Liveright, 1908), 171.
18. *New York Times,* September 30, 1862, 2; *Portland (ME) Daily Advertiser,* October 20, 1863; John Burroughs, "Manifold Nature," *North American Review* (August 1916): 253.
19. Granville Hicks, *The Great Tradition: An Interpretation of American Literature since the Civil War* (New York: Macmillan, 1933), 3; Holmes, *Ralph Waldo Emerson,* 152. See also Brooks Atkinson, *Henry Thoreau: The Cosmic Yankee* (New York: Alfred A. Knopf, 1927), 3; *Philadelphia Inquirer,* September 24, 1866; *New York Daily Tribune,* September 12, 1873; Canby, *Thoreau,* 444; and William Sloane Kennedy, "A New Estimate of Thoreau," in *Recognition of Thoreau,* ed. Glick, 92-93.
20. Krastin, "He Took to the Woods," 79. See also Franklin W. Hamilton, *Thoreau on the Art of Writing* (Ann Arbor: University Microfilms, 1962), 77, box 328, Thoreau Fellowship Collection (hereafter TFC), Raymond H. Fogler Library, Special Collections Department, University of Maine, Orono; Lucy Lockwood Hazard, "Thoreau: The Intensive Pioneer," in *The Frontier in American Literature* (New York: Barnes & Noble, 1941), 168; and Edwin S. Smith, "A Thoreau for Today," pt. 2, *Mainstream* 13 (May 1960): 4-5.
21. Emerson quoted in Carl Bode, *The Anatomy of American Popular Culture, 1840-1861* (1959; reprint, Carbondale: Southern Illinois University Press, 1970), 207; Holmes,

Ralph Waldo Emerson, 294; E. C. Gale, "The Walden Recluse," *Yale Literary Magazine* (January 1883): 138; "New Books," *New York Times,* November 23, 1863, 2. See also A. B., "Souls in Bundles," *Oneida (NY) Circular* 10 (October 6, 1873): 324; B. Smith, *Forces in American Criticism,* 76; and A. G. Sedgwick, "Sanborn's Thoreau," *Nation* 35 (July 13, 1882): 34.

22. Daniel Walker Howe, "The Market Revolution and the Shaping of Identity in Whig-Jacksonian America," in *The Market Revolution in America: Social, Political, and Religious Expressions, 1800–1880,* ed. Melvyn Stokes and Stephen Conway (Charlottesville: University Press of Virginia, 1996), 270, 271 (quote).

23. Hicks, *Great Tradition,* 4.

24. Ibid., 30–31; Canby, *Thoreau,* 447; Henry James quoted in Scharnhorst, *Annotated Bibliography,* 97. See also B. Smith, *Forces in American Criticism,* 230–31; and Atkinson, *Cosmic Yankee,* 4.

25. Alcott, *Journals,* 374. See also Daniel Gregory Mason, "The Idealistic Basis of Thoreau's Genius," in *New England Writers and the Press,* ed. Kenneth W. Cameron (Hartford, CT: Transcendental Books, 1980), 75; *New York Daily Tribune,* April 27, 1865; and *New York Commercial Advertiser,* August 27, 1866.

26. *Albion* 41 (November 7, 1863): 537 (first quote); *Boston Recorder,* October 23, 1863 (second quote); Thomas Storrow Higginson, "Henry D. Thoreau," in *Pertaining to Thoreau: A Gathering of Ten Significant Nineteenth-Century Opinions,* ed. Samuel Arthur Jones (Hartford, CT: Transcendental Books, 1970), 39 (third quote).

27. Robert Sattelmeyer, "*Walden:* Climbing the Canon," in *More Day to Dawn: Thoreau's "Walden" for the Twenty-First Century,* ed. Sandra Harbert Petrulionis and Laura Dassow Walls (Amherst: University of Massachusetts Press, 2007), 12–13, 25 (quote); Philip G. Hubert Jr., "Concord and Thoreau," *Zion's Herald,* August 18, 1897, 33.

28. George Eliot, "Review of *Walden,*" in *Recognition of Thoreau,* ed. Glick, 12 (first quote); James Playsted Wood, "English and American Criticism of Thoreau," *New England Quarterly* 6 (December 1933): 738 (second quote). See also Francis B. Dedmond, "100 Years of *Walden,*" *Concord Journal,* June 24, 1954, *Walden,* E, Miscellaneous, iii, j, Centenary, series II, WHC; W. Barksdale Maynard, *Walden Pond: A History* (New York: Oxford University Press, 2004), 220; and "An American Rousseau," *Saturday Review* (London) 18 (December 3, 1864), 694–95.

29. Henry Seidel Canby, "Thoreau: The Great Eccentric," *Saturday Review of Literature* 4 (November 1927): 338; Edward Carpenter, *England's Ideal, and Other Papers on Social Subjects* (New York: Scribner's, 1919), 95–96. See also John Edwards quoted in Lonnie L. Willis, "The Thoreau Centenary in Britain," *American Studies International* 37 (June 1999): 64; George Hendrick, "Henry S. Salt, the Late Victorian Socialists, and Thoreau," *New England Quarterly* (September 1977): 416–22; Oehlschlaeger and Hendrick, *Thoreau's Modern Reputation,* 20–24; Leary, "Century of *Walden,*" 114–15; Robert Stowell, "Thoreau's Influence on an English Socialist," *Thoreau Society Bulletin* (Winter 1967): 1–3; Wood, "English and American Criticism," 740–41; and Walter Harding, "Thoreau's Fame Abroad," in *Recognition of Thoreau,* ed. Glick, 316–18, 322.

30. *Boston Daily Advertiser,* April 9, 1878 (first quote); *Quincy (IL) Whig,* February 4, 1871 (second and third quotes); Alcott, *Journals,* 359 (fourth quote). See also Lawrence Buell, "The Thoreauvian Pilgrimage: The Structure of an American Cult," *American Literature* 61 (May 1989): 194; and Krutch, "Steady Fascination of Thoreau," in *Recognition of Thoreau,* ed. Glick, 298.

31. A. Bronson Alcott, "Thoreau," *Independent* 24 (September 5, 1872): 1; Alcott, *Concord Days* (Boston: Roberts Brothers, 1872), 12–13, 16.
32. Julian Hawthorne, *The Memoirs of Julian Hawthorne,* ed. Edith Garrigues Hawthorne (New York: Macmillan, 1938), 58; Wilson Flagg, "Concord Philosophy," *Boston Transcript,* August 20, 1880; Bronson Alcott, "Thoreau," in *Recognition of Thoreau,* ed. Glick, 48–49. See also Alcott, "Thoreau," *Independent,* September 5, 1872, 1; and Alcott, *Concord Days,* 16.
33. William Ellery Channing quoted in Sanborn, *Life of Thoreau,* 488. See also F. B. Sanborn, *Sixty Years of Concord, 1855–1915,* ed. Kenneth Walter Cameron (Hartford, CT: Transcendental Books, 1976), 17–18; William Ellery Channing, "Life," *Nation* (November 20, 1902): 403; "Thoreau," *Literary World* 4 (September 1, 1873): 49; and *New York Daily Tribune,* October 14, 1871.
34. William Ellery Channing quoted in A. H. P., "In Winter with Thoreau," 79 (first quote); William Ellery Channing, *Thoreau: The Poet-Naturalist, with Memorial Verses* (Boston: Roberts Brothers, 1873), 10 (second quote), 34, 218, 243.
35. "New Publications," *New York Times,* October 25, 1873, 11; Channing, *Poet-Naturalist,* 50. See also Horatio N. Powers, "Thoreau," *Dial* 3 (August 1882): 70; and Edith Kellogg Dunton, "An Old and a New Estimate of Thoreau," *Dial* (December 16, 1902): 465.
36. "Thoreau," *Literary World* (September 1, 1873): 49 (first quote); Canby, *Thoreau,* 444 (second quote). See also *Portland (ME) Daily Press,* September 20, 1873; *Boston Daily Advertiser,* September 6, 1873; *Cincinnati Daily Gazette,* September 11, 1873; *Massachusetts Spy* (Worcester), September 19, 1873; *New York Daily Tribune,* September 12, 1873; and *New York Evening Post,* September 5, 1873.
37. "New Publications," *New York Times,* October 25, 1873, 11 (first quote); *New York Evening Post,* September 5, 1873 (second quote).
38. Ralph Waldo Emerson, "Thoreau," *Atlantic Monthly,* August 1862, 245 (first quote); Channing in "New Publications," *New York Times,* October 25, 1873, 11 (second quote); A. D. Anderson, "Henry David Thoreau," *Nassau Literary Magazine* (March 1878): 262 (third quote); Leila S. Taylor, "Thoreau's Individualness," *Springfield (MA) Republican,* September 5, 1880 (fourth quote). See also Francis H. Underwood, "Henry David Thoreau," *Good Words* 29 (July 1888): 451; Mary Hosmer Brown, "Memories of Concord," in *Thoreau in His Own Time,* ed. Petrulionis, 204; James T. Fields, "Our Poet-Naturalist," in *Papyrus Leaves,* ed. William Fearing Gill (New York: Worthington, 1879), 31–35; and *Montpelier (VT) Argus and Patriot,* July 3, 1872.
39. "Contemporary Literature," *North American Review* (May–June 1878): 547 (first quote); James Leonard Corning, "Henry Thoreau," *Independent,* August 1, 1872, 11 (second quote); Thomas Wentworth Higginson, *Short Studies of American Authors* (Boston: Lee & Shepard, 1880), 24 (third quote), 28–30. See also John Nichol, *American Literature: An Historical Sketch* (Edinburgh: Adam & Charles Black, 1882), 315; *Springfield (MA) Republican* quoted in Franklin Benjamin Sanborn, ed., *Literary Studies and Criticism: Evaluations of the Writers of the American Renaissance* (Hartford, CT: Transcendental Books, 1980), 25; Pendleton King, "Notes of Conversations with Emerson," *New York Herald Tribune,* December 27, 1883; and *Springfield (MA) Republican,* May 2, 1878.
40. James Russell Lowell quoted in *New York Times,* September 20, 1885. See also *Boston Journal,* September 14, 1885.

41. George W. Cooke, "The Two Thoreaus," *Independent*, December 10, 1896, 3; John Weiss and Thomas Wentworth Higginson quoted in Gilbert Payson Coleman, "Thoreau and His Critics," *Dial* (June 1, 1906): 352–53.
42. Albert Line, *Concord Authors at Home* (Concord, MA: Erudite Press, 1902), 11 (quote), 16. See also, for example, Mary J. Stafford, "American Mecca," *Belford's Magazine* (August 1891): 413; *Boston Daily Advertiser*, September 3, 1894; B. W. Ball, "Old Concord—Sleepy-Hollow Cemetery," *Lowell (MA) Daily Citizen and News*, December 9, 1865; and *Springfield (MA) Weekly Republican*, May 1, 1869.
43. Winthrop Packard, *Literary Pilgrimages of a Naturalist* (Boston: Small, Maynard, 1911), 92; Robert A. Gross, introduction to *Traditions and Reminiscences of Concord, Massachusetts, 1779–1878*, by Edward Jarvis, ed. Sarah Chapman (Amherst: University of Massachusetts Press, 1993), xvi–ix; Annie Russell Marble, "Where Thoreau Worked and Wandered," *Critic* (June 1902): 513–16; *Philadelphia Inquirer*, April 21, 1895.
44. Theodore F. Wolfe, *Literary Shrines: The Haunts of Some Famous American Authors* (Philadelphia: Lippincott, 1895), 18. See also Harriet Mulford Lothrop, *Old Concord: Her Highways and Byways* (Boston: D. Lothrop, 1888), 28; Hannah R. Hudson, "Concord Books," *Harper's New Monthly Magazine* 71 (June 1875): 19; Buell, "Thoreauvian Pilgrimage," 197, 199; "Emerson: A Literary Interview," in *Annotated Bibliography*, by Scharnhorst, 275; Line, *Concord Authors at Home*, 9, 27–28; and *New York Times*, August 23, 1891, 11.
45. Hudson, "Concord Books," 30; Rufus Rockwell Wilson, *New England in Letters* (New York: A. Wessels, 1904), 100; Gary Scharnhorst, *Henry David Thoreau: A Case Study in Canonization* (Columbia, SC: Camden House, 1993), 28; Salt, *Life of Thoreau*, 189. See also Philip G. Hubert Jr., "Thoreau's Concord," *New York Herald Tribune*, September 13, 1896; *Boston Daily Journal*, August 22, 1883; M. Starr, "In and About Concord," *Chicago Inter Ocean*, December 25, 1878; Marble, "Where Thoreau Worked and Wandered," 509, 514–16; and Hamilton W. Mabie, "A May Day in Concord," *Christian Union* 29 (June 5, 1884): 533.
46. Maynard, *Walden Pond: A History*, 155; Hubert, "Thoreau's Concord." See also Line, *Concord Authors at Home*, 6; and Mark W. Sullivan, *Picturing Thoreau: Henry David Thoreau in American Visual Culture* (Lanham, MD: Lexington Books, 2015), 35.
47. Alcott, *Journals*, 358 (first quote); Alcott quoted in Maynard, *Walden Pond: A History*, 156 (second quote) 157, 164–65. See also "A Visit to Thoreau's Haunts," *Genius* 1 (January 1888): 21–23, W6, Walden Pond, c, series III, WHC; and Walter Harding, introduction to *Discovery at Walden*, by Roland W. Robbins (Concord, MA: R. Robbins, 1947), x–xvi.
48. Alcott, *Journals*, 452. See also James Dawson, "A History of the Cairn," *Thoreau Society Bulletin* (Summer 2000): 1–3; Raymona Hull, "The Cairn at Walden Pond," *Thoreau Society Bulletin* (Winter 1968): 5–6; Alcott, *Concord Days*, 259; *New York Herald Tribune* (June 17, 1878); and Maynard, *Walden Pond: A History*, 174.
49. "Visit to Thoreau's Haunts," 22 (first quote); *New York Tribune*, August 21, 1866 (second quote); ibid., July 28, 1869 (third quote). See also *Lowell (MA) Daily Citizen and News*, July 28, 1868; *New York Daily Tribune*, September 3, 1870; Maynard, *Walden Pond: A History*, 34, 216–17; and S. R., "More Concord Days," *Friends' Intelligencer* 38 (August 27, 1881): 434.
50. Sophia Thoreau quoted in Maynard, *Walden Pond: A History*, 164; Wilson Flagg, *The Woods and By-Ways of New England* (Boston: James R. Osgood, 1872), 392.
51. Rose Hawthorne Lathrop, "Glimpses of Force: Thoreau and Alcott, 1891," in *Thoreau*

in His Own Time, ed. Petrulionis, 146 (first quote); Mabie, "May Day in Concord," 533 (second quote). See also C. T. Ramsey, "Pilgrimage to the Haunts of Thoreau," *New England Magazine* 50 (November 1913): 378-79; and *Kansas Semi-Weekly Capital,* November 9, 1894.

52. Ariana, "The Concord School of Philosophy," *Critic* (April 28, 1882): 195. See also Sanborn, *Sixty Years of Concord,* 49-50.
53. "Philosophy at Concord," pt. 2, *Nation* 31 (September 2, 1880): 164 (first quote); *Worcester (MA) Daily Spy,* July 29, 1879 (second quote); *Boston Daily Journal,* July 24, 1883 (third quote); *New York Herald,* February 28, 1881 (fourth quote). See also *Springfield (MA) Republican,* August 11, 1879, July 23, 1880, August 31, 1881; and *Boston Daily Journal,* July 13, 1880, July 14, 1881.
54. *Springfield (MA) Republican,* August 4, 1881 (first quote); "Philosophy at Concord," 165 (second and third quotes). See also Alcott, *Journals,* 506; *Boston Daily Advertiser,* August 7, 1879; and *Boston Journal,* July 28, 1883.
55. John Burroughs, "Henry D. Thoreau," *Century Illustrated Magazine* 24 (July 1882): 369 (first quote); Charles Abbott, "Thoreau," in *Recognition of Thoreau,* ed. Glick, 128 (second quote); Abbott, "Thoreau," *Lippincott's Monthly Magazine,* June 1895, 853 (third quote). See also Coleman, "Thoreau and His Critics," 354.
56. H. A. Page [J. A. Japp], *Thoreau: His Life and Aims, a Study* (Boston: J. R. Osgood, 1877), x. See also *Boston Daily Advertiser,* November 28, 1877.
57. Page, *Thoreau,* 91-92, 95, 114 (quote), 224-25, 233. See also *Athenaeum* (November 3, 1877): 562, box 978, TFC; "Recent Literature," *Atlantic Monthly,* May 1878, 672-73.
58. Robert Burns quoted in Page, *Thoreau,* 7. See also ibid., ix, 7, 10, 12-14, 49-51, 109; and *North American Review* (May 1878): 546-48.
59. Page, *Thoreau,* 1, 5, 50-51, 225, 233. See also Mrs. [Margaret] Oliphant, *Francis of Assisi* (London: R. Clay, Sons, and Taylor, 1887).
60. *North American Review* (May 1878): 548; J. V. O'Connor, "Thoreau and New England Transcendentalism," *Catholic World* 27 (June 1878): 298; William Sharp, "Fascinating Henry Thoreau," *American Transcendental Quarterly* (1977): 9-10 (from *Encyclopedia Britannica*). See also Thomas Hughes quoted in *Academy* (November 17, 1877), J, 6, Japp, series III, WHC; and Arthur Compton-Rickett, *The Vagabond in Literature* (1906; reprint, Port Washington, NY: Kennikat Press, 1968), 105-6.
61. George William Curtis, "Editor's Easy Chair," *Harper's Monthly,* March 1878, 624. See also Thomas Hughes, "A Study of Thoreau," *Eclectic Magazine of Foreign Literature* 27 (January 1878): 116.
62. Alcott, *Journals,* 357-58, 431 (first quote); *Lowell (MA) Daily Citizen and News,* August 25, 1869 (second quote). See also Thomas Wentworth Higginson, *Cheerful Yesterdays* (Boston: Houghton Mifflin, 1898), 170; Elizabeth Hall Witherell, "The Availability of Thoreau's Texts and Manuscripts from 1862 to the Present," in *Thoreau's World and Ours: A Natural Legacy,* ed. Edmund A. Schofield and Robert C. Baron (Golden, CO: North American Press, 1993), 109-11, 115; Sanborn, *Sixty Years of Concord,* 17; and J. S. Wade, "Henry Thoreau and His Journal," *Nature Magazine* 10 (July 1927): 53.
63. Canby, "Thoreau in History," 3; Alcott, *Journals,* 451. See also Alcott to Ricketson, February 12, 1865, in *Letters of Alcott,* ed. Herrnstadt, 362-63; and Alcott, *Concord Days,* 264.
64. *New York Times,* September 20, 1880 (first quote); H. G. O. Blake, introduction to *Early Spring in Massachusetts* (Boston: Houghton Mifflin, 1881), iv (second quote). See also *Springfield (MA) Republican,* December 17, 1887.

65. *Boston Daily Advertiser,* June 16, 1884 (first quote); Isabella King, *Harvard Register* 3 (April 1881): 233, Journal, C, Editions, *Early Spring in Massachusetts,* series II, WHC (second quote). See also "Thoreau in Summer," *Literary World* 15 (July 12, 1884): 223; *Nation* (January 5, 1888): 19; *San Francisco Daily Evening Bulletin,* December 17, 1887; and *Springfield (MA) Republican,* June 15, 1884.
66. *New York Herald,* February 28, 1881 (first quote); Hudson, "Concord Books," 29 (second quote). See also "Thoreau's 'Autumn,'" in *Annotated Bibliography,* by Scharnhorst, 292–93; "Thoreau's Portrait—by Himself," *Literary World* (March 24, 1881), Journal, C. Editions, Early Spring in Massachusetts, series II, WHC; *New York Times,* March 12, 1881; *Boston Daily Advertiser,* June 16, 1884; and *Nation* 39 (July 31, 1884): 98–99.
67. "Thoreau's Winter Journal," *Literary World* (January 7, 1888) (first quote); "Thoreau in Summer," *Literary World* (July 12, 1884): 223 (second quote). See also *New York Times,* March 12, 1881.
68. Odell Shepard, introduction to *The Heart of Thoreau's Journals,* by Henry David Thoreau, ed. Shepard (Boston: Houghton Mifflin, 1927), ix (first quote); E. D. McCreary, "A Worshiper of Nature," *National Repository* 5 (June 1879): 533 (second quote). See also Walter Hardy, "Some Forgotten Reviews of *Walden,*" *Thoreau Society Bulletin* (Winter 1954): 3; and Bode, *Anatomy of American Popular Culture,* 208.
69. H. G. O. Blake, *Selections from the Writings of Henry David Thoreau* (Boston: Houghton Mifflin, 1890), iii, v; Henry Salt to S. A. Jones, June 30, 1890, in *Thoreau's Modern Reputation,* ed. Oehlschlaeger and Hendrick, 75. See also George S. Hellman, review of *The Maine Woods,* by Thoreau, *New York Times Book Review,* October 22, 1909 631; Norman Foerster, "Humanism of Thoreau," *Nation* (July 5, 1917): 9; and *Cleveland Plain Dealer,* November 16, 1890.
70. *New York Times,* September 20, 1880, 4.
71. Franklin Sanborn quoted in George William Curtis, *Harper's Monthly,* September 1882, 632 (first quote); Sedgwick, "Sanborn's Thoreau," 34 (second quote); R. A. Oakes, "Thoreau," *Independent,* August 26, 1883, 6 (third quote). See also "Literature," *Christian Advocate* (July 13, 1882); *New York Times,* September 13, 1891; *New York Herald Tribune,* July 25, 1882; S. A. Jones to A. W. Hosmer, July 23, 1893, in *Thoreau's Modern Reputation,* ed. Oehlschlaeger and Hendrick, 178; Powers, "Thoreau," 70; and Sanborn, *Sixty Years of Concord,* 13, 42.
72. *New York Times,* September 20, 1880, 4 (first quote); *Nation* (October 18, 1894): 292 (second quote). See also Sanborn, *Henry D. Thoreau,* 242; "Concord and Thoreau," *Literary World* (July 15, 1882): 227; and Louis J. Block, "Thoreau's Letters," *Dial* (October 16, 1894): 229–30.
73. Salt, *Life of Thoreau,* 11, 77, 98, 101, 156–60, 162, 194, 205; Hendrick, "Salt, the Late Victorian Socialists, and Thoreau," 410–13, 418; John T. Flanagan, "Henry Salt and His *Life of Thoreau,*" *New England Quarterly* 28 (June 1955): 237; Samuel Arthur Jones, "Thoreau and His Biographers," *Lippincott's Monthly Magazine,* August 1891, 225–26; Fritz Oehlschlaeger, "Henry Salt's Third Biography of Thoreau," *Thoreau Society Bulletin* (Winter 1979): 3.
74. Sanborn, *Life of Thoreau,* 315 (first quote); Annie Russell Marble, *Thoreau: His Home, Friends and Books* (1902; reprint, New York: AMS Press, 1969), 183 (second quote); Underwood, "Henry David Thoreau," 445.
75. Maynard, *Walden Pond: A History,* 175 (first quote); Powers, "Thoreau," 71 (second quote); A. H. P., "In Winter with Thoreau," 74 (third quote); Henry S. Salt, "Thoreau in Twenty Volumes," *Living Age* (July–September 1908): 135 (fourth quote).

76. Dunton, "Old and New Estimate," 464; Sattelmeyer, "*Walden*," 15; "Thoreau's Winter Journal," *Critic* (March 3, 1888): 101; Oehlschlaeger and Hendrick, *Thoreau's Modern Reputation*, 20, 53.
77. Donald G. Mitchell quoted in *The Library of Literary Criticism of English and American Authors*, ed. Charles Wells Moulton (Buffalo: Moulton, 1901), 6:277. See also Coleman, "Thoreau and His Critics," 355; and "A Worshiper of Nature," *National Repository* (June 1879): 528.
78. *New York Herald Tribune*, May 31, 1878 (from *Catholic World*). See also Corning, "Thoreau," 11.
79. Jones, "Thoreau and His Biographers," 227. See also *Lippincott's Magazine* (August 1890): 277, *Anti-slavery and Reform Papers*, Criticism, series II, WHC; Abbott, "Thoreau," *Lippincott's Monthly Magazine*, 854; and *Cleveland Plain Dealer*, February 3, 1879.
80. A. H. P., "In Winter with Thoreau," 82.

Chapter 3: The Cult of Nature and the Age of Progress, 1890-1917

1. A. S. Clark, "Notes of a Recent Visit to Walden Pond," *New York Times Book Review*, December 23, 1899, 902; Edward Waldo Emerson, *Henry Thoreau: As Remembered by a Young Friend* (1917; reprint, Concord, MA: Thoreau Foundation, 1968), 48.
2. Clifton Johnson, introduction to *Walden*, by Henry David Thoreau (New York: Thomas Y. Crowell, 1910), x–xi; Winthrop Packard, *Literary Pilgrimages of a Naturalist* (Boston: Small, Maynard, 1911), 66, 69; C. T. Ramsey, "Pilgrimage to the Haunts of Thoreau," *New England Magazine* 50 (November 1913): 375.
3. *In American Fields and Forests: Henry D. Thoreau, John Burroughs, John Muir, Bradford Torrey, Dallas Lore Sharp, Olive Thorne Miller* (Boston: Houghton Mifflin, 1909), vi; Brander Matthews, "Concerning Out-Door Books," *Cosmopolitan*, June 1981, 252; *New York Herald*, July 23, 1882; *Albuquerque Morning Journal*, March 8, 1918.
4. Joseph Wood Krutch, *Henry David Thoreau* (New York: W. Sloane Associates, 1948), 250–54; Lawrence Buell, "The Thoreauvian Pilgrimage: The Structure of an American Cult," *American Literature* 61 (May 1989): 187–88.
5. P. Anderson Graham, *Nature in Books: Some Studies in Biography* (London: Methuen, 1891), 71. See also Norman Foerster, *Nature in American Literature: Studies in the Modern View of Nature* (New York: Russell & Russell, 1923), 75.
6. Millard C. Davis, "The Influence of Emerson, Thoreau, and Whitman on the Early American Naturalists—John Muir and John Burroughs," *Living Wilderness* (Winter 1966–67): 23, box 331, Thoreau Fellowship Collection, Raymond H. Fogler Library, Special Collections Department, University of Maine, Orono. See also Eric Christopher Lupfer, "The Emergence of American Nature Writing, 1860–1909: John Burroughs, Henry David Thoreau, and Houghton, Mifflin and Company" (PhD diss., University of Texas, 2003), 78, 158, 189–90; and Lawrence Buell, *The Environmental Imagination: Thoreau, Nature Writing, and the Formation of American Culture* (Cambridge, MA: Harvard University Press, 1995), 23–25, 342.
7. Stanton Kirkham, *East and West: Comparative Studies in Nature in Eastern and Western States* (New York: G. P. Putnam's Sons, 1911), 1; Wallace Stegner, review of *Speaking for Nature: How Literary Naturalists from Henry Thoreau to Rachel Carson Have Shaped America*, by Paul Brooks, *Sierra* (January 1981): 109. See also Dallas Lore Sharp, *The Lay of the Land* (1908; reprint, Boston: Houghton Mifflin, 1922), 119–20.
8. Hans Huth, *Nature and the American* (Berkeley: University of California Press, 1957), 152, 156, 159; Edward Foster, *The Civilized Wilderness* (New York: Macmillan, 1975), 111.

9. S. H. Hammond and L. W. Mansfield, *Country Margins and Rambles of a Journalist* (New York: J. C. Derby, 1855), 40; Foster, *The Civilized Wilderness,* 102; Norman Foerster, "The Nature Cult To-Day," *Nation* (April 11, 1912): 358.
10. Edith Dickson, "A Ramble among the Critics," *New York Times Book Review,* August 18, 1900, 9; Leonard Gray, "The Growth of Thoreau's Reputation," *Thoreau Society Bulletin* (Winter 1953): 3–4.
11. Frank Norris, "The 'Nature' Revival in Literature," in *The Responsibilities of the Novelist* (Garden City, NY: Grant Richards, 1928), 137–38, 140 (quote), 141.
12. *Springfield (MA) Republican,* November 8, 1890.
13. John Macy, *The Spirit of American Literature* (New York: Boni and Liveright, 1908), 191 (quote), 192.
14. *New York Times* quoted in Edward J. Renehan Jr., *John Burroughs: An American Naturalist* (Post Mills, VT: Chelsea Green, 1992), 104. See also Lorenzo Sears, *American Literature in the Colonial and National Periods* (Boston: Little, Brown, 1902), 338; Peter J. Schmitt, *Back to Nature: The Arcadian Myth in Urban America* (Baltimore: Johns Hopkins University Press, 1990), 78–79; Kevin C. Armitage, *The Nature Study Movement: The Forgotten Popularizer of America's Conservation Ethic* (Lawrence: University Press of Kansas, 2009), 3, 5, 43, 62; Henry Chester Tracy, *American Naturists* (New York: E. P. Dutton, 1930), 210, 214; Francis Halsey, "The Rise of the Nature Writers," *American Monthly Review of Reviews* 26 (1910): 567–71; and Ernest Ingersoll, "Outdoor Books," *New York Times,* April 30, 1898, 281.
15. Arthur Compton-Rickett, *The Vagabond in Literature* (1906; reprint, Port Washington, NY: Kennikat Press, 1968), 10, 19, 30, 52, 61; Henry Stephens Salt, *Life of Henry David Thoreau* (London: W. Scott, 1896), 11–12; Armitage, *Nature Study Movement,* 27; Philip G. Hubert Jr., *Liberty and a Living* (New York: Putnam's, 1889), 173–81; *In American Fields and Forests,* vi; *New York Times,* June 13, 1897, 22.
16. Maurice Thompson, *By-Ways and Bird Notes* (New York: John B. Alden, 1885), 44. See also Huth, *Nature and the American,* 146, 149, 188, 204.
17. Reginald L. Cook, *Passage to Walden* (Boston: Houghton Mifflin; New York: Russell & Russell, 1966), 19; Walter Besant, *The Eulogy of Richard Jefferies* (New York: Longman's, Green, 1888), 214, 228–29; "One of the Very Greatest of God's Naturalists," *Current Literature* (November 1909): 516–17; *New York Times,* May 10, 1879, 6; *New York Herald Tribune,* December 5, 1888.
18. George H. Ellwanger, "The Sphere of Thoreau," in *Idyllists of the Country-Side* (New York: Dodd, Mead, 1896), 177; Besant, *Eulogy of Jefferies,* 120, 165, 173, 206, 221–22, 227; Henry S. Salt, *Richard Jefferies: A Study* (London: Swan Sonnenschein, 1893), 9, 10–11, 19–20, 78, 188–90; "Two Books by Naturalists," *Critic* 15 (January 3, 1891): 3; Compton-Rickett, *The Vagabond in Literature,* 146, 156.
19. Jefferies quoted in Besant, *Eulogy of Jefferies,* 130–31. See also H. S. Salt, "Richard Jefferies," *Littell's Living Age* (July 18, 1891): 186.
20. Fred Lewis Pattee, "Rise of the Nature Writers," in *A History of American Literature since 1870* (New York: Century, 1915), 144 (first and third quotes); Thomas Wentworth Higginson, *Out-Door Papers* (1863; reprint, Boston: Lee & Shepard, 1886), 251 (second quote).
21. Paul Brooks, *Speaking for Nature: How Literary Naturalists from Henry Thoreau to Rachel Carson Have Shaped America* (Boston: Houghton Mifflin, 1980), 62–65. See also Huth, *Nature and the American,* 100.
22. Wilson Flagg, *The Woods and By-Ways of New England* (Boston: James R. Osgood,

1872), v, ix–xi, xiii, xv, 21, 23–25, 134 (quote). See also W. G. Barton, "Thoreau, Flagg, and Burroughs," in *Songs and Saunterings by a Poet and Naturalist* (Salem, MA: Salem Press, 1892), 5.
23. "Outdoor Life in Books," *New York Times Book Review,* June 2, 1900, 8.
24. Bernard Smith, *Forces in American Criticism: A Study in the History of American Literary Thought* (New York: Harcourt, Brace, 1939), 231; Sharp, *Lay of the Land,* 111, 124 (quote), 125. See also Thompson, *By-Ways and Bird Notes,* 111.
25. Lupfer, "Emergence of American Nature Writing," 13, 18, 54, 77–81, 121 (quote), 127, 131, 166, 197; W. Barksdale Maynard, *Walden Pond: A History* (New York: Oxford University Press, 2004), 220. See also Henry Steele Commager, "At the Center of the Flowering of New England," *New York Times Book Review,* October 6, 1963, 293; Eric Christopher Lupfer, "Before Nature Writing: Houghton, Mifflin and Company and the Invention of the Outdoor Book, 1800–1900," *Book History* 14 (2001): 181; *Boston Daily Journal,* December 20, 1870; and *New York Times Book Review,* September 30, 1899, 648.
26. Armitage, *Nature Study Movement,* 2.
27. George Cotkin, *Reluctant Modernism: American Thought and Culture, 1880–1900* (New York: Twayne, 1992), 18, 133 (quote), 145–46.
28. Sharp, *Lay of the Land,* 101; William Beebe, *The Log of the Sun: A Chronicle of Nature's Year* (New York: Henry Holt, 1906), 265–66; Bradford Torrey, *A Rambler's Lease* (Cambridge, MA: Riverside Press, 1889), 32, 48–49, 52, 103–5 (quote). See also Armitage, *Nature Study Movement,* 1, 11, 27, 31; Henry Childs Merwin, "Books about Nature," *Scribner's Magazine,* April 1903, 430; and "Thoreau's Life," *Spectator,* October 18, 1890, 527, S, 3, Salt, Henry S, series III, Walter Harding Collection (hereafter WHC), Thoreau Institute, Lincoln, MA.
29. Schmitt, *Back to Nature,* 21–22.
30. Halsey, "Rise of the Nature Writers," 568; Tracy, *American Naturists,* 190–92; Schmitt, *Back to Nature,* 34–35; Brooks, *Speaking for Nature,* 169–76.
31. *Macon (GA) Telegraph,* February 18, 1889. See also Bradford Torrey, *Birds in the Bush* (Cambridge, MA: Riverside Press, 1885); review of *Birds in the Bush,* by Torrey, *Literary World* (June 13, 1885): 203; Brooks, *Speaking for Nature,* 140, 141, 143–46; and Ernest Ingersoll, "Four Outdoor Books," *New York Times Book Review,* January 14, 1899, 22.
32. Caroline A. Creevey, *Flowers of Field, Hill, and Swamp* (New York: Harper and Brothers, 1897), 18 (first quote); Joel Benton, "150 Books for Summer Reading," *New York Times Book Review,* June 25, 1898, 409 (second quote). See also F. Schuyler Mathews, *Familiar Life in Field and Forest: The Animals, Birds, Frogs, and Salamanders* (New York: D. Appleton, 1898), 3.
33. *Montpelier (VT) Argus and Patriot,* February 6, 1889 (first quote); Sharp, *Lay of the Land,* 2, 8, 38–39, 45, 46 (second quote), 161–62, 208–9. See also Beebe, *Log of the Sun,* vii, 10–11, 113, 134–35, 179–81 191; Mabel Osgood Wright, "Hudson's 'Hampshire Days,'" *New York Times Book Review,* November 14, 1903, 1; Torrey, *A Rambler's Lease,* 22, 46; Paul Burnill Jenkins, "Nature for Nature's Sake," *Nassau Literary Magazine* (June 1891): 108–10; Merwin, "Books about Nature," 430–32, 437; Thompson, *By-Ways and Bird Notes,* 106–7, 110; *New York Times Book Review,* June 22, 1913, 373; "New England Nature Studies: Thoreau, Burroughs, Whitman," *Edinburgh Review* 208 (October 1908): 343, 346; and *Springfield (MA) Sunday Republican,* May 27, 1894.
34. Charles C. Abbott, *A Naturalist's Rambles about Home* (New York: D. Appleton, 1885);

New York Times, March 7, 1886, 12. See also John Burroughs, "Manifold Nature," *North American Review* (August 1916): 249; Thompson, *By-Ways and Bird Notes,* 42; and Paul Elmer More, *Shelburne Essays* (New York: G. P. Putnam's Sons, 1904), 4.

35. Beebe, *Log of the Sun,* 128, 310, 317 (quote). See also Merwin, "Books about Nature," 430; Armitage, *Nature Study Movement,* 6–7, 44; and *Mooney's Magazine* quoted in *Kansas City Times,* June 9, 1921.

36. Buell, *Environmental Imagination,* 34, 346 (quote); Henry A. Beers, *An Outline Sketch of American Literature* (New York: Chautauqua Press, 1887), 145. See also Gary Scharnhorst, *Henry David Thoreau: A Case Study in Canonization* (Columbia, SC: Camden House, 1993), 47; Frederick Miller Smith, "Thoreau," *Critic* (July 1900): 60–67; John R. Spears, review of *Walden,* by Thoreau, *New York Times Book Review,* October 4, 1902, 12; Ellwanger, "The Sphere of Thoreau," 178; "The Riverside Thoreau," *Outlook,* February 10, 1894, 283; "The Love of Nature," *Current Literature* (November 1902): 519–20; and "Thoreau's Journal," *Independent,* July 13, 1905, 103.

37. "The Diary of a Poet-Naturalist," *Current Literature* (November 1905): 510–12. See also William Howarth, "The Journal of Henry D. Thoreau, 1906–2006," *Princeton University Library Chronicle* (Summer 2006): 642–43.

38. Buell, *Environmental Imagination,* 341; F. B. Sanborn, "Thoreau in His Journals," *Dial* (February 17, 1907): 107, Journal, C, Editions, Writings of Henry David Thoreau, series II, WHC; Paul Elmer More quoted in Howarth, "Journal of Thoreau," 637, 653. See also Mark Van Doren, *Henry David Thoreau: A Critical Study* (Boston: Houghton Mifflin, 1916), 1; Buell, *Environmental Imagination,* 27; Norman Foerster, "Humanism of Thoreau," *Nation* (July 5, 1917): 9; Henry S. Salt, "Thoreau in Twenty Volumes," *Living Age* (July–September 1908): 131–39; and "Thoreau's Works in New Edition," *New York Times Book Review,* July 6, 1907, 427.

39. Bradford Torrey quoted in Wendell Glick, ed., *The Recognition of Henry David Thoreau: Selected Criticism since 1848* (Ann Arbor: University of Michigan Press, 1969), 142 (first quote); Emerson, *As Remembered by a Young Friend,* vii (second quote); Barrett Wendell quoted in Glick, *Recognition of Thoreau,* 151–52 (third quote); Graham, *Nature in Books,* 86 (fourth quote). See also Hamilton W. Mabie, "Thoreau: A Prophet of Nature," *Outlook,* June 3, 1905, 282; Tracy, *American Naturists,* 73; Van Doren, *Henry David Thoreau,* 67; "The Centenary of Thoreau," *Outlook,* September 12, 1917, 44; and "A Worshiper of Nature," *National Repository* 5 (June 1879): 525.

40. Salt, "Thoreau in Twenty Volumes," 136 (first quote); Daniel Gregory Mason, "The Idealistic Basis of Thoreau's Genius," *Harvard Monthly* (December 1897): 83 (second quote); Macy, *Spirit of American Literature,* 171, 174 (third quote); H. S. Canby, "Thoreau in History: The Story of a Literary Reputation," *Saturday Review of Literature* (July 15, 1939): 4 (fourth quote). See also Paul Elmer More, "A Hermit's Notes on Thoreau," in *Thoreau: A Century of Criticism,* ed. Walter Roy Harding (Dallas: Southern Methodist University Press, 1954), 98; Michael Curtis Meyer, *Several More Lives to Live: Thoreau's Political Reputation in America* (Westport, CT: Greenwood Press, 1977), 18–19; and Scharnhorst, *Case Study in Canonization,* 44, 56–57.

41. Dallas Lore Sharp, *The Seer of Slabsides* (Boston: Houghton Mifflin, 1910), 46–47; *Boston Evening Journal,* January 19, 1889; Renehan, *John Burroughs,* 65; Hamilton Wright Mabie, "John Burroughs," *Century,* August 1897, 560–66; Schmitt, *Back to Nature,* 24–25; Henry Litchfield West, "John Burroughs," *Outing and the Wheelman,* January 1885, 280–85; *Anaconda (MT) Standard,* March 30, 1921; *Baltimore American,* March 30, 1921.

42. Clara Barrus, *The Life and Letters of John Burroughs* (New York: Russell & Russell, 1968), 1:247; Pattee, "Rise of the Nature Writers," 151; Barton, "Thoreau, Flagg, and Burroughs," 14. See also Frederick Perkins, "Nature in Thoreau and Burroughs," *Collegian* (February 1889): 123, B, 105, Burroughs File, series III, WHC; West, "Burroughs," 284–85; and *New York Times*, January 14, 1876, 2.
43. Burroughs quoted in Pattee, "Rise of the Nature Writers," 148; Sharp, *The Seer of Slabsides*, 50; W. Sloane Kennedy, "John Burroughs," *Californian* (August 1882): 187. See also Burroughs quoted in Renehan, *John Burroughs*, 4; Barrus, *Life and Letters of Burroughs*, 2:2, 5–6, 247, 327–28, 334; Herbert S. Gorman, "John Burroughs Lacked the True Touch of Greatness," *New York Times Book Review*, January 3, 1926, 3; Cook, *Passage to Walden*, 29; W. Sloane Kennedy, *The Real John Burroughs: Personal Recollection and Friendly Estimate* (New York: Funk & Wagnalls, 1924), 6; Lupfer, "Emergence of American Nature Writing," 24–26; "An Estimate of Burroughs," *Current Literature* (September 1897): 203; and *New York Times*, May 2, 1886: 12.
44. John Burroughs quoted in Gorman, "Burroughs Lacked the True Touch of Greatness," 3 (also quoted in Barrus, *Life and Letters of Burroughs*, 2:564); Thomas Wentworth Higginson, "Henry David Thoreau," in *American Prose*, ed. George Rice Carpenter (New York: Macmillan, 1898), 341. See also John L. Hervey quoted in "The Strength and the Weakness of John Burroughs," *Current Opinion* (July 1921): 74; Burroughs quoted in Kennedy, *Real John Burroughs*, 77, 223–24, 189; Schmitt, *Back to Nature*, 24; "An Estimate of Burroughs," 203; and *New York Times*, May 8, 1881, 10.
45. John Burroughs, "Critical Glance into Thoreau," 783; Kennedy, *Real John Burroughs*, 225. See also John Burroughs, "Henry D. Thoreau," *Century Illustrated Magazine*, July 1882, 376, 377; John Burroughs, "Henry David Thoreau," *Chautauquan* (June 1889): 533; James Perrin Warren, *John Burroughs and the Place of Nature* (Athens: University of Georgia Press, 2006), 15, 19; and John Burroughs, *Indoor Studies* (Boston: Houghton, Mifflin, 1902), 9–11.
46. John Burroughs quoted in Barrus, *Life and Letters of Burroughs*, 2:335–36.
47. Burroughs, "Critical Glance into Thoreau," 781 (first quote); Barton, "Thoreau, Flagg, and Burroughs," 15 (second quote), 7 (third quote).
48. John Burroughs quoted in Hildegarde Hawthorne, "John Burroughs's Last Book," *New York Times Book Review*, December 17, 1922, 53 (first quote); John Burroughs, "Thoreau's Wildness," *Critic* (March 26, 1881): 74 (second quote); Kennedy, *Real John Burroughs*, 222 (third quote); Ellwanger, "The Sphere of Thoreau," 192 (fourth quote). See also Sharp, *The Seer of Slabsides*, 48–49, 59; and William Lyon Phelps, *Henry David Thoreau: A Study* (New York: Macmillan, 1924), 32.
49. Otis B. Wheeler, *The Literary Career of Maurice Thompson* (Baton Rouge: Louisiana State University Press, 1965), 3–4, 39 (first quote), 42; Thompson, *By-Ways and Bird Notes*, 26, 84, 87, 93 (second quote), 103, 116; W. H. Hudson, *Idle Days in Patagonia* (London: Chapman & Hall, 1893), 221 (third quote), 226 (fourth quote). See also Brooks, *Speaking for Nature*, 44, 202; Enos Mills, *The Adventures of a Nature Guide* (Garden City, NY: Doubleday, Page, 1923), ix; Charles C. Abbott, *Recent Rambles; or, In Touch with Nature* (Philadelphia: J. B. Lippincott, 1892), 49–50; and Beebe, *Log of the Sun*, 172–73.
50. Kirkham, *East and West*, 3, 9 (first quote), 10, 31, 51 (second quote), 105, 193–94, 246–47.
51. Hudson, *Idle Days in Patagonia*, 228; W. T. Worth, "Thoreau: A Study," *Zion's Herald*,

September 4, 1901, 1130; Lincoln Adams, "A Faithful Lover of Nature," *Frank Leslie's Popular Monthly* 33 (May 1892): 574.
52. Archibald MacMechan, "Thoreau," in *The Cambridge History of American Literature*, ed. William Peterfield Trent (New York: G. P. Putnam's Sons, 1917), 10, 12 (first quote); Norman Foerster, "Thoreau and 'the Wild,'" *Dial* (June 28, 1917): 8, 9 (second quote), in Excursions, C, Individual Titles, 7, "Walking," c, series II, WHC.
53. Mary Austin, *The Land of Little Rain* (Boston: Houghton Mifflin, 1904), 3; Theodore Watts-Dunton, *Henry Thoreau and Other Children of the Open Air* (Cedar Rapids, IA: Torch Press, 1910), 33.
54. Nicholas Roosevelt, "Muir of the Western Mountains," *New York Times Book Review*, December 28, 1924, 1; Edmund Way Teale, introduction to *The Wilderness World of John Muir*, by John Muir (Boston: Houghton Mifflin, 1954), xviii.
55. Edith Franklin Wyatt, "Two Woodsmen," *North American Review* 204 (September 1916): 436. See also Stephen R. Fox, *John Muir and His Legacy: The American Conservation Movement* (Boston: Little, Brown, 1981); and Donald Worster, *A Passion for Nature: The Life of John Muir* (New York: Oxford University Press, 2008).
56. Muir, *Wilderness World*, 100.
57. Kennedy, *Real John Burroughs*, 166 (first quote); Pattee, "Rise of the Nature Writers," 154, 156 (second and third quotes).
58. Muir, *Wilderness World*, 169 (first and fourth quotes), 170, 182 (third quote), 185 (second quote), 186, 221.
59. *In American Fields and Forests*, 193–94, 195, 210, 213 (first quote); Muir, *Wilderness World*, 48–49, 151 (second quote), 155–56.
60. Roosevelt, "Muir of the Western Mountains,"1; Muir, *Wilderness World*, 104–5, 163–64; "The Agassiz of the Pacific Slope," *Current Literature* (July 1899): 40; Raymond Holden, "Search for the Untouched," *New York Times Book Review*, September 26, 1954, 7.
61. Pattee, "Rise of the Nature Writers," 155; Thomas Wentworth Higginson, *Short Studies of American Authors* (Boston: Lee and Shepard, 1888), 24; Wyatt, "Two Woodsmen," 435–36; Cook, *Passage to Walden*, 34; Teale, introduction to *Wilderness World*, xi.
62. Teale, introduction to *Wilderness World*, xv. See also Brooks, *Speaking for Nature*, 18.
63. Muir, *Wilderness World*, 231. See also *New York Times Book Review*, January 4, 1902, 4; Teale, introduction to *Wilderness World*, xiii; and Roosevelt, "Muir of the Western Mountains," 24.
64. Davis, "Influence of Emerson, Thoreau, and Whitman," 19, 22 (quote).
65. Hiram M. Stanley, "Thoreau as a Prose Writer," *Dial* 21 (October 1, 1896): 179, 181 (first quote); "Birds and Laws," *Miami Herald*, August 29, 1921 (second quote). See also "An Estimate of Burroughs," 203.
66. Schmitt, *Back to Nature*, 45. See also Ralph H. Lutts, *The Nature Fakers: Wildlife, Science & Sentiment* (Charlottesville: University Press of Virginia, 1990).
67. Kirkham, *East and West*, 141 (quotes), 143; Torrey, *A Rambler's Lease*, 118 (second quote); Dallas Lore Sharp, "The Nature Writer," *Outlook*, April 30, 1910, 994 (third quote), 998–99, 1000. See also Schmitt, *Back to Nature*, 36, 45; and Charles C. Abbott, *Outings at Odd Times* (New York: D. Appleton, 1890), 27.
68. Brooks, *Speaking for Nature*, 207. See also Tracy, *American Naturists*, 240–42.
69. Schmitt, *Back to Nature*, 54. See also William J. Long, *Ways of the Wood Folk* (Andover, MA: by the author, 1899), vi.

70. Sharp, "The Nature Writer," 997 (first quote); John Burroughs quoted in Kennedy, *Real John Burroughs,* 147, 149 (second quote), 151; William J. Long quoted in Renehan, *John Burroughs,* 233–35, 238 (third quote).
71. Renehan, *John Burroughs,* 232–33, 239; Brooks, *Speaking for Nature,* 209–10; Kennedy, *Real John Burroughs,* 156.
72. Foerster, *Nature in American Literature,* 89 (first quote), 90 (second quote); Bradford Torrey, introduction *The Writings of Henry David Thoreau: Journal,* ed. Torrey, vol. 1, *1837–1846* (Boston: Houghton Mifflin, 1906), xliv (fourth quote), xlv (third quote). See also "Thoreau's Works in New Edition," *New York Times Book Review,* July 6, 1907, 427.
73. H. W. Boynton, "Mr. Torrey's 'Thoreau,'" *New York Times Book Review,* October 20, 1906, 681.
74. John Burroughs quoted in *New York Times,* November 10, 1894 (first quote); Fannie Hardy Eckstorm, "Thoreau's *Maine Woods,*" in *Thoreau,* ed. Harding, 106 (second quote), 110 (third quote), 115. See also Burroughs, "Critical Glance into Thoreau," 778; and Burroughs quoted in Barrus, *Life and Letters of Burroughs,* 2:264.
75. Francis H. Allen, "Thoreau's Knowledge of Birds," *Nation* 150 (September 22, 1910): 261; Charles C. Abbott, *Notes of the Night, and Other Outdoor Sketches* (New York: Century, 1896), 223; Charles F. Richardson, *American Literature, 1607–1885* (New York: G. P. Putnam's Sons, 1891), 1:387. See also "Widening Influence of Thoreau," *Current Literature* (August 1908): 170–71.
76. Joshua W. Caldwell, "Ten Volumes of Thoreau," *New Englander and Yale Review* (November 1891): 422 (first quote), 423 (second quote); More, *Shelburne Essays,* 15.
77. Caldwell, "Ten Volumes of Thoreau," 421 (first quote), 422 (second quote).
78. Lawrence Buell, "Henry Thoreau and the American Canon," in *New Essays on "Walden,"* ed. Robert F. Sayre (New York: Cambridge University Press, 1992), 37 (first quote); Buell, *Environmental Imagination,* 353 (second quote); Charles Abbott quoted in Glick, *Recognition of Thoreau,* 129 (third quote). See also Abbott, "Thoreau," *Lippincott's Monthly Magazine* (June 1895): 855; Paul Elmer More quoted in Glick, *Recognition of Thoreau,* 156–57; and Marble, *Thoreau,* 276.
79. Pattee, "Rise of the Nature Writers," 139.
80. Foerster, *Nature in American Literature,* 89 (first quote); Thoreau quoted in "New England Nature Studies," 353 (second quote); Van Doren, *Henry David Thoreau,* 112 (third quote). See also Armitage, *Nature Study Movement,* 32; Odell Shepard, "Paradox of Thoreau," *Scribner's Magazine,* September 1920, 342; and Bradford Torrey, *Friends on the Shelf* (Boston: Houghton Mifflin, 1906), 134–35, 143.
81. Foerster, "The Nature Cult To-Day," 358. See also Foerster, "Humanism of Thoreau," 11; A. H. P., "In Winter with Thoreau," *Unitarian Review* (July 1888): 81; Pattee, "Rise of the Nature Writers," 140; and Joseph Wood Krutch, *Great American Nature Writing* (New York: Sloane, 1950), 5.
82. Edward Waldo Emerson, "Centenary of Henry David Thoreau: Personal Recollections," *Bookman* 52 (June 1917): 82 (first quote), 84; *Cleveland Plain Dealer,* July 15, 1917 (second quote). See also *Philadelphia Inquirer,* October 16, 1917; *London Times* quoted in *New York Times,* August 26, 1917, 63; *Portland Oregonian,* July 22, 1917; and Lonnie L. Willis, "The Thoreau Centenary in Britain," *American Studies International* 37 (June 1999): 43–44, 47–48.
83. Henry David Thoreau quoted in Wyatt, "Two Woodsmen," 426. See also Burroughs, "Manifold Nature," 245–46.

Chapter 4: Thoreau for the Ages, Thoreau for the Times, 1920-1960

1. Raymond B. Fosdick, "The Individual's Place in the Age of Machines," *New York Times,* June 22, 1930, E4.
2. Walter Fuller Taylor, *A History of American Letters* (Boston: American Book, 1936), 166; Donald Culross Peattie, "Is Thoreau a Modern?," *North American Review* (Spring 1938): 159-61. See also Henry Steele Commager, "The Roaring Forties," *New York Times Sunday Magazine,* March 30, 1941, 14; Gerald Carson, "An American Heretic," *Bookman* (January 1928): 581-82; and Charles G. Walcutt, "Thoreau in the Twentieth Century," *South Atlantic Quarterly* 39 (1940): 168.
3. Robert Sattelmeyer, "Walden: Climbing the Canon," in *More Day to Dawn: Thoreau's Walden for the Twenty-First Century,* ed. Sandra Harbert Petrulionis and Laura Dassow Walls (Amherst: University of Massachusetts Press, 2007), 20 (first quote), 18 (second quote). See also Henry Seidel Canby, "Thoreau: A New Estimate," *Saturday Review of Literature* (December 3, 1949): 15-16; Randall Stewart, "The Growth of Thoreau's Reputation," *College English* 17 (January 1946): 208, 210-11; and Leonard Gray, "The Growth of Thoreau's Reputation," *Thoreau Society Bulletin* (Winter 1953): 3.
4. Henry W. Nevison, *Essays in Freedom and Rebellion* (New Haven, CT: Yale University Press, 1921), 112 (quote), 113-14; Walcutt, "Thoreau in the Twentieth Century," 168; Russell Blankenship, *American Literature as an Expression of the National Mind* (New York: Henry Holt, 1931), 311; Thomas L. Collins, "Thoreau's Coming of Age," *Sewanee Review* 49 (1941): 59. See also Gilbert Seldes, "Thoreau," in *The Recognition of Henry David Thoreau: Selected Criticism since 1848,* ed. Wendell Glick (Ann Arbor: University of Michigan Press, 1969), 273-74.
5. Raymond B. Fosdick, *The Old Savage in the New Civilization* (Garden City, NY: Doubleday Doran, 1928), 10-11. See also George Shelton Hubbell, "*Walden* Revisited: A Grammar of Dissent," *Sewanee Review* 27 (July 1929): 283-87.
6. James Mackaye, ed., *Thoreau: Philosopher of Freedom: Writings on Liberty by Henry David Thoreau* (New York: Vanguard Press, 1930), xii; Brooks Atkinson, "Two or Three Ideas," *New York Times,* December 27, 1931, 89. See also Michael Curtis Meyer, *Several More Lives to Live: Thoreau's Political Reputation in America* (Westport, CT: Greenwood Press, 1977), 68.
7. Cornelia James Cannon, "The New Leisure," *North American Review* (September 1, 1926): 498-500; Henry Seidel Canby, "Thoreau: The Great Eccentric," *Saturday Review of Literature* (November 1927): 338. See also Ralph Henry Gabriel quoted in George Frisbie Whicher, ed., *The Transcendentalist Revolt* (Lexington, MA: Heath, 1968), 25.
8. Charles A. Beard and Mary R. Beard, *The Rise of American Civilization* (New York: Macmillan, 1927), 715, 786 (quote), 794, 800. See also Meyer, *Several More Lives to Live,* 21, 25.
9. Lewis Mumford, *The Brown Decades* (1931; reprint, New York: Dover, 1966), 62-65.
10. Brooks Atkinson (paraphrasing Mumford), "Looking towards the Future from a Study of the Past," *New York Times Book Review,* December 19, 1926, 2 (first quote); Lewis Mumford, "Renewal of the Landscape," 71 (second and fourth quote); Mumford, *The Golden Day: A Study in American Experience and Culture* (New York: Horace Liveright, 1926), 114 (third quote).
11. Sattelmeyer, "Walden: Climbing the Canon," 19 (first quote); Vernon Louis Parrington, *Main Currents in American Thought: An Interpretation of American Literature*

from the Beginnings to 1920 (1927; reprint, New York: Harcourt, Brace, 1930), 406 (second quote), 400 (third quote).
12. Léon Bazalgette, *Henry Thoreau: Bachelor of Nature* (London: Jonathan Cape, 1925), 78, 89 (quote), 248, 243–44. See also Waldo Frank, "Bazalgette and Thoreau," *Dial* (March 1925): 232.
13. "Bachelor of Nature and Hermit of Walden Pond," *New York Times Book Review*, December 7, 1924 (first quote); Gordon Hall Gerould, "Interpreting Thoreau," *Bookman* (February 1925): 768, B21, Bazalgette, series III, Walter Harding Collection (hereafter WHC), Thoreau Institute, Lincoln, MA (second quote); Norman Foerster, "A French Estimate of Thoreau," *New York Sun*, December 13, 1824, quoted ibid. (third quote).
14. Bazalgette, *Henry Thoreau*, 138.
15. Brooks Atkinson, *Henry Thoreau: The Cosmic Yankee* (New York: Alfred A. Knopf, 1927), 2–3, 8, 49–50 (quote), 51–52. See also Odell Shepard, introduction to *The Heart of Thoreau's Journals*, ed. Shepard (Boston: Houghton Mifflin, 1927), viii; and Brooks Atkinson, "Thoreau: 'Cracking the Hard Facts,'" *New York Times Book Review*, October 3, 1948, 4.
16. Henry Seidel Canby, "American Challenge," *Saturday Review of Literature* (September 2, 1939): 12. See also Canby, "Men of Concord and Some Others as Portrayed in the Journal of Henry David Thoreau," *Saturday Review of Literature* 15 (December 5, 1936): 16, Journals, C, Editions, series II, WHC; and Canby, *Thoreau* (Boston: Houghton Mifflin, 1939), 383–84.
17. Howard Zahniser, *Nature* 35 (1939): 551, C7, Canby, series III, E, WHC; Walcutt, "Thoreau in the Twentieth Century," 168; Clifton Fadiman, review of *Thoreau*, by Henry Canby, *New Yorker*, December 7, 1939, C7, Canby, series III, WHC.
18. *Reader's Digest* quoted in Sattelmeyer, "*Walden*: Climbing the Canon," 20; Sinclair Lewis, "One Man Revolution," in *Thoreau: A Century of Criticism*, ed. Walter Roy Harding (Dallas: Southern Methodist University Press, 1954), 148–49. See also Sinclair Lewis quoted in Mark W. Sullivan, *Picturing Thoreau: Henry David Thoreau in American Visual Culture* (Lanham, MD: Lexington Books, 2015), 53; and Lucy Lockwood Hazard, "Thoreau: The Intensive Pioneer," in *The Frontier in American Literature* (New York: Barnes & Noble, 1941), 168.
19. Stewart, "Growth of Thoreau's Reputation," 211–12, 213 (quote).
20. Gary Scharnhorst, *Henry David Thoreau: Case Study in Canonization* (Columbia, SC: Camden House, 1993), 51 (first quote); John Edwards, "Henry David Thoreau," *Socialist Review* 14 (1917): 422, E12, series III, WHC (second quote). See also John Macy, *The Spirit of American Literature* (New York: Boni and Liveright, 1908), 174; and Richard Tuerk, "Recreating American Literary Tradition: Michael Gold on Emerson and Thoreau," *Markham Review* 15 (Fall–Winter 1985–86): 9, G22, series III, WHC.
21. V. F. Calverton quoted in Glick, *Recognition of Thoreau*, 344 (first quote); Calverton, *The Liberation of American Literature* (New York: Charles Scribner's Sons, 1932), xi–xii, 27, 50, 225, 232, 235, 245, 264 (second and third quotes), 255, 262–64, 269, 270.
22. Granville Hicks, *The Great Tradition: An Interpretation of American Literature since the Civil War* (New York: Macmillan, 1933), 10 (quote), 212–14.
23. F. O. Matthiessen, *American Renaissance: Art and Expression in the Age of Emerson and Whitman* (New York: Oxford University Press, 1941), 86.
24. Irwin Edman, *Fountainheads of Freedom* (New York: Reynal and Hitchcock, 1942), 3

(first quote), 150–53; Collins, "Thoreau's Coming of Age," 58–60, 63 (second quote), 64–66. See also Scharnhorst, *Case Study in Canonization,* 62.
25. Walter Harding, "Century of Thoreau," *Audubon* (March 1945): 84. See also Alice Felt Tyler, *Freedom's Ferment* (Minneapolis: University of Minnesota Press, 1944), 58; and Francis B. Dedmond, "100 Years of *Walden,*" *Concord (MA) Journal,* June 24, 1954, E, Miscellaneous, iii, series II, WHC.
26. *New York Times,* June 17, 1945, *Walden,* E, Miscellaneous, iii, j, Centenary, series II, WHC.
27. Harding, "Century of Thoreau," 80–84; Charles A. Madison, *Critics and Crusaders: A Century of American Protest* (New York: Henry Holt, 1947), 163–73.
28. T. Morris Longstreth, review of *"Walden" Revisited: A Centennial Tribute to Henry David Thoreau,* by George Frisbie Whicher, *Christian Science Monitor,* July 11, 1945, W41, E, Miscellaneous, iii, j, Centenary, series II, WHC; Jacques Ducharme, "An American Classic," *Think* (November 1954): 28, *Walden,* E, Miscellaneous, iii, j, Centenary, series II, WHC. See also C. R. B. Combellack, "Two Critics of Society—Marx and Thoreau," *Pacific Spectator* (Autumn 1949): 440, 445; R. N. Stromberg, "Thoreau and Marx: A Century After," *Social Studies* (February 1949): 53–56; Joseph Wood Krutch, "Thoreau's Literary Reputation," *Christian Science Monitor,* May 1949, K45, Krutch, Joseph Wood, series III, WHC; "Thoreau's *Walden* Is Now 100," *Des Moines (IA) Sunday Register,* July 8, 1945, *Walden,* E, Miscellaneous, iii, j, Centenary, series II, WHC; Rev. Leonard B. Gray, "Written 100 Years Ago: Thoreau's Famed *Walden,*" *Worcester (MA) Sunday Telegram,* July 4, 1954, *Walden,* E, Miscellaneous, iii, j, Centenary, series II, WHC; and Elizabeth Keiper, "Thoreau's Pen, a Century Ago, Wrote Truths for Today," *Rochester (NY) Times-Union,* July 16, 1954.
29. Fosdick, *Old Savage,* 23.
30. Joseph Wood Krutch, *Human Nature and the Human Condition* (New York: Random House, 1959), 142–43.
31. Henry Miller, preface to *Life without Principle: Three Essays by Henry David Thoreau* (Stanford, CA: James Ladd Delkin, 1946), 3; Herbert Faulkner West, "Strange Interlude—Thoreau Voice of America," in *Rebel Thought* (Boston: Beacon, 1953), 210; John Haynes Holmes, "Thoreau's *Civil Disobedience,*" *Christian Century* 66 (January–June 1949): 789.
32. Wendell Glick, "*Civil Disobedience:* Thoreau's Attack upon Relativism," *Western Humanities Review* 7 (Winter 1952–53): 35, *Anti-slavery and Reform Papers,* Criticism, C, Individual Titles, series II, WHC; Waldo Frank, "Thoreau's *Walden:* One Hundred Years," *New York Times Book Review,* August 8, 1954, 7. On Richard Boyer, see *New York Herald Tribune,* April 20, 1949, *Civil Disobedience,* Miscellaneous Clippings file, 1849–1959, series II, WHC. See also Samuel Sillen, "Thoreau in Today's America," *Masses and Mainstream* (December 1954): 9; and Isabel Paterson, "Henry David Thoreau, Native of Concord," *New York Herald Tribune,* October 23, 1945, Whicher, George, viii, series III, WHC.
33. Nick Aaron Ford, "Henry David Thoreau, Abolitionist," *New England Quarterly* 19 (September 1946): 360, 362–63, 365, 371 (quote); G. M. Ostrander, "Emerson, Thoreau, and John Brown," *Mississippi Valley Historical Review* 39 (March 1953): 713 (quotes), 714, 720, 722, 726; Samuel Middlebrook, "Henry David Thoreau," in *Great American Liberals,* ed. G. R. Mason (Boston: Stars King, 1956), 69. See also Kelsey Guilfoil, "The Thoreau Cultists—Are They Insane?," *Chicago Tribune,* December 1, 1946, D18, Denunciations of Thoreau, series III, WHC.

34. C. C. Hollis, "Thoreau and the State," *Commonweal* (September 9, 1949): 530, 531 (quote), 532; Vincent Buranelli, "The Case against Thoreau," *Ethics* 67 (1957): 257–58, 261 (quote), 262; Robert LaForte, "The Political Thought of Henry D. Thoreau: A Study in Paradox," *Educational Leader* (July 1959): 49, L.3, series III, WHC; Robert Ludlow, "Thoreau and the State," *Commonweal* (September 23, 1949): 581–82 (response to Hollis); Holmes, "Thoreau's Civil Disobedience," 788 (quote). See also Ralph L. Ketcham, "Reply to Buranelli's Case against Thoreau," *Ethics* 69 (April 1959): 206–8.
35. Alexandra Krastin, "He Took to the Woods 100 Years Ago," *Saturday Evening Post*, June 30, 1945, 79; Alfred Kazin, "Dry Light and Hard Expressions," *Atlantic Monthly*, July 1957, 74.
36. Stanley Edgar Hyman, *The Promised End: Essays and Reviews, 1942–1962* (Freeport, NY: Books for Libraries Press, 1963), 63; Scharnhorst, *Case Study in Canonization*, 75 See also Sattelmeyer, "*Walden:* Climbing the Canon," 20.
37. George S. Hellman, "'They Are the Mountains in Our Range of Letters,'" *New York Times Book Review*, June 15, 1941, 4. See also Matthiessen, *American Renaissance*, 77–78; Scharnhorst, *Case Study in Canonization*, 70; and Raymond W. Adams and Henry S. Canby, "Henry David Thoreau," in *Dictionary of American Biography*, vol. 18 (New York: Charles Scribner's Sons, 1936).
38. Howard Mumford Jones, *Theory of American Literature* (Ithaca, NY: Cornell University Press, 1949), 4 (first quote); Sherman Paul, *The Shores of America: Thoreau's Inward Exploration* (New York: Russell & Russell, 1958); 75 (second quote), 106; Robert Paul Cobb, "Thoreau and 'the Wild,'" *Emerson Society Quarterly* 18 (1960): 5 (third quote). See also Sherman Paul, preface to *"Walden" and "Civil Disobedience,"* by Henry David Thoreau (Boston: Houghton Mifflin, 1957), viii–xvi, xxxvi; Meyer, *Several More Lives to Live*, 68–70, 72, 78, 96, 102, 119, 121; Sherman Paul, "Resolution at Walden," in *Interpretations of American Literature*, ed. Charles Feidelson Jr. and Paul Brodtkorb Jr. (New York: Oxford University Press, 1959), 66–69; Lauriat Lane Jr., "On the Organic Structure of *Walden*," *College English* 21 (January 1960): 195–202; and James C. McKusick, *Green Writing: Romanticism and Ecology* (New York: St. Martin's Press, 2000), 13–14.
39. See also Paul F. Runge, "Discover Your Own Walden," *Audubon* (May 1949): 142; Eunice Fuller Barnard, "We Turn Again to a Life in the Open," *New York Times Sunday Magazine*, July 8, 1934, 6; Nona Balakian, "The Lures of Nature," *New York Times Book Review*, March 28, 1943, 25; Donald Culross Peattie, "The Joy of Walking," *New York Times Sunday Magazine*, April 5, 1942, 10; and Frederick Boyd, "Knowing the Art of Walking Rewards the Rationed Motorist," *New York Times*, April 19, 1942, D10.
40. *Time*, July 29, 1957, 9, T34, Thoreau Society, q, Save Walden Committee, 1957, series III, WHC.
41. John Kieran quoted in Robert Gorham Davis, "Nature-Lover's Notebook," *New York Times Book Review*, July 20, 1947, 6; William Beebe, *Unseen Life of New York: As a Naturalist Sees It* (New York: Duell, Sloan, and Pearce, 1953), 8 (quote), 10, 94–96, 121, 134–40. See also Joseph Wood Krutch, "The Cockroach Likes Us," *New York Times Book Review*, December 13, 1953, 54.
42. Joseph Wood Krutch, *The Modern Temper* (New York: Harcourt, Brace, 1929), 61, 76 (first quote), 78–79; Krutch, *Human Nature and the Human Condition*, 44–45 (second quote), 47, 49, 56; Krutch, *Henry David Thoreau* (New York: W. Sloane Associates,

1948), 10 (fourth quote), 172 (third quote). See also Paul Brooks, *Speaking for Nature: How Literary Naturalists from Henry Thoreau to Rachel Carson Have Shaped America* (Boston: Houghton Mifflin, 1980), 193–94; Francis H. Allen, review, *Bulletin of the Massachusetts Audubon Society* (November 1949): K45, Krutch, Joseph Wood, series III, WHC; Meyer, *Several More Lives to Live*, 126–27, 131; and Brooks Atkinson, *New York Times Book Review*, October 3, 1948, 4.

43. Edwin W. Teale, ed., *The Thoughts of Thoreau* (New York: Dodd, Mead, 1962), xiii (first quote); Teale, *North with the Spring* (New York: Dodd, Mead, 1951), 1 (second quote). See also Teale, *The Lost Woods: Adventures of a Naturalist* (New York: Dodd, Mead, 1945), 3, 5; Joan Cook, "Edwin Way Teale Is Dead at 81," *New York Times Book Review*, October 21, 1980, 10; Roger Tory Peterson, "Time of Rest, Rebirth and Hope," *New York Times Book Review*, October 24, 1965, 1; and Paul O. Williams, "The Influence of Thoreau on the American Nature Essay," *Thoreau Society Bulletin* (Fall 1978): 4.

44. Carl Bode, "Thoreau Finds a House," *Saturday Review of Literature*, July 20, 1946, 15. See also Benson Young Landis, "Decentralist at Walden Pond," *Christian Century*, July 11, 1945, 811; and T. Morris Longstreth, "The Man Who Sought Peace with Himself," *New York Times*, July 1, 1945, 56.

45. Henry Beston, *Northern Farm: A Glorious Year on a Small Maine Farm* (1948; reprint, New York: Henry Holt, 1976), 4–5 (quotes), 7.

46. Lewis Gannett, *Cream Hill: Discoveries of a Week-End Countryman* (New York: Viking Press 1949), 13–14. See also Hal Borland, "Two Urban(e) Authors Record Their Relations with Nature," *New York Times Book Review*, May 15, 1949, 3.

47. Landis, "Decentralist at Walden Pond," 110–11. See also Dona Brown, "New England Farms and the Back-to-the-Land Movement of the 1930s," in *A Landscape History of New England*, ed. Blake Harrison and Richard W. Judd (Cambridge, MA: MIT Press, 2011), 163–78; and Benson Y. Landis, "The Squatter at Walden Pond," *Advance* (July 1945): 16, *Walden*, E, Miscellaneous, xii, l, a, clippings and articles, series II, WHC.

48. Rebecca Kneale Gould, *At Home in Nature: Modern Homesteading and Spiritual Practice in America* (Berkeley: University of California Press, 2005), 181–82.

49. Borland, "Two Urban(e) Authors," 3. See also Hal Borland, *An American Year: Country Life and Landscapes through the Seasons* (New York: Simon and Schuster, 1946), 38–39, 122, 136–37; and Borland, "Phases of U.S. Life," *New York Times Book Review*, November 7, 1948, 36.

50. David McCord, "Turner, Thoreau and Debussy Together," *New York Times*, July 19, 1970, 198 (first quote); Hal Borland quoted in Joseph Wood Krutch, "Windows on the World of Nature," *New York Times*, June 9, 1957, 229 (second quote); C. P. Gorely, "Thoreau and the Land," *Landscape Architecture* 24 (April 1934): 147 (third quote), 148–49, 151–52. See also Paul H. Oehser, "Pioneers in Conservation," *Nature* (April 1945): 189–90; and Krutch, *Human Nature and the Human Condition*, 141–42.

51. Borland, *American Year*, 54; Paul, "Resolution at Walden," 166 (quotes), 168–69.

52. Donald Culross Peattie, *An Almanac for Moderns* (New York: G. P. Putnam's Sons, 1935), 3 (first quote), 19 (second and third quotes).

53. Ibid., 27 (first quote), 28 (second quote), 29 (third quote).

54. Ibid., 32 (first and second quotes), 123 (third and fourth quotes).

55. Krastin, "He Took to the Woods," 79 (first quote); Henry Seidel Canby, "Man Who Did What He Wanted," *Saturday Review of Literature* (December 26, 1936): 4 (second quote).

Chapter 5: Thoreau in a Changing Political World, 1960-1970

1. Lewis Leary, "Century of *Walden*," *Nation* 179 (August 7, 1954): 115 (first quote); Henry David Thoreau, *Civil Disobedience* (New York: New York Thoreau Fellowship, 1946), 20 (second quote). See also "Supreme Individualist," *Christian Science Monitor*, July 12, 1967.
2. Louis B. Salomon, "The Practical Thoreau," *College English* 17 (January 1956): 229 (first quote), 232, 229-32; Wade Thompson, "The Impractical Thoreau," *College English* 19 (November 1957): 67 (second quote), 68-70. On Thoreau's use of paradox, see Joseph J. Moldenhauer, "The Extra-vagant Maneuver: Paradox in *Walden*," in *Critical Essays on Henry David Thoreau's Walden*, ed. Joel Myerson (Boston: G. K. Hall, 1988), 96-97; Richard H. Dillman, "The Psychological Rhetoric of *Walden*," *Emerson Society Quarterly* 25 (1979): 80, *Walden*, D, Criticism, iv, D, f, series II, Walter Harding Collection (hereafter WHC), Thoreau Institute, Lincoln, MA; C. C. Hollis, "Thoreau and the State," *Commonweal* 50 (September 9, 1949): 530; Saul K. Padover, *The Genius of America: Men Whose Ideas Shaped our Civilization* (New York: McGraw-Hill, 1960), 198-99; and Paul Lauter, "Thoreau's Prophetic Testimony," *Massachusetts Review* 4 (Autumn 1962): 121-23.
3. Lawrence Buell, *The Environmental Imagination: Thoreau, Nature Writing, and the Formation of American Culture* (Cambridge, MA: Harvard University Press, 1995), 361.
4. Odell Shepard, introduction to *The Heart of Thoreau's Journals*, by Henry David Thoreau, ed. Shepard (Boston: Houghton Mifflin, 1927), ix-x (first quote); John Davies, *Vegetarian Messenger* (February 1947): 40, V6, Vegetarianism, series III, WHC (second quote). See also Lawrence MacDonald, "Henry Thoreau—Liberal, Unconventional, Nudist," *Sunshine and Health* (January 1943): N45, Nudism, series III, WHC; William White, "Thoreau among the Nudists," *Thoreau Society Bulletin* 104 (Summer 1968): 5; Robert Epstein, "Thoreau's 'Higher Laws' and the Heroics of Vegetarianism," *Between the Species* (Summer 1985): V6, Vegetarianism, series III, WHC; and Theodore Baird, "Corn Grows in the Night," *Massachusetts Review* 4 (Autumn 1962): 93-94.
5. Richard Drinnon, "Thoreau's Politics of the Upright Man," *Massachusetts Review* 4 (Autumn 1962): 135, 137-38; Kenneth J. Smith, "Henry David Thoreau: America's Hippie Existentialist Philosopher," *Existentialism and Ethical Humanism* (1969): 49-50; Walter Harding, "Five Ways of Looking at Walden," *Massachusetts Review* 4 (Autumn 1962): 149.
6. *Boston Daily Journal*, October 26, 1895; *Boston Daily Advertiser*, October 28, 1895, February 29, 1896.
7. *Gateway*, July 1941, T34, Thoreau Society, ii, Press Clippings/Miscellaneous Papers, series III, WHC. See also *Concord (MA) Herald*, July 17, 1941, quoted ibid.; K. W. Cameron, "A Brief Glance at the Thoreau Society," *Emerson Society Quarterly* (Second Quarter 1957), 48; L. Greenfield, "Followers of Thoreau Form Organization Called the Thoreauans," *Saturday Review of Literature* 24 (July 26, 1941): 20; *New York Times*, January 20, 1938, 17; July 22, 1948, 25; August 16, 1948, 17; and Brooks Atkinson, "Value of the Thoreau Society," *New York Times*, July 11, 1961, 28.
8. Brooks Atkinson, "Century after Thoreau's Death, America Knows How 'Great a Son It Has Lost,'" *New York Times*, May 8, 1962, 36; Hall of Fame director (unidentified) quoted in Atkinson, "Spirit of Frugal Thoreau," *New York Times*, January 19, 1962, 28. See also Howard Mumford Jones, "Thoreau and Human Nature," *Atlantic Monthly*, September 1962, 56; Atkinson, "Thoreau's Accession to the Hall of Fame

Took Long," *New York Times,* October 3, 1961, 36; October 11, 1900, 14; October 26, 1930, N1; June 30, 1935, N1; November 3, 1935, N1; November 15, 1940, 23; and W. Barksdale Maynard, *Walden Pond: A History* (New York: Oxford University Press, 2004), 266.
9. Carl Bode, "Smaller and Larger than Life," *New York Times Book Review,* December 26, 1965, box 331, "News Clippings, Book Reviews," Thoreau Fellowship Collection (hereafter TFC), Raymond H. Fogler Library, Special Collections Department, University of Maine, Orono (first two quotes); Howard Mumford Jones, "Facts Tell Story," *Boston Globe,* February 20, 1966, box 331, "News Clippings, Book Reviews," TFC (third quote); Sterling North, "Frog's-Eye View at Walden Pond," *Saturday Review* (January 15, 1966): 39 (fourth quote). See also Walter Harding, *The Days of Henry Thoreau* (New York: Alfred A. Knopf, 1962), 194–94; Paul H. Oehser, "From the Thoreauvian Well," *Living Wilderness* (Autumn 1966): 27–29, box 326, TFC; John J. McAleer, *America* (January 1, 1966), box 331, "News Clippings, Book Reviews," TFC; and Joel Porte, "The Sociable Hermit," *Christian Science Monitor,* February 10, 1966, box 331, "News Clippings, Book Reviews," TFC.
10. John J. McAleer, "The Therapeutic Vituperations of Thoreau," *American Transcendental Quarterly* 11 (Summer 1971): 82 (first quote), 84 (second quote), 85; Leo A. Bressler, "*Walden:* Neglected American Classic," *English Journal* 51 (January 1962): 14 (third quote). See also "A Baker's Dozen of Writers Comment on *Civil Disobedience,*" *New York Times Magazine,* November 26, 1967; Robert Dickens, *Thoreau, the Complete Individualist: His Relevance—and Lack of It—for Our Time* (New York: Exposition Press, 1974), 5; Leo Stoller, "Civil Disobedience: Principle and Politics," *Massachusetts Review* 4 (Autumn 1962): 86; and Brent Powell, "Henry David Thoreau, Martin Luther King Jr., and the American Tradition of Protest," *OAH Magazine of History* (Winter 1995): 29.
11. Herbert F. West, "Thoreau and the Younger Generation," *Thoreau Society Bulletin* 56 (Summer 1956): 1; Delbert L. Earisman, *Hippies in Our Midst* (Philadelphia: Fortress, 1968), 106–7.
12. Abe Fortas, *Concerning Dissent and Civil Disobedience* (New York: Signet, 1968), 59–60, 73. See also Emmet John Hughes, "From the New Frontier to the New Revolution: The Politics of the Sixties," *New York Times Sunday Magazine,* April 4, 1971, 24.
13. Lewis P. Simpson, "The Short, Desperate Life of Henry Thoreau," *Emerson Society Quarterly* 42, no. 1 (1966): 51; Charles W. White, "A Protest against the Thoreau Society's Annual Meeting," *Thoreau Society Bulletin* (Fall 1970): 4; Truman Nelson, "A Society Not Yet Formed," in "Thoreau and the New Radicals," ed. Holley Cantine et al., special issue, *Liberation* (April 1963): 23; J. Lyndon Shanley, "Thoreau: His 'Lover's Quarrel with the World,'" in *Four Makers of the Modern Mind,* ed. T. E. Crawley (Durham, NC: Duke University Press, 1976), 25. See also Nathaniel Seefurth, "Thoreau: How Relevant Today?," *American Transcendental Quarterly* 32 (Fall 1976): 10; and Betty Schechter, *The Peaceable Revolution* (Boston: Houghton Mifflin, 1963), 8.
14. Willard Uphaus, "Conscience and Disobedience," *Massachusetts Review* 4 (Autumn 1962): 105, 106 (quote), 107–8. See also William Henry Nelson, "Thoreau and the Current Non-violent Struggle for Integration," *Thoreau Society Bulletin* (Summer 1964): 2; and Pyarelal, "Thoreau, Tolstoy and Gandhiji," *New Outlook,* May 1957, 3, box 329, TFC.
15. Shirley Cochell, "Thoreau: A Man for Our Times," *Senior Scholastic* (teachers' edition) (February 15, 1968): 9; Max Lerner, "Thoreau: No Hermit," in *Thoreau: A*

Collection of Critical Essays, ed. Sherman Paul (Englewood Cliffs, NJ: Prentice Hall, 1962), 20. See also Baird, "Corn Grows in the Night," 93, 95; "Henry Thoreau: An American Rebel," *Arts and Man* (n.d. [1953?]), A39, a, Anarchism, series III, WHC; and Kingsley Widmer, *The Literary Rebel* (Carbondale: Southern Illinois University Press, 1965), 23–24.

16. Martin Luther King Jr., *Stride toward Freedom* (New York: Ballantine Books, 1958); 50 (first quote), 51 (second quote), 52; King, "A Legacy of Creative Protest," *Massachusetts Review* 4 (Autumn 1962): 45 (third quote). See also Robert Bingham Downs, *Books That Changed the World* (Chicago: American Library Association, 1956), 72–75; and Michael Curtis Meyer, *Several More Lives to Live: Thoreau's Political Reputation in America* (Westport, CT: Greenwood Press, 1977), 157–58.

17. Sharon Todd, "Thoreau's Night in Jail Study of Man, Philosophy," *Greenville (SC) News and Piedmont,* June 11, 1977, D42, Drama, Items Relating to *Night Thoreau Spent in Jail,* series III, WHC (first quote); *Ohio State Lantern,* April 23, 1970, Lawrence and Lee, Night in Jail, box 329, TFC (second quote); "The Night Thoreau Spent in Jail," *Literary Cavalcade* (April 1972): D42, Drama, Items Relating to *Night Thoreau Spent in Jail,* series III, WHC (third quote). See also Howard Taubman, "On Stage, Thoreau Speaks to Today," *New York Times,* December 23, 1970, 16; and Jay Carr, "Thoreau Play Means Well but the Action Is Diffuse," *Detroit News,* October 10, 1970, D42, Drama, Items Relating to *Night Thoreau Spent in Jail,* series III, WHC.

18. Barry Kritzberg, "Thoreau the Man," *Chicago Sun-Times,* February 14, 1971, D42, Drama, Items Relating to *Night Thoreau Spent in Jail,* series III, WHC (first quote); Charles Clerc, "The Now Thoreau: Caveat Emptor," *Midwest Quarterly* 16 (Summer 1975): 380 (second quote), 381 (third quote).

19. *Ohio State Lantern,* April 23, 1970; Irving H. Bartlett, *The American Mind in the Mid-Nineteenth Century* (New York: Crowell, 1967), 46; Townsend Scudder, "Henry David Thoreau," in *Literary History of the United States,* ed. Robert E. Spiller et al. (New York: Macmillan, 1963–72), 1:411; Truman Nelson, "Thoreau and the Paralysis of Individualism," *Ramparts* (March 1966): 20, in *Anti-slavery and Reform Papers,* E, John Brown Essays, 1, o, series II, WHC. See also Sherman Paul quoted in Henry David Thoreau, *"Walden" and "Civil Disobedience"* (Boston: Houghton Mifflin, 1957), 232; and Shanley, "'Lover's Quarrel with the World,'" 25.

20. Staughton Lynd, *Intellectual Origins of American Radicalism* (New York: Pantheon, 1968), 8, 68–69, 92–93, 94. See also Eugene D. Genovese, "Abolitionist," *New York Review of Books,* September 26, 1968.

21. Stoughton Lynd, "Henry Thoreau: The Admirable Radical," *Liberation* (February 1963): 21 (first and second quotes); Lynd, "Admirable Radical," 26 (third quote).

22. Bob Dickens, "Thoreau on Slavery, Economy & Alienation," *Anarchy* (London) (1972): 22, A39, f, series III, WHC; Nelson, "Society Not Yet Formed," 25. See also Dickens, *Thoreau, the Complete Individualist,* 5–6, 62, 67, 96, 78–79, 99; and Gordon Rohman, review of *Thoreau: The Complete Individualist,* by Robert Dickens *American Literature* (March 1976): 84, 85, A39, Anarchism, d, series III, WHC.

23. Dachine Rainer, "Who Are the Anarchists?," in "Thoreau and the New Radicals," ed. Cantine et al., 26. See also E. M. Schuster, "Native American Anarchism," *Smith College Studies in History* 17 (October 1931–July 1932): 47–50; Joseph L. Blau, *Men and Movements in American Philosophy* (New York: Prentice Hall, 1952), 131–41; Saul K. Padover, "American as Anarchist," in *Genius of America,* 196–97; Schechter, *The Peaceable Revolution,* 23; Holley Cantine, "The Direct Actionists and the Bird

Watchers," in "Thoreau and the New Radicals," ed. Cantine et al., 22; and Victor Richman, "More than Our Minds Can Map," ibid., 27–28.
24. Charles R. Anderson, *The Magic Circle of Walden* (New York: Holt, Rinehart & Winston, 1968), 19. See also Alfred Kazin, "Writing in the Dark," in *Henry David Thoreau: Studies and Commentaries,* ed. Walter Harding, George Brenner, and Paul A. Doyle (Madison, NJ: Fairleigh Dickinson University Press, 1972), 19; and Jonathan Bishop, *Catholic Worker* (September 1964): box 331, "News Clippings, Book Reviews," TFC.
25. Earisman, *Hippies in Our Midst,* 136 (first quote), 15 (second quote), 143. See also Kenneth Kurtz, "Thoreau and Individualism Today," *Emerson Society Quarterly* 18 (1960): 14.
26. Jack Kerouac, *On the Road* (1957; reprint, New York: Penguin Books, 1976), 5. See also Earisman, *Hippies in Our Midst,* 99, 101, 104–5, 109, 111–12; and Rod Phillips, *"Forest Beatniks" and "Urban Thoreaus": Gary Snyder, Jack Kerouac, Lew Welch, and Michael McClure* (New York: P. Lang, 2000), 2, 50–51, 138 (quote).
27. Paul H. Wild, "Flower Power: A Student's Guide to Pre-hippie Transcendentalism," *English Journal* 58 (January 1969): 62, 63 (first quote); Earisman, *Hippies in Our Midst,* 128–29, 130 (second quote); John T. McCutcheon Jr., "Was Thoreau a Hippy?," *Chicago Tribune,* July 27, 1967, H53, Hippies, D, Newspaper Articles/Clippings, WHC, series III (third quote); Smith, "America's Hippie Existentialist Philosopher," 44 (fourth quote), 52 (fifth quote). See also Morgan Bulkeley, "Beatnik with a Difference," *Berkshire Eagle* (Pittsfield, MA), July 13, 1967, H53, Hippies, D, Newspaper Articles/Clippings, series III, WHC.
28. Mark W. Sullivan, *Picturing Thoreau: Henry David Thoreau in American Visual Culture* (Lanham, MD: Lexington Books, 2015), 86 (quote, paraphrasing Baskin), 90. See also "Hall of Fame Issues a Thoreau Medal," *Audubon* (November 1963): 374–75; and *Western Stamp Collector* (April 22, 1967): S96, Stamp, series III, WHC.
29. Raymond Adams quoted in *Concord (MA) Journal,* n.d., ca. July 1967, and *New York Times,* July 17, 1967, both in box 329, "Commemorative Stamp," TFC; John Chamberlain, "Thoreau: A Hippie or Not?," *Tulsa (OK) Tribune,* July 17, 1967, H53, Hippies, D, Newspaper Articles/Clippings, series III, WHC.
30. *Boston Globe,* May 4, 1967 (first quote); *Concord (MA) Journal,* n.d., ca. July 1967 (second quote); *Columbus (OH) Dispatch,* May 29, 1967, S.96, Stamp, series III, WHC (third quote); Mary P. Sherwood, "Thoreau Stamp Is a Disgrace," *Concord (MA) Journal,* n.d. (fourth quote); Raymond Adams in *Concord Journal,* n.d., ca. July 1967 (fifth quote); unidentified post office representative in *Washington Evening Star,* May 8, 1967, WHC (sixth quote); Leonard Baskin in Jean Caldwell, "Artist: My Thoreau 'Real,'" *Boston Globe,* June 7, ibid., WHC (seventh quote). See also *East Village Other* quoted in *New York Times,* July 17, 1967; *Washington Evening Star,* May 8, 1967; *Chicago Daily News,* May 5, 1967; Brooks Atkinson, "Thoreau's Message after 150 Years," *New York Times,* July 15, 1967, 17; and Assistant Postmaster General Richard J. Murphy quoted in *Concord (MA) Journal,* July 13, 1967, "Commemorative Stamp," all in box 239, TFC.
31. Henry David Thoreau quoted in Michael C. Johnson, "Thoreau on Drugs," *Thoreau Society Bulletin* (Winter 1976): 4; Lee A. Burress III, "Thoreau on Ether and Psychedelic Drugs," *American Notes and Queries* 12 (1974): 99–100; *Boston Herald,* July 6, 1967.
32. William K. Bottorff and David G. Hoch, "Thoreau and Ether," *Thoreau Society Bulletin* (Summer 1976): 6; Guy Wright, "Thoreau the Square," *San Francisco Examiner,* May 16, 1968, H53, Hippies, D, Newspaper Articles/Clippings, series III, WHC. See

also Dorothy Brant Brazier, "Was Thoreau First Hippie?," *Seattle Times,* n.d., ibid.; Paul Woodring, "A View from Campus: Was Thoreau a Hippie?," *Saturday Review* (December 16, 1967): 68; "Rutgers Professor [F. T. McGill] Contends Thoreau Was Not a Hippie," *New York Times,* January 5, 1968, 24; Chamberlain, "Hippie or Not?"; and Smith, "America's Hippie Existentialist Philosopher," 43.
33. Joseph Wood Krutch, "If You Don't Mind My Saying So," *American Scholar* 37 (Winter 1967): 17 (both quotes). See also Cecelia Tichi, *Embodiment of a Nation: Human Form in American Places* (Cambridge, MA: Harvard University Press, 2001), 72–86.
34. Alexander Kern, "Thoreau and Individualism Today," *Emerson Society Quarterly* 18 (1960): 12; William A. Herr, "Thoreau: A Civil Disobedient?," *Ethics* 85 (October 1974): 87, 89 (quote), 90. See also Herr, "A More Perfect State: Thoreau's Concept of Civil Government," *Massachusetts Review* 16 (Summer 1975): 471, 473–75, 478; John Morris, "America's Gentle Anarchist," *Religious Humanism* 3 (Spring 1969): 64–65; Bartlett, *American Mind,* 46; Drinnon, "Thoreau's Politics of the Upright Man," 131–33; and William Stuart Nelson, "Thoreau and American Non-violent Resistance," *Massachusetts Review* 3 (Autumn 1962): 56, 57.
35. Heinz Eulau, "Wayside Challenger: Some Remarks on the Politics of Henry David Thoreau" (1949), in *Collection of Critical Essays,* ed. Paul, 120 (first quote), 127, 129; Lewis H. Van Dusen Jr., "Civil Disobedience: Destroyer of Democracy," *American Bar Association Journal* 55 (February 1969): 123, in *Anti-slavery and Reform Papers,* Criticism, C, Individual Titles, series II, WHC (second quote); Richard Revere, "Freedom: Who Needs It?," *Atlantic Monthly,* May 1968, 41–42, 43 (third quote); Frederick K. Sanders, "Mr. Thoreau's Timebomb," *National Review,* June 4, 1968, 544 (fourth quote), 546. See also Hannah Arendt, "Reflections: Civil Disobedience," *New Yorker,* September 12, 1970, 70, 72, 78; Fred DeArmond, "Can Dissenters Really Claim Thoreau?," *Human Events* (May 25, 1968): 330; and James Lundquist, "An Apology for Henry" (response to Sanders), *National Review,* August 13, 1968, 806, 818–19, in *Anti-slavery and Reform Papers,* Criticism, C, Individual Titles, series II, WHC.
36. Erwin N. Griswold, 'The Right to Differ . . . Has Limits,'" *Christian Science Monitor,* July 20, 1968. See also Fortas, *Concerning Dissent and Civil Disobedience,* 49–51, 53, 55; George Moneyhun, "Civil Disobedience: Shape of Debate," *Christian Science Monitor,* July 20–22, 1968, in *Anti-slavery and Reform Papers,* Criticism, C, Individual Titles, series II, WHC; Carl Bode, *The Young Rebel in American Literature* (New York: Praeger, 1960), 12; and Raymond Tatalovich, "Thoreau on Civil Disobedience: In Defense of Morality or Anarchy?," *Southern Quarterly* 11 (January 1973): 107–9, in *Anti-slavery and Reform Papers,* Criticism, C, Individual Titles, series II, WHC.
37. Winfield Townley Scott, "Walden Pond in the Nuclear Age," *New York Times Magazine,* May 6, 1962, 84. See also Herr, "Thoreau: A Civil Disobedient," 90; and West, "Thoreau and the Younger Generation," 1.
38. Gorham B. Munson, "Dionysian in Concord," *Outlook,* August 29, 1928, 692.
39. Ludwig Lewisohn, *Expression in America* (New York: Harper & Brothers, 1932), 138–39; Irwin Edman, *Saturday Review of Literature* (October 7, 1939), C7, in Canby, series III, WHC; F. O. Matthiessen, unattributed, ibid.; Clifton Fadiman, review of *Thoreau,* by Henry Canby, *New Yorker,* December 7, 1939, ibid.; Thomas Lyle Collins, "Thoreau's Coming of Age," *Sewanee Review* 49 (January 1941): 57–66. See also Henry Seidel Canby, *Thoreau* (Boston: Houghton Mifflin, 1939), 127; and Canby, "Thoreau in History: The Story of a Literary Reputation," *Saturday Review of Literature* (July 15, 1939): 4.

40. Tyrus Hillway, "The Personality of H. D. Thoreau," *College English* 6 (March 1945): 330; Stanley Hyman quoted in Thompson, "The Impractical Thoreau," 70.
41. David Kalman, "A Study of Thoreau," *Thoreau Society Bulletin* (January 1948): 2 (first and second quotes); Raymond D. Gozzi, "A Freudian View of Thoreau," in *Thoreau's Psychology: Eight Essays*, ed. Gozzi (Lanham. MD: University Press of America, 1983), 2 (third quote), 4 (fourth quote), 6 (fifth quote), 8, 16 (sixth quote). For a more balanced assessment of Thoreau's sexuality, see Maxwell Geismar, "Thoreau: The Private Man," *New Republic* (May 7, 1951): 26; Robert D. Richardson Jr., *Henry Thoreau: A Life of the Mind* (Berkeley: University of California Press, 1986), 58; and Laura Dassow Walls, *Henry David Thoreau: A Life* (Chicago: University of Chicago Press, 2017), 241.
42. R. R. W., "Perry Miller Writes *Consciousness in Concord*," *Concord (MA) Journal*, n.d., ca. June 1958, Journals, C, Editions, series II, WHC; *New York Times*, October 3, 1956, 35; *Time*, July 7, 1958, box 331, "News Clippings, Book Reviews," TFC.
43. Perry Miller, *The Transcendentalists: An Anthology* (Cambridge, MA: Harvard University Press, 1950), 5, 12–13.
44. Perry Miller, introduction to *Consciousness in Concord: The Text of Thoreau's Hitherto "Lost Journal," 1840–1841*, by Henry David Thoreau, ed. Perry Miller (Boston: Houghton Mifflin, 1958), 94 (both quotes).
45. Ibid., 82–85, 86 (quote), 87, 95–96, 127, 205.
46. Ibid., 127 (first quote), 126 (second quote), 119 (third and fourth quotes). See also Raymond D. Gozzi, "Some Aspects of Thoreau's Personality," in *Henry David Thoreau: A Profile*, ed. Walter Roy Harding (New York: Hill and Wang, 1971), 165; Hyman, "Thoreau Once More," 166; and Walls, *Henry David Thoreau*, 172.
47. Lance Newman, *Our Common Dwelling: Henry Thoreau, Transcendentalism, and the Class Politics of Nature* (New York: Palgrave Macmillan, 2005), 37; Henry Pochmann, review of *Consciousness in Concord*, by Perry Miller, *American Literature* 31 (May 1959): 198, Journals, C, Editions, WHC, series II. See also Gary Scharnhorst, *Henry David Thoreau: A Case Study in Canonization* (Columbia, SC: Camden House, 1993), 80.
48. Stephen Whicher, review of *Consciousness in Concord*, by Miller, *American Scholar* 28 (Winter 1958–59): 119; Walter Harding, "Afterword: Some Random Thoughts on Thoreau's Personality," in *Thoreau: A Profile*, ed. Harding, 247. See also Quentin Anderson, "Thoreau on July 4," *New York Times Book Review*, July 4, 1971, 17, box 331, "News Clippings—Book Reviews," TFC; Walter Harding, "Henry Thoreau and Ellen Sewall," *South Atlantic Quarterly* 64 (Winter 1965): 100–106; Richard Lebeaux, *Young Man Thoreau* (Amherst: University of Massachusetts Press, 1977), 3; Lebeaux, "From Canby to Richardson: The Last Half-Century of Thoreau Biography," in *Thoreau's World and Ours: A Natural Legacy*, ed. Edmund A. Schofield and Robert C. Baron (Golden, CO: North American Press, 1993), 131; and Paul Lauter, "New Light on Thoreau," *New Leader* (June 15, 1959), L, 11, series III, WHC.
49. Leo Stoller in *South Atlantic Quarterly*, n.d., ca. 1958, 326, Journals, C, Editions, Consciousness in Concord, series II, WHC. See also J. Lyndon Shanley, "Years of Decay and Disappointment?," in *Thoreau: A Profile*, ed. Harding, 191–92; Henry Beetle Hough, "The Lost Volume," *Saturday Review* (July 5, 1958): 30; and Albert Gilman and Roger Brown, "Personality and Style in Concord," in *Transcendentalism and Its Legacy*, ed. Myron Simon and Thornton H. Parsons (Ann Arbor: University of Michigan Press, 1966), 93–94.
50. Charles Poore, "Books of the Times," *New York Times*, June 26, 1958; Bernard R.

Carman, "Thoreau Is as Thoreau Does," *Berkshire Eagle* (Pittsfield, MA), June 21, 1958; Robert Taylor, "The 'Lost' Journal of Henry Thoreau, *Boston Herald*, July 28, 1958; and *Concord (MA) Journal*, n.d., ca. June 1958, all in Journals, C, Editions, Consciousness in Concord, series II, WHC.

51. Odell Shepard, "Perry Miller's Thoreau," *Nation* 187 (December 6, 1958): 428 (first and second quotes), 429 (third quote), 430; Shepard, "Unconsciousness in Cambridge: The Editing of Thoreau's 'Lost Journal,'" *Emerson Society Quarterly* 13 (1958): 19 (fourth quote).
52. Atkinson, "Century after Thoreau's Death," 36 (first quote); Quentin Anderson, "The Writings of Henry D. Thoreau," *New York Times Book Review*, July 4, 1971, 1 (second quote); Henry David Thoreau in Hyman, "Thoreau Once More," 165 (third quote); Carl Bode, "The Half-Hidden Thoreau," *Massachusetts Review* 4 (Autumn 1962): 68 (fourth, fifth, and sixth quotes), 78; Herbert S. Bailey, "Thoreau Changed the World—and the World Changed Him," *Princeton Alumni Weekly* (October 1, 1968): 22 (seventh quote). See also Baird, "Corn Grows in the Night," 100–101.
53. Leon Edel, "Walden: The Myth and the Mystery," *American Scholar* 44 (Spring 1975): 280 (first quote); Edel, "Reappraisals: *Walden*—the Myth and the Mystery," *American Scholar* 44 (Spring 1975): 275, in *Walden*, D. Criticism: v. E, b, series II, WHC (third and fourth quotes); Edel, *Henry D. Thoreau*, University of Minnesota Pamphlets on American Writers, no. 90 (Minneapolis: University of Minnesota Press, 1970), 20 (fifth and sixth quotes), 39 (seventh quote); John Shirigian (reply to Edel), *American Scholar* 44 (Autumn 1975): 689 (eighth quote), 90 (includes Elaine Cogswell quote), E7, Edel, Leon, WHC, series III.
54. Mark Elkins Moller, "Thoreau, Womankind, and Sexuality," *Emerson Society Quarterly* 22 (1976): 123–24, 125 (first quote), 126, 128 (second quote).
55. James McIntosh, *Thoreau as Romantic Naturalist: His Shifting Stance toward Nature* (Ithaca, NY: Cornell University Press, 1974), 73 (all quotes).
56. John Kenneth Galbraith, "*The Affluent Society* after Ten Years," *Atlantic Monthly*, July 1957, 44. See also Adam Rome, "'Give Earth a Chance': The Environmental Movement and the Sixties," *Journal of American History* 90 (September 2003): 535–54.
57. Henry David Thoreau quoted in Padover, *Genius of America*, 200; Joseph Wood Krutch, *Human Nature and the Human Condition* (New York: Random House, 1959), 21, 22 (quote), 31–32, 37–38. See also Elwyn Brooks White, "Walden, 1954," *Yale Review* (September 1954): 13–14; and William Barrett, "Machine-Made Man," *New York Times Book Review*, September 6, 1959, 3.
58. Box 331, clipping, "Hippies," "unidentified clippings," TFC.
59. Governor Thomas P. Salmon quoted in Roy Reed, "Back-to-Land Movement Seeks Self-Sufficiency," *New York Times*, June 9, 1975, 63.
60. Rebecca Kneale Gould, *At Home in Nature: Modern Homesteading and Spiritual Practice in America* (Berkeley: University of California Press, 2005), 3, 38 (first quote), 39 (second quote).
61. Bennett M. Berger, "Total Loss Farm," *New York Times Book Review*, November 14, 1971, 6 (first quote); Hugh Kenner, "The Last Whole Earth Catalogue," *New York Times Book Review*, November 14, 1971, 7 (second quote); Reed, "Back-to-Land Movement," 63 (third quote). See also Nelson Bryant, "The Foxfire Book," *New York Times Book Review*, March 19, 1972, 20; and Walter J. Ong, "Religion, Scholarship, and the Restitution of Man," *Daedalus* 91 (Spring 1962): 421, 422–25.
62. Reed, "Back-to-Land Movement," 63 (first quote); Victor A. Croley, "The Freedom

Way, *Mother Earth News* (January 1970): 46 (second quote), 47; Willard Uphaus quoted in "Meditation on Concord River," *Boston Globe,* July 15, 1961, box 331 "Individualist," TFC (third quote); Bressler, "*Walden:* Neglected American Classic," 15 (fourth quote). See also Stanley Carr, "Getting Away from It All," *New York Times,* July 9, 1972, XX13; and D. W. Kleine, "Civil Disobedience: The Way to Walden," *Modern Language Notes* 75 (April 1960): 298.
63. Kleine, "Civil Disobedience," 297 (first quote), 300 (second quote).
64. Philip Booth, "Walden in the World of Today: A Way of Talking about Freedom," *Christian Science Monitor,* June 22, 1961, in *Walden,* E, Miscellaneous, iii, j, series II, WHC.

Chapter 6: An Environmental Icon

1. David Cushman Coyle, "To Keep the Wilderness Wild," *New York Times,* August 11, 1957, 174.
2. Olaus J. Murie, "Wild Country as a National Asset," 127, 129, and "Speech of Hon. John P. Saylor, of Pennsylvania in the House of Representatives, July 12, 1956," 73, both in "National Wilderness Preservation Act: Hearings before the Committee on Interior and Insular Affairs," U.S. Senate, 85 Cong., sess. 1, on S. 1176, June 19–20, 1957. See also Howard Zahniser, "A Statement on Wilderness Preservation in Reply to a Questionnaire," 168, ibid.; and Reginald L. Cook, *Passage to Walden* (Boston: Houghton Mifflin; New York: Russell & Russell, 1966), 10–12.
3. Ray Mungo, "If Mr. Thoreau Calls, Tell Him I've Left the Country," *Atlantic Monthly,* May 1970, 73, 79 (quote), box 331, "Papers, News Clippings," Thoreau Fellowship Collection (hereafter TFC), Raymond H. Fogler Library, Special Collections Department, University of Maine, Orono.
4. Mark W. Sullivan, *Picturing Thoreau: Henry David Thoreau in American Visual Culture* (Lanham, MD: Lexington Books, 2015), 104; William J. Wolf, *Thoreau: Mystic, Prophet, Ecologist* (Philadelphia: Pilgrim Press, 1974), 14; Robert Paul Cobb, "Thoreau and 'the Wild,'" *Emerson Society Quarterly* 18 (1960): 5–6; "Thoreau: Wilderness Saint," *Sports Afield* (June 1976), S92, series III, Walter Harding Collection (hereafter WHC), Thoreau Institute, Lincoln, MA.
5. Elizabeth Keiper, "Thoreau's Pen, a Century Ago, Wrote Truths for Today," *Rochester (NY) Times-Union,* July 16, 1954, Miscellaneous, Walden, B, series II, WHC.
6. Leo Stoller, *After Walden: Thoreau's Changing Views on Economic Man* (Stanford, CA: Stanford University Press, 1957), 8, 83 (second quote), 90–93, 105, 106 (first quote), 108–15, 121, 156, 164, 445–46, 451–52.
7. Stewart L. Udall, *The Quiet Crisis* (New York: Holt, Rinehart, and Winston, 1963), 59 (first quote), 64 (second and third quotes). See also William M. Condry, *Thoreau* (New York: Philosophical Library, 1954); August William Derleth, *Concord Rebel: A Life of Henry D. Thoreau* (Philadelphia: Chilton, 1962); and William M. Condry, "A Hundred Years of Walden," *Dublin Magazine* 31 (January–March 1955): 71.
8. Brooks Atkinson, "Century after Thoreau's Death, America Knows How 'Great a Son It Has Lost,'" *New York Times,* May 8, 1962, 36; Horace Taylor, "Thoreau Scientific Interests as Seen in His Journal," *McNeese Review* (1962): 47–49, 52, 56 (first quote), 59, in S25, Science, ee, series III, WHC; Charles David Stewart, "Word for Thoreau," *Atlantic Monthly,* July 1935, 114. See also Leo Stoller, "A Note on Thoreau's Place in the History of Phenology," *ISIS* 47, no. 2 (1956), in S25, Science, cc, series III, WHC; Theodore Baird, "Corn Grows in the Night," *Massachusetts Review* 4

(Autumn 1962): 101-3; Joseph Wood Krutch, "A Little Fishy Friend," *Nation* (October 8, 1949): 350, in K45, series III, WHC; Henry Beetle Hough, *Thoreau of Walden: The Man and His Eventful Life* (New York: Simon and Schuster, 1956), 210; and Robin S. McDowell, "Thoreau in the Current Scientific Literature," *Thoreau Society Bulletin* (Spring 1978): 2.
9. Stoller, *After Walden*, 75.
10. Edward S. Deevey Jr., "A Re-examination of Thoreau's *Walden*," *Quarterly Review of Biology* 17 (March 1942): 9; Aldo Leopold and Sara Elizabeth Jones, "A Phenological Record for Sauk & Dane Counties, Wisconsin, 1935-1945," *Ecological Monographs* 18 (January 1947): 83; Philip Whitford and Kathryn Whitford, "Thoreau: Pioneer Ecologist and Conservationist," *Scientific Monthly*, November 1951, 291-96; Kathryn Whitford, "Thoreau and the Woodlots of Concord," *New England Quarterly* 23 (September 1950): 293, 295, 300; Henry Hayden Clark, *Transitions in American Literary History* (Durham, NC: Duke University Press, 1954), 281; Charles R. Metzger, "Thoreau on Science," *Annals of Science* (September 1956): 206-11; Raymond Adams, "Thoreau's Science," *Scientific Monthly*, May 1945, 379-82.
11. Henry Thomas Schnittkind and Dana Lee Schnittkind, "Thoreau's Adventure into the Simple Life," in *Living Adventures in Philosophy*, ed. Schnittkind and Schnittkind (New York: Hanover House, 1954), 234 (quote), 235. See also Alec Lucas, "Thoreau, Field Naturalist," *University of Toronto Quarterly* 23 (1954): 227; and Kevin P. Van Anglen, "True Pulpit Power: 'Natural History of Massachusetts' and the Problem of Cultural Authority," *Studies in the American Renaissance* (1990): 122.
12. Paul Brooks, *Speaking for Nature: How Literary Naturalists from Henry Thoreau to Rachel Carson Have Shaped America* (Boston: Houghton Mifflin, 1980), 238-40, 241 (quote). See also Stuart Chase, *Rich Land, Poor Land: A Study of Waste in the Natural Resources of America* (New York: McGraw-Hill, 1936), 103.
13. Paul B. Sears, "The Inexorable Problem of Space," in *The Subversive Science: Essays toward an Ecology of Man*, ed. Paul Shepard and Daniel McKinley (Boston: Houghton Mifflin, 1969), 81 (quote), 82, 91; Fairfield Osborn quoted in Brooks, *Speaking for Nature*, 243; William Vogt quoted ibid., 246.
14. George M. Woodwell, W. M. Malcolm, and R. H. Whittaker, "A-Bombs, Bug Bombs, and Us," in *Subversive Science*, ed. Shepard and McKinley, 230 (quote), 231, 234-35, 238-39. See also Robert Gottlieb, *Forcing the Spring: The Transformation of the American Environmental Movement* (Washington, DC: Island Press, 1993), 35-38.
15. Frank Graham Jr., *Since "Silent Spring"* (Boston: Houghton Mifflin, 1970), 69 (first quote), 268 (second quote). See also Linda J. Lear, *Rachel Carson: Witness for Nature* (New York: Henry Holt, 1997); Lear, "Rachel Carson's *Silent Spring*," *Environmental History Review* 17 (Summer 1993): 23; and Daniel J. Kevles, "Contested Earth: Science, Equity & the Environment," *Daedalus* (Spring 2008): 87.
16. Woodwell, Malcolm, and Whittaker, "A-Bombs, Bug Bombs, and Us," 230 (quote). See also Sears, "Inexorable Problem of Space," 77, 79; LaMont C. Cole, "The Impending Emergence of Ecological Thought," in *Subversive Science*, ed. Shepard and McKinley, 268; and Daniel McKinley, "The New Mythology of 'Man in Nature,'" ibid., 351-52, 359.
17. Mark Hamilton Lytle, *The Gentle Subversive: Rachel Carson, "Silent Spring," and the Rise of the Environmental Movement* (New York: Oxford University Press, 2007), 199 (first quote), 201 (second quote).
18. Nina Baym, "Thoreau's View of Science," *Journal of the History of Ideas* 26 (April

1965): 222, 224–26, 228–31; Van Anglen, "True Pulpit Power," 123; Peter A. Fritzell, "Walden and Paradox: Thoreau as Self-Conscious Ecologist," *New England Review* 3 (1980): 52.
19. Donald Worster, *Nature's Economy: A History of Ecological Ideas* (Cambridge: Cambridge University Press, 1977), 63, 66 (first quote), 82 (second quote).
20. Kevles, "Contested Earth," 85–86.
21. Samuel P. Hays and Barbara D. Hays, *Beauty, Health, and Permanence: Environmental Politics in the United States, 1955–1985* (New York: Cambridge University Press, 1987); Kevles, "Contested Earth," 84–86.
22. *New York Times,* August 11, 1970, 32; Richard W. Judd and Christopher S. Beach, *Natural States: The Environmental Imagination in Maine, Oregon, and the Nation* (Washington, DC: Resources for the Future, 2003), 95–101.
23. Kent Curtis, "The Virtue of Thoreau: Biography, Geography, and History in the Walden Woods," *Environmental History* (January 2010): 31. See also John J. McAleer, "The Therapeutic Vituperations of Thoreau," *American Transcendental Quarterly* 11 (Summer 1971): 82–83.
24. "Walden Pond—'a Literary Shrine,'" *Newsweek,* May 18, 1960, W6, Walden Pond, x, Walden Pond, series III, WHC. See also Truman Nelson, "Shores of Strife," *New York Times Sunday Magazine,* April 27, 1958, 79; Edward Weeks, "What Happened to Walden," in *In Friendly Candor* (Boston: Little, Brown, 1959), 246–49; John H. Fenton, "A Battle Rages at Walden Pond," *New York Times,* July 21, 1957, 42; and *New York Times,* September 23, 1957, 50.
25. Robert Whitcomb, "The Thoreau 'Country,'" *Bookman* (July 1931): 461; E. B. White in Michael Francis Moloney, "Walden: A Centenary," *America* (March 27, 1954): 683; Edwin Way Teale, *North with the Spring* (New York: Dodd, Mead, 1951), 303. See also Raymond Nadeau, "Walden Raped," *New England Review* 1 (July–August 1969): 15; E. B. White, "One Man's Meat: Pilgrimage to Walden Pond," *Harper's,* August 1939, 329–32; George Frisbie Whicher, preface to *Walden Revisited: A Centennial Tribute to Henry David Thoreau* (Chicago: Packard, 1945), n.p.; and Gilbert Byron, "An 'Open Letter to Thoreau,'" *Saturday Review of Literature* (June 5, 1948): 47.
26. *Boston Traveler,* May 3, 1960. T34, Thoreau Society, q, Save Walden Committee 1960, series III, WHC. See also Truman Nelson, "The Battle of Walden Pond," pt. 1, *National Parks Magazine* (December 1960): 4–6, T34, Thoreau Society, q, Save Walden Committee, series III, WHC; Mary P. Sherwood, "Renaissance at Walden," *Arnoldia* (Summer 1986): 47–58; and Walter Cameron, "The Little Pond—What It Means to Us," *Emerson Society Quarterly* 13 (1958): 2–3, W6, Walden Pond, k, series III, WHC.
27. Nelson, "Battle of Walden Pond," pt. 1, 5 (first quote); *Saturday Review* (August 17, 1957), T34, Thoreau Society, q, Save Walden Committee, 1957, series III, WHC (second quote); Brian Cahill, "Concord Musters to New 'Battle,'" *Ottawa Gazette,* August 3, 1957, W6, Walden Pond, q, Articles, Walden Pond, series III, WHC (third quote); *Concord (MA) Journal,* April 16, 1959, T34, Thoreau Society, q, Save Walden Committee, 1959, series III, WHC (fourth quote). See also *Concord (MA) Journal,* April 2, 1959, ibid.; W. Barksdale Maynard, *Walden Pond: A History* (New York: Oxford University Press, 2004), 256–58; Walter Harding, preface to *Thoreau's World and Ours: A Natural Legacy,* ed. Edmund A. Schofield and Robert C. Baron (Golden, CO: North American Press, 1993), xvi; *Concord (MA) Journal,* July 25, August 1, 8, 1957, April 16, December 10, 1959; *Saturday Review* (August 17, 1957); *New York*

Times Magazine Section, May 11, 1958; "Plea to 'Save Walden' Voiced in 1875," *Boston Herald,* October 4, 1959; letter to the editor, *Boston Globe,* August 2, 1957; "Concord Up in Arms Again over Walden Pond," *Boston Globe,* August 21, 1960; *Boston Globe,* August 3, 1957; and *New York Times,* August 3, 1957, all in T34, Thoreau Society, q, Save Walden Committee, WHC, series III.

28. Morris Longstreth and Frederic Babcock in "The 'Save Walden' Campaign," *Thoreau Society Bulletin* (Fall 1957): 1; Russell Nye in *Michigan State News,* May 15, 1958, T34, Thoreau Society, q, Save Walden Committee, series III, WHC. See also Perry Miller in Maynard, *Walden Pond: A History,* 258; Brooks Atkinson in *New York Times,* August 19, 1957, T34, Thoreau Society, q, Save Walden Committee, series III, WHC; Babcock quoted in *Chicago Tribune,* August 25, 1946, pt. 4, 4; Truman Nelson, "Battle of Walden Pond," pt. 2, *National Parks Magazine* (January 1961): 4–6, T34, Thoreau Society, s, Save Walden Committee, series III, WHC; Hough, *Thoreau of Walden,* 263; and Truman Nelson, "Walden on Trial," *Nation* (July 19, 1958): 30, 33.
29. *Philadelphia Inquirer,* May 5, 1960; Albert D. Hughes, "Court Rules to Preserve Walden Pond," *Christian Science Monitor,* May 3, 1960, both in T34, Thoreau Society, q, Save Walden Committee, series III, WHC; *New York Times,* July 24, 1957, 28, September 15, 1957, 74; March 30, 1958; May 4, 1960, 51; March 26, 1961, 22; Maynard, *Walden Pond: A History,* 261–62, 280, 289; Sherwood, "Renaissance at Walden," 47–48, 50–54, 57.
30. *Boston Herald,* March 18, 1960, T34, Thoreau Society, q, Save Walden Committee, series III, WHC (first quote); John B. Oakes, "The Uses of Conservation," *New York Times,* June 5, 1960, 31, ibid. (second quote). See also *New Haven (CT) Journal-Courier,* May 16, 1960, and *Providence (RI) Journal,* May 7, 1960; and Albert D. Hughes, "Walden Ruling Applauded by Antiquarians," *Christian Science Monitor,* May 4, 1960, all ibid.
31. Local citizen quoted in Howard Whitman, "Thoreau's Concord Is Willing to Leave Nature's Work Alone," *New York Times,* September 17, 1972, XX1. See also Joan Merrick Neider, "The Coming Siege of Concord," *New York Times,* March 2, 1975, 349; D. F. Clow, letter to the editor, *New York Times,* March 23, 1975, 336, W40, Wheeler, Ruth Robinson, D ii, series III, WHC; Peter Arnold, "In Thoreau's Woods," *Massachusetts Audubon* (Spring 1968): 2–9, box 326, TFC; Harold H. Blanchard, "Thoreau's Concord," *Tuftonian* (Fall 1944): 117, ibid.; and "Estabrook Country," ibid.
32. *New York Times,* February 1, 1962, 16; February 15, 1965, 26.
33. Henry David Thoreau, *Wild Fruits: Thoreau's Rediscovered Last Manuscript,* ed. Bradley P. Dean (New York: W. W. Norton, 2000), 238. See also John H. Fenton, "Towns Enacts Law to Save Streams," *New York Times,* May 14, 1967, 6; and Adeline Pepper, "The Battle to Preserve a Jersey Pond," *New York Times,* May 12, 1968, XX16.
34. John Hildebidle, "Thoreau at the Edge," *Prose Studies* 15 (December 1992): 344. See also Howard Mumford Jones, "Thoreau and Human Nature," *Atlantic Monthly,* September 1962, 57–59.
35. Oscar Godbout, "On Wheels and in Tents," *New York Times,* March 22, 1964, "Family Camping" section, 1; John C. Miles, "Wilderness as a Learning Place," *Journal of Environmental Education* 18 (Winter 1986–87): 34–35; Joseph Wood Krutch, "Windows on the World of Nature," *New York Times,* June 9, 1957, 229.
36. Michael Frome, "After 50 Years, the American Wilderness Still Stands—in Peril," *New York Times,* June 2, 1974, I:1, 20–21; Sigurd F. Olson, "The Preservation of Wilderness in the Space Age," *Appalachia* (December 1962): 198–99; Gary Snyder, *The Practice of the Wild* (San Francisco: North Point Press, 1990), 18.

37. Roderick Nash, *Wilderness and the American Mind*, 3rd ed. (1967; reprint, New Haven, CT: Yale University Press, 1982), 84 (first [Thoreau] and second quotes), 102 (third and fourth quotes).
38. Henry D. Thoreau, *The Maine Woods*, ed. Joseph J. Moldenhauer (Princeton, NJ: Princeton University Press, 1972), 80, 152, 219, 235, 275 (quote). See also Paul H. Oehser, "Wild Man of Walden," *Living Wilderness* (Summer 1949): 19–20, in K45, Krutch, Joseph Wood, series III, WHC; James McIntosh, *Thoreau as Romantic Naturalist: His Shifting Stance toward Nature* (Ithaca, NY: Cornell University Press, 1974), 190; Sherman Paul, "Thoreau, The Maine Woods, and the Problem of Ktaadn," in *A Century of Early Ecocriticism*, ed. David Mazel (Athens: University of Georgia Press, 2001), 332; Annie Russell Marble, introduction to *The Maine Woods*, by Henry David Thoreau (New York: Thomas Y. Crowell, 1906), ix–x; and Kent C. Ryden, *Landscape with Figures: Nature & Culture in New England* (Iowa City: University of Iowa Press, 2001), 120–21.
39. Lewis Leary, "Beyond the Brink of Fear: Thoreau's Wilderness," *Studies in the Literary Imagination* (Spring 1974): 70 (first and second quotes), 72; R. D. Richardson Jr., *Myth and Literature in the American Renaissance* (Bloomington: Indiana University Press, 1978), 106 (third quote). See also Robert Francis, "Thoreau on the Benevolence of Nature," *Thoreau Society Bulletin* (Summer 1977): 2; and Robert Kuhn McGregor, *A Wider View of the Universe: Henry Thoreau's Study of Nature* (Urbana: University of Illinois Press, 1997), 74, 80–82.
40. John G. Blair and Augustus Trowbridge, "Thoreau on Katahdin," *American Quarterly* 12 (Winter 1960): 510 (Thoreau quote), 511.
41. Thoreau, *The Maine Woods*, 70–71 (first quote), 156 (second quote). See also Bradford Torrey, "Thoreau's Attitude toward Nature," *Atlantic Monthly*, November 1899, 708.
42. Victor C. Friesen, "Alexander Henry and Thoreau's Climb of Mount Katahdin," *Thoreau Society Bulletin* (Spring 1973): 5–6; Blair and Trowbridge, "Thoreau on Katahdin," 514; McIntosh, *Thoreau as Romantic Naturalist*, 189; Leo Stoller in Stanley Edgar Hyman, "Henry Thoreau Once More," *Massachusetts Review* 4 (Autumn 1962): 164. For more recent interpretations, see Kent Curtis, "The Virtue of Thoreau: Biography, Geography, and History in the Walden Woods," *Environmental History* (2010): 34; Daniel Botkin, *No Man's Garden: Thoreau and a New Vision for Civilization and Nature* (Washington, DC, and Covelo, CA: Island Press / Shearwater Books, 2001), 10; Lawrence Buell, *The Environmental Imagination: Thoreau, Nature Writing, and the Formation of American Culture* (Cambridge, MA: Harvard University Press, 1995), 12; and Robert D. Richardson Jr., *Henry Thoreau: A Life of the Mind* (Berkeley: University of California Press, 1986), 258.
43. Thoreau, *Maine Woods*, 71.
44. Paul H. Oehser, "From the Thoreauvian Well," *Living Wilderness* 30 (Autumn 1966): 28, box 326, TFC.
45. Condry, *Thoreau*, 91 (first quote), 92 (second quote, paraphrasing Léon Bazalgette's *Henry Thoreau, Bachelor of Nature*). See also Michael Frome, "*The Maine Woods*: Thoreau, the Essential Guide, Now as in His Own Time," in *Promised Land: Adventures and Encounters in Wild America* (New York: William Morrow, 1985), 81, *The Maine Woods*, D, Criticism, WHC, series II (entire file).
46. Henry David Thoreau in Joseph Wood Krutch, "Wilderness as a Tonic," *Saturday Review* (June 8, 1963): 17; Philip F. Gura, "Thoreau's Maine Woods Indians: More Representative Men," *American Literature* 49 (November 1977), 363; John K. Terres,

"Seven for Birdwatchers and Friends," *New York Times Book Review*, December 6, 1964, 70.
47. Richard Fleck, "Thoreau and Wilderness," *Appalachia* (December 1964): 289–91; Jonathan Fairbanks, "Thoreau: Speaker for Wilderness," *South Atlantic Quarterly* 70 (1971): 493, 501, 503, 505; Reginald L. Cook, "Thoreau in Perspective," *University of Kansas City Review* 14 (1947): 120; Jack Schwartzman in Walter Harding, George Brenner, and Paul A. Doyle, *Henry David Thoreau: Studies and Commentaries* (Madison, NJ: Fairleigh Dickinson University Press, 1972), 151.
48. Philip Slater, *The Pursuit of Loneliness: American Culture at the Breaking Point*, rev. ed. (1970; reprint, Boston: Beacon Press, 1976), 1, 2, 8–9; 15 (all quotes).
49. B. F. Skinner, "Walden (One) and Walden Two," *Thoreau Society Bulletin* (Winter 1973): 3–4. See also Thornton Wilder, "The American Loneliness," *Atlantic Monthly*, August 1952, 65–69; and Richard Todd, "'Walden Two': Three? Many More?," *New York Times*, March 15, 1970, 229.
50. Edwin S. Smith, "A Thoreau for Today," pt. 2, *Mainstream* (May 1960): 18; McAleer, "Therapeutic Vituperations," 86; Henry Beston in Charles B. Seib, *The Woods: One Man's Escape to Nature* (Garden City, NY: Doubleday, 1971), 4. See also Joseph Wood Krutch, "Epitaph for an Age," *New York Times*, July 30, 1967, 170; and Peter E. Hartley, "Ecological Vision in American Literature," *Ecologist* 5 (March–April 1975): 94.
51. Thoreau, *The Maine Woods*, 71; Stanley A. Tag, "Growing Outward into the World: Henry David Thoreau and the Maine Woods Narrative Tradition, 1804–1886" (PhD diss., University of Iowa, 1994), 277–78. See also McIntosh, *Thoreau as Romantic Naturalist*, 188, 205–9; Cobb, "Thoreau and 'the Wild,'" 6–7; Gura, "Thoreau's Maine Woods Indians," 372, 379–81, 383; and Kelli Olson, "A Cultural Study of Henry D. Thoreau's *The Maine Woods*" (PhD diss., University of Iowa, 2000), 95–96, 104–8, 112).
52. Olson, "Preservation of Wilderness," 198, 199 (first quote), 200, 201 (second quote), 202, 206 (third [Thoreau] quote).
53. Stewart L. Udall, "To Save the Wonder of the Wilderness," *New York Times Sunday Magazine*, May 27, 1962, 12 (first quote), 40 (second quote). See also Frome, "After 50 Years," 20.
54. Botkin, *No Man's Garden*, 156.
55. Henry David Thoreau, "A Winter Walk," in *The Natural History Essays*, by Thoreau, ed. Robert Sattelmeyer (Salt Lake City: Peregrine Smith, 1980), 55 (first quote); 476; Thoreau, *Walden* (New York: Thomas Y. Crowell, 1910), 377 (second quote); "Walking," in *The Natural History Essays*, by Thoreau, ed. Sattelmeyer, 93 (third quote); Thoreau, *A Week on the Concord and Merrimack Rivers: The Writings of Henry David Thoreau*, Riverside Press ed. (Boston: Houghton Mifflin, 1893), 1:395–96.
56. McIntosh, *Thoreau as Romantic Naturalist*, 95; Leo Marx, "Walden as Transcendental Pastoral," *Emerson Society Quarterly* 18 (1960): 16. See also Fairbanks, "Thoreau: Speaker for Wilderness," 495–96; and Theodore Haddin, "Thoreau's Reputation Once More," *Thoreau Journal Quarterly* 4 (January 15, 1972): 13.
57. Jacob Deschin, "The Theme Is Nature," *New York Times*, May 29, 1963, XX21.
58. Eliot Porter, *In Wildness Is the Preservation of the World* (San Francisco: Sierra Club, 1962), 7 (first quote); Brooks Atkinson, "'Place No One Knew' Is Photographic Elegy on Demise of a Western Canyon," *New York Times*, June 11, 1963, 34 (second quote). See also Jacob Deschin, "Porter's Camera Looks at Nature," *New York Times*, July 23, 1967, 88.

59. Joseph Wood Krutch in Porter, *In Wildness,* 9 (first quote), 10, 11 (second quote). See also Eliot Porter, *Summer Island: Penobscot Country* (San Francisco: Sierra Club / Ballantine Books, 1976).
60. Howard Zahniser, "Thoreau and the Preservation of Wildness," *Thoreau Society Bulletin* 60 (1957): 2. See also Henry G. Bugbee, "Wilderness in America," *Journal of the American Academy of Religion* 42 (December 1974): 614.
61. Sandra Harbert Petrulionis and Laura Dassow Walls, afterword to *More Day to Dawn: Thoreau's "Walden" for the Twenty-First Century,* ed. Petrulionis and Walls (Amherst: University of Massachusetts Press, 2007), 242 (first quote); Baird, "Corn Grows in the Night," 99 (second quote); Walter Harding, "Century of Thoreau," *Audubon* (March 1945): 80 (third quote).
62. Joseph Wood Krutch, "The Wilderness at Our Doorstep," *New York Times Book Review,* June 21, 1953, 1.
63. Wendell Berry, "Getting along with Nature," in *Home Economics* (San Francisco: North Point Press, 1987), 11 (first and third quotes); Berry, "Preserving Wildness," ibid., 140 (second quote), 144 (fourth quote).

Epilogue: Thoreau in the Millennial Age

1. Kathryn Schulz, "Pond Scum," *New Yorker,* October 19, 2015, 40. For a more nuanced description of the *St. John* scene, see Laura Dassow Walls, *Henry David Thoreau: A Life* (Chicago: University of Chicago Press, 2017), 278; Jedediah Purdy, "In Defense of Thoreau," *Atlantic,* October 20, 2015; and Sandra Harbert Petrulionis and Laura Dassow Walls, afterword to *More Day to Dawn: Thoreau's Walden for the Twenty-First Century,* ed. Petrulionis and Walls (Amherst: University of Massachusetts Press, 2007), 245.
2. Richard Lebeaux, *Young Man Thoreau* (Amherst: University of Massachusetts Press, 1977); Richard Bridgman, *Dark Thoreau* (Lincoln: University of Nebraska Press, 1982), x (first quote), xi (second quote), 119; Robert Milder, *Reimagining Thoreau* (New York: Cambridge, 1995), 5 (quote), 99–102, 134.
3. Robert Sullivan, *The Thoreau You Don't Know: How Reevaluating the Dean of Green Makes Us Rethink Our World* (New York: Bloomsbury, 2012), 5, 10–14, 144 (quote), 160, 173–74; David Gessner, "Wild and Crazy Guy," *New York Times Book Review,* April 19, 2009, 26. See also Petrulionis and Walls, afterword to *More Day to Dawn,* 246.
4. Scott A. Sandage, *Born Losers* (Cambridge, MA: Harvard University Press, 2005), 2, 20 (Thoreau and Sandage quotes), 21.
5. Bill McKibben, "The End of Nature," *New Yorker,* September 11, 1989, 70, 72–73, 79, 104 (both quotes).
6. Albert Southwick, "Thoreau's Drumbeat Is Still Being Heard," *Boston Globe,* July 7, 1991, A20. See also Ian Box, "Why Read Thoreau?," *Dalhousie Review* 75 (Spring 1995): 5–6.
7. Elizabeth Hall Witherell, "Henry David Thoreau," in *Prospects for the Study of American Literature: A Guide for Scholars and Students,* ed. Richard Kopley (New York: New York University Press, 1997), 21; Stephen Fender, "The Environmental Imagination: *Walden* and Its Readers," *Journal of American Studies* 31 (August 1997): 313; Petrulionis and Walls, afterword to *More Day to Dawn,* 241.
8. Monika Elbert, "(S)exchanges: Julia Ward Howe's *The Hermaphrodite* and the Gender Dialectics of Transcendentalism," in *Toward a Female Genealogy of Transcendentalism,* ed. Jana L. Argersinger and Phyllis Cole (Athens: University of Georgia Press, 2014),

238; Jane Bennett, *Thoreau's Nature, Ethics, Politics and the Wild* (Lanham, MD: Rowman & Littlefield, 1994), 17. See also Lawrence Buell, "American Pastoral Ideology Reappraised," *American Literary History* 1 (Spring 1989): 3.
9. Gary Scharnhorst, *Henry David Thoreau: A Case Study in Canonization* (Columbia, SC: Camden House, 1993), 1. Other books that trace his status in the canon include Michael T. Gilmore, *American Romanticism and the Marketplace* (Chicago: University of Chicago Press, 1985); Raymond Jackson Wilson, *Figures of Speech: American Writers and the Literary Marketplace* (New York: Alfred A. Knopf, 1989); Steven Fink, *Prophet in the Marketplace: Thoreau's Development as a Professional Writer* (Princeton, NJ: Princeton University Press, 1992); and Lawrence Buell, *The Environmental Imagination: Thoreau, Nature Writing, and the Formation of American Culture* (Cambridge, MA: Harvard University Press, 1995).
10. Donald Worster, *Nature's Economy: A History of Ecological Ideas* (Cambridge: Cambridge University Press, 1977), 65–66; Kent Curtis, "The Virtue of Thoreau: Biography, Geography, and History in the Walden Woods," *Environmental History* (2010): 37.
11. Bennett, *Thoreau's Nature*, xx, xxii (quote), 89. See also Michael Curtis Meyer, *Several More Lives to Live: Thoreau's Political Reputation in America* (Westport, CT: Greenwood Press, 1977), 9, 20, 25, 44; Bob Pepperman Taylor, *America's Bachelor Uncle: Thoreau and the American Polity* (Lawrence: University Press of Kansas, 1996), 1–2, 13; and John S. Pipkin, "Hiding Places: Thoreau's Geographies," *Annals of the Association of American Geographers* 91, no. 3 (2001): 527–28.
12. Sandra Harbert Petrulionis, *To Set This World Right: The Antislavery Movement in Thoreau's Concord* (Ithaca, NY: Cornell University Press, 2006), 2 (quote) 3–4, 54, 59, 103, 141; Michael Bennett, *Democratic Discourses: The Radical Abolition Movement and Antebellum American Literature* (New Brunswick, NJ: Rutgers University Press, 2005), 105. See also J. J. Donahue, "'Hardly the Voice of the Same Man': Civil Disobedience and Thoreau's Response to John Brown," *Midwest Quarterly* 48 (Winter 2007): 247–55, 261–62, 264; and Barry Kritzberg, "Thoreau, Slavery, and Resistance to Civil Government," *Massachusetts Review* 30 (Winter 1989): 535–39, 547, 550, 562.
13. Jay Parini, *Promised Land: Thirteen Books That Changed America* (New York: Doubleday, 2008), 131; Brent Powell, "Henry David Thoreau, Martin Luther King Jr., and the American Tradition of Protest," *OAH Magazine of History* 9 (Winter 1995): 29; Chad Montrie, *Making a Living: Work and Environment in the United States* (Chapel Hill: University of North Carolina Press, 2008), 130. See also Sandra Harbert Petrulionis, "The 'Higher Law': Then and Now," *Thoreau Society Bulletin*, no. 262 (Spring 2008): 6–7; Taylor, *America's Bachelor Uncle*, 73, 84, 91; Bennett, *Thoreau's Nature*, 97, 99–100; Len Gougeon, "Thoreau and Reform," in *Cambridge Companion to Henry David Thoreau*, ed. Joel Myerson (New York: Cambridge University Press, 1995), 194–214; Lance Newman, "Thoreau's Materialism: From *Walden* to *Wild Fruits*," in *More Day to Dawn*, ed. Petrulionis and Walls, 101, 107; and Box, "Why Read Thoreau?," 9.
14. Southwick, "Thoreau's Drumbeat Is Still Being Heard."
15. Gary Paul Nabhan, foreword to *Faith in a Seed: The Dispersion of Seeds, and Other Late Natural History Writings*, by Henry D. Thoreau, ed. Bradley P. Dean (Washington, DC: Island Press, 1993), xiii; Robert D. Richardson Jr., introduction to ibid., 8; Peter A. Fritzell, *Nature Writing and America: Essays upon a Cultural Type* (Ames: Iowa State University Press, 1990), 189; Petrulionis and Walls, afterword to *More Day to Dawn*,

243; William Rossi, "Thoreau's Transcendental Ecocriticism," in *Thoreau's Sense of Place: Essays in American Environmental Writing,* ed. Richard J. Schneider (Ames: University of Iowa Press, 2000), 28, 33, 36; Laura Dassow Walls in "Thoreau's *Walden* in the Twenty-First Century," *Concord Saunterer,* n.s., 12–13 (2004–5): 16.

16. Max Oelschlaeger, *The Idea of Wilderness from Prehistory to the Age of Ecology* (New Haven, CT: Yale University Press, 1991), 162 (quote), 171; Nabhan, foreword to *Faith in a Seed,* by Thoreau, xiv (quote). See also Richardson, introduction to ibid., 13; and Newman, "Thoreau's Materialism," 103. In her 2017 biography of Thoreau, Laura Dassow Walls traces Thoreau's pre-Darwinian thought back to his reading of Charles Lyell's evolutionary geology. See also Walls, *Henry David Thoreau,* 275, 459.

17. Leo Marx, "The Struggle over Thoreau," pt. 1, *New York Review of Books* 46, no. 11 (1999): 60; Richardson, introduction to *Faith in a Seed,* by Thoreau, 3, 5–7; Nina Baym, "Region and Environment in American Literature," *New England Quarterly* 77 (June 2004): 301.

18. Lawrence Buell, "Henry Thoreau and the American Canon," in *New Essays on "Walden,"* ed. Robert F. Sayre (New York: Cambridge University Press, 1992), 46. See also Buell, *Environmental Imagination,* 365; Baym, "Region and Environment," 305; Timothy Sweet and Daniel Philippon, "Projecting Early American Environmental Writing: Is Early American Environmental Writing Sustainable? A Response to Timothy Sweet," *Early American Literature* 45, no. 2 (2010): 404; John Cumbler, review of *Environmental Imagination,* by Buell, *American Studies* 38 (Spring 1997): 165; Lawrence Buell, "Thoreau and the Natural Environment," in *Cambridge Companion to Thoreau,* ed. Myerson, 171–93; and Buell, "American Pastoral Ideology Reappraised," 20.

19. Matthew F. Child, "The Thoreau Ideal as a Unifying Thread in the Conservation Movement," *Conservation Biology* 23 (April 2009): 241. See also Mark Hamilton Lytle, *The Gentle Subversive: Rachel Carson, "Silent Spring," and the Rise of the Environmental Movement* (New York: Oxford University Press, 2007), 199; Bennett, *Thoreau's Nature,* 81; David M. Robinson, *Natural Life: Thoreau's Worldly Transcendentalism* (Ithaca, NY: Cornell University Press, 2004), 26, 94, 100, 102, 108; Oelschlaeger, *Idea of Wilderness,* 150; and Newman, "Thoreau's Materialism," 116.

20. Don Mortland, "Henry David Thoreau: Deep Ecologist?," *Between the Species* 10 (Summer–Fall 1994): 131 (quote), 134; Curtis, "Virtue of Thoreau," 32 (quote), 33. See also Don Scheese, *Nature Writing: The Pastoral Impulse in America* (New York: Twayne, 1996), 41. The original interpretation of Thoreau as a pastoralist is Leo Marx, *The Machine in the Garden: Technology and the Pastoral Ideal in America* (1964; reprint, New York: Oxford University Press, 2000), 15, 23. See also Marx, "*Walden* as Transcendental Pastoral," *Emerson Society Quarterly* 18 (1960): 17; Lawrence Buell and Leo Marx, "An Exchange on Thoreau," *New York Review of Books,* December 2, 1999, 64; and Lawrence Buell, "American Pastoral Ideology Reappraised," 21.

21. Daniel Botkin, *No Man's Garden: Thoreau and a New Vision for Civilization and Nature* (Washington, DC: Island Press / Shearwater Books, 2001), xv, xvi, 20, 38–39, 107, 117, 125. See also Philip Cafaro, review of *No Man's Garden, Conservation Biology* 15 (October 2001): 1472.

22. David R. Foster, *Thoreau's Country: Journey through a Transformed Landscape* (Cambridge, MA: Harvard University Press, 1999).

23. Michelle Nijhuis, "Teaming Up with Thoreau," *Smithsonian Magazine* 38 (October 2007): 62–63, 64 (quote). See also Robert Lee Hotz, "Another Thoreau Lesson: His

Notes from 1850s Help Study of Climate Change," *Wall Street Journal,* June 13, 2008, A10; Richard B. Primack, Abraham J. Miller-Rushing, and Kiruba Dharaneeswaran, "Changes in the Flora of Thoreau's Concord," *Biological Conservation* 142, no. 3 (2009): 502, 506; Miller-Rushing and Primack, "Global Warming and Flowering Times in Thoreau's Concord: A Community Perspective," *Ecology* 89 (February 2008): 332–33, 238, 340; Cornelia Dean, "Thoreau Is Rediscovered as a Climatologist," *New York Times,* October 28, 2008, D1; and Walls, *Henry David Thoreau,* xvi.

24. Anne LaBastille, "If Thoreau Could See It Now," *Boston Globe,* May 6, 1990, B21 (first quote), B22 (second quote). See also Leslie Allen, "Thoreau's Soggy Beach Trek," *New York Times,* October 31, 1999, TR8; and Ethan Gilsdorf, "Tracking Thoreau through a Land 'Grim and Wild,'" *New York Times,* September 19, 1008, F4.

25. Scheese, *Nature Writing,* 56 (quote), 57, 60; James A. Papa Jr., "Reinterpreting Myths: The Wilderness and the Indian in Thoreau's Maine Woods," *Midwest Quarterly* 40 (Winter 1999): 216, 217 (quote), 218–22. See also J. Parker Huber, *The Wildest Country: A Guide to Thoreau's Maine* (Boston: Appalachian Mountain Club, 1981); Jeffrey Meyers, "Seeking New Terrain: Thoreau's 'Preservation of the World,'" in *Converging Stories: Race, Ecology, and Environmental Justice in American Literature* (Athens: University of Georgia Press, 2005); and John R. Knott, *Imagining Wild America* (Ann Arbor: University of Michigan Press, 2002), 68.

26. William Cronon, "The Trouble with Wilderness; or, Getting Back to the Wrong Nature." *Environmental History* 1 (January 1996): 7 (Thoreau quote and first Cronon quote), 10 (second quote) 11, 15 (third quote), 17, 21, 25.

27. Donald Worster, "Thoreau and the American Passion for Wilderness," *Concord Saunter,* n.s., 10 (2002): 5, 8 (first quote), 9 (second quote), 11–12.

28. Edward M. Kennedy in *Heaven Is Under Our Feet,* ed. Don Henley and Dave Marsh (Stamford, CT: Longmeadow Press, 1991), 45. See also Bennett, *Thoreau's Nature,* 80–81; and Papa, "Reinterpreting Myths," 215.

29. Sullivan, *Thoreau You Don't Know,* 3; Bradley P. Dean in "Thoreau's Walden in the Twenty-First Century," 7; Bennett, *Thoreau's Nature,* 81; SueEllen Campbell in "Thoreau's Walden in the Twenty-First Century," 7. See also Petrulionis and Walls, afterword to *More Day to Dawn,* 242; Box, "Why Read Thoreau?," 12; and Alex Beam, "Thoreau Makes More Sense as the Years Go By," *Boston Globe,* July 12, 2008, E8.

30. Parini, *Promised Land,* 128; Petrulionis and Walls, afterword to *More Day to Dawn,* 245; Southwick, "Thoreau's Drumbeat Is Still Being Heard."

INDEX

abolitionism, 20–22
Adams, Raymond, 110, 119, 137
Alcott, Bronson, 8–9, 20, 25, 36, 37–38, 43–44, 45, 48–49
Alger, William Rounseville, 31
American literature, development of, 2, 3, 4, 11, 18, 27, 29, 34–35, 58–61
anarchism, 116
Anti-slavery and Reform Papers, 35
Atkinson, Brooks, 88, 91, 110, 136
"Autumnal Tints," 32–33

Bazalgette, Léon, *Henry Thoreau, Bachelor of Nature*, 90–91, 98
Beard, Charles, 89
Beard, Mary, 89
Bennett, Jane, 163–64, 169
Berry, Wendell, 158–59
Beston, Henry, 57, 102, 103, 152
Blake, Harrison, 46, 49, 50, 51, 54, 67, 68
Bode, Carl, 102, 111, 127
Borland, Hal, 103, 104
Borsodi, Ralph, 103
Botkin, Daniel, 154–55, 166
Brown, John, 21–22, 79
Buell, Lawrence, 2, 67–68, 82, 93, 108, 165
Burroughs, John, 33, 46, 58, 63, 69–73, 74, 79, 80, 83

Calverton, V. F., 3, 93, 98
Canby, Henry, 27, 35, 37, 49, 88, 91, 97, 98, 122, 164
Cape Cod, 35
Carson, Rachel, *Silent Spring*, 139–41, 165
Channing, Ellery, 8, 9, 37; *Thoreau, The Poet Naturalist: With Memorial Verses*, 38–40, 43
"Civil Disobedience," 20–21, 111, 132
Civil War, 33
Cold War, 96–99, 102–3, 122–23
Colonial Revival, 41–43, 45
Concord, 7–10, 13–14, 42–46, 145
Concord Days (Alcott), 38
Concord School of Philosophy, 45–46, 49
Condry, William, 12, 136, 150
Cronon, William, 163, 168
Curtis, Kent, 142, 163, 166

Darwinism, 64
Dean, Bradley, 20, 165

Eckstorm, Fannie Hardy, 80–81, 82
ecology, 137–41
Edel, Leon, 127–28
Emerson, Edward, 1, 56, 66, 68, 83–84
Emerson, Ralph Waldo, 8–10, 12, 13, 14, 17, 22, 26, 27–29, 33–34, 36, 40, 45–46

215

environmental movement, 133–35, 141–42, 146–47, 152–55
eulogies to Thoreau, 28, 36, 40
Excursions, 36

Flagg, Wilson, 62
Foerster, Norman, 59, 73, 80, 82, 83, 90
Fosdick, Raymond, 85, 86, 88, 91, 96
Freud, Sigmund. *See* psychoanalysis

Galbraith, John Kenneth, 129
Gandhi, Mahatma, 113–14
Gilded Age, 55
Great Depression, 91–93

Hall of Fame for Great Americans, 109–11, 118
Harding, Walter, *Days of Henry Thoreau*, 3, 6–7, 95, 110–11, 125, 157
Henley, Don, 169
Higginson, Thomas Wentworth, 3–4, 8, 9, 12, 26, 36, 40–41, 62, 66, 70, 71
hippies, 117–20
homesteading movement, 130–31

individualism, 34, 116
Industrial Revolution, 33–34, 55, 89, 90

Japp, Alexander Hay, *Thoreau: His Life and Aims*, 46–47
Jefferies, Richard, 61
Jones, Howard Mumford, 99, 111, 146

Kalman, David, 123, 124
Katahdin, 147–49
King, Martin Luther, Jr., 114
Kirkham, Stanton, 58, 72, 78
Krutch, Joseph Wood, 96, 100–101, 120, 129–30, 150, 156, 158

Lawrence, Jerome, *The Night Thoreau Spent in Jail*, 114
Lear, Linda, 139
Leary, Lewis, 31, 107, 109, 111, 121, 131
Lee, Robert E., *The Night Thoreau Spent in Jail*, 114
Lowell, James Russell, 2, 15, 16–17, 29–31, 37, 40–41, 59, 60, 69, 110
Lynd, Stoughton, *Intellectual Origins of American Radicalism*, 115–16, 121
Lytle, Mark Hamilton, 140, 165

Macy, John, 60, 68, 93, 98
Maine Woods, The, 15–16, 147–49, 150–51, 153

Matthiessen, Francis O., 94, 99, 122, 127
Maynard, Barksdale, 43, 53, 63
McAleer, John J., 111, 152
McCarthy hearings, 96–97, 113
McGregor, Robert Kuhn, 12–13
McIntosh, James, 128, 149
McKibben, Bill, 162
Miller, Perry, *Consciousness in Concord*, 123–25, 126, 144
Montrie, Chad, 164
Muir, John, 73–77
Mumford, Lewis, 4, 89–90
Murie, Olaus, 133–34, 149

Nash, Roderick, 147
nature, literary depictions, 4–5, 10, 27, 32–33, 36–37, 57–67, 71–73, 77–80, 84, 102–4, 146–47, 157
Nearing, Helen and Scott, 130–31
Night Thoreau Spent in Jail, The, 114–15

Oelschlaeger, Max, 165
outdoor recreation, 99–100

Paul, Sherman, 99, 104–5, 115
Peattie, Donald Culross, 105–6
Porter, Eliot, *In Wildness Is the Preservation of the World*, 155–57
posthumous publications, 36, 48–49, 67–68
psychoanalysis, 122–24, 126–28

religion. *See* Thoreau, Henry David: religious views
reviews. *See* Thoreau, Henry David: book reviews
Richardson, R. D., 4, 12, 148, 165
romanticism, 10–11

Salomon, Louis, 108
Salt, Henry S., *Life of Thoreau*, 42, 51, 52–53, 68
Sanborn, Franklin, *Henry D. Thoreau and Personality of Thoreau*, 52, 53
Sattelmeyer, Robert, 17, 36, 86, 90
Schulz, Kathryn, 160–61, 170
Scudder, Townsend, 6, 8, 15, 115
Sewall, Ellen, 6–7, 124, 125
Shepard, Odell, 91, 126
Sherwood, Mary, 119, 144
Skinner, B. F., *Walden II*, 152
Slater, Philip, *Pursuit of Loneliness*, 151–52
slavery. *See* abolitionism
Sleepy Hollow. *See* Concord
social criticism, 86–90, 93

socialism, 47, 92–93
Stevenson, Robert Louis, 31–32
Stoller, Leo, 125, 135–36, 137, 149, 167

Teale, Edwin Way, 100, 101–2, 104, 143
Thompson, Maurice, 61, 72, 83
Thoreau, Cynthia Dunbar (mother), 5
Thoreau, Henry David: biographies of, 9, 11–13, 16, 27, 38–39, 46–48, 51–53, 90–91, 110–11, 122, 127, 128, 136; book reviews, 49–50, 68, 80–82, 107; British reception of, 36–37; contemporary opinions of, 13–15, 16–17, 18–20, 25–26; death, 22–23, 27; friends, 8–9; journal, 13, 48–51, 67–68, 80–81, 91, 136; lectures and lecturing, 14–15, 22; religious views, 26, 30, 54; youth, 5–7
Thoreau, John (brother), 6
Thoreau, John (father), 5–6
Thoreau, Sophia (sister), 23, 29, 36, 44, 49, 67
Thoreau Society, 110–11, 143
Torrey, Bradford, 64, 65, 67, 68, 78, 80
transcendentalism, 10–11, 33

Udall, Stewart, 136, 154
Unitarianism, 11, 31
Uphaus, Willard, 113, 131

Walden (book), 3, 13, 18–20, 27, 37, 85–86, 94–95, 98–99, 107–8, 117–18, 129–32, 134, 157
Walden Pond, 11–12, 25–26, 29, 43–44, 56–57, 142–45
"Walking" (essay), 155
Walls, Laura Dassow, 16, 22, 157
Watts-Dunton, Theodore, 73
Week on the Concord and Merrimack Rivers, A, 12, 16–17, 30, 31, 146
wilderness preservation. *See* environmental movement
World War II, 94–96
Worster, Donald, 141, 163, 168–69
Wright, Mabel Osgood, 65, 66–67

Yankee in Canada, A, 35

Zahniser, Howard, 91, 146, 157

www.ingramcontent.com/pod-product-compliance
Lightning Source LLC
Chambersburg PA
CBHW030136240426
43672CB00005B/150